The Magdalen Manuscript

The Alchemies of Horus &
The Sex Magic of Isis

by Tom Kenyon
and Judi Sion

Sounds True, Inc., Boulder CO 80306

Published 2006
Printed in Canada

ISBN 1-59179-455-5

Library of Congress Control Number 2005936046

Previously published by ORB Communications, 2002 as *The Magdalen
Manuscript: The Alchemies of Horus and The Sex Magic of Isis*.

TABLE OF CONTENTS

The Magdalen Manuscript

Internal Alchemy

One Woman's Story

The Magdalen
Manuscript

Invocation
to the
Cosmic Mother

Oh, Great Mother, divine feminine, birther of the cosmos, lover unto Spirit, Creatrix of all matter and queen of all worlds within worlds and those without, we call you to us in this hour.

We are your children; hear our call.

We are the daughters and sons of your divine union, the flesh of your passion for life. You, who lay with Spirit, our Father, in the beginning of time, and brought us forth from the blessed union of Spirit and Matter, we are your children, the sons and daughters of your flesh and your heart, and we remember your touch and the fragrance of your essence, and we long for you.

Come to our hearts and gift us the remembering. Come to our minds and open our genius.

Enlighten us with your presence.

Draw back the veils that we might see, and harken the doors to open, that beauty and ecstasy may live in our homes and hearts more fully.

This is our hour of greatest need. We call you through fire and water, through earth and wind, through all that bears your name. We call all your lineages and all your names. Come unto us. Come into us. So be it.

—Judi Sion

Tom's Introduction to The Magdalen Manuscript

Personally, I have tremendous challenges with this manuscript. For one, it is channeled, and I thought that I had left that kind of writing behind me after I finished the Hathor Material* (Orb Publishing Group).

For me, channeling is a questionable activity. It reminds me of the seine nets people cast in the waterways of the Carmargue in southern France, an area believed by many to be where Magdalen came ashore. Along the banks, large nets sit in the river. Occasionally someone cranks a hoist and pulls the net out of the water to see what got caught. I think channeling is a lot like this.

There are currents within our psyches. They carry a hodgepodge of things, some of them interesting, some of them worthless, and some of them downright strange. Sometimes the channeling net catches something of unquestionable value, but often it is mixed in with a bunch of junk.

My first experience with channeling was in the late seventies. A friend of mine happened to be a medical researcher at Duke University, and we conducted a series of informal experiments on the phenomenon. Since I worked with hypnosis in my psychotherapy practice, we decided to see what might emerge from hypnotic states in relation to channeled material.

The very first evening we made "contact" with an immense intelligence that we euphemistically called "Big Dude." I have quite an irreverent streak, and anyone who knows me will attest to this.

* The Hathors are a group of interdimensional beings who offer information regarding personal and planetary transformation.

Big Dude spoke in a characteristically grand style typical of channeled entities or intelligences. It spoke about possible earth changes, and it spoke about the interconnectedness of the universe. While the transcripts of the talks were intriguing, both my friend and I agreed that there was nothing of real substance, and after three months of meeting once every two weeks or so, we dropped the experiment.

As a psychotherapist working in the area of Transpersonal Psychology for many years, I have seen a lot of clients who channeled. Some of them were quite comfortable with it. Some were quite disturbed by it— like the woman in her late forties who was awakened at three every morning for the last year. She would sit, pen in hand, and scribble out messages from the other side. The other side of what is the question. Her transcriptions talked about the power of love to heal; sometimes they offered some decent solutions to problems; sometimes, quite frankly, they said some very strange things.

Strange is, of course, a relative term. What is strange to one person may seem quite reasonable to another. The cultural filters we use to sieve our experiences are often arbitrary and based on inherited nonsense.

My task as a psychotherapist was to help my channeling clients make sense out of their transpersonal babble. I use these words on purpose. The collective unconscious is filled with all sorts of things. The psychological entities that reside there are varied, like the characters in real life. Some of these denizens from the collective are brilliant and well-intentioned. Some of them are idiots masquerading as spiritual beings.

There is a tremendous increase in channeling among both laypersons and professionals alike. I think it is just a sign that as a collective, we are beginning to gain access to our psychological and spiritual depths. Many people are having spiritual emergencies in which their views of the world are quickly and radically altered by peak spiritual experiences. I believe that we will be seeing even more of these psycho-spiritual crises over the next several decades as the new mythos within our collective mind begins to surface.

Channeling, within this context, is nothing more than a message from the deep. But like the summer fishing holes of my youth, some of the things down there are not worth fishing for. But still they come to the surface of the mind, like an old shoe or a rusted beer can.

One of the tasks for anyone faced with channeling is to separate the valuable from the inane, the uplifting from the dangerous. Just because the information is coming from the other side should not imbue it with any more authority than the words from someone down the street.

In fact, when someone hands me something and tells me that it has been channeled, my guard goes up. And when a being from the other world shows up on my doorstep, so to speak, I look for logical inconsistencies. I lay traps. If they pass these tests, I am more likely to consider what they are telling me. But I am the final judge. If what they say does not make sense to me, I dismiss it.

And so, in the midst of my immense resistance to the channeling phenomena, Magdalen showed up one night in Zurich, Switzerland. My partner, Judi, had asked me to see if I could get anything about the Magdalen since we were shortly going to be in Sainte Maries de la Mer, the site where Magdalen supposedly landed after the crucifixion.

I closed my eyes and entered a light hypnotic trance. Immediately, a being appeared in my mind's eye, and announced that she was the Magdalen herself. She began to dictate the manuscript you now hold in your hands. Over many sessions she spoke with an undeniable clarity and urgency. Every word was precise, and the feeling in the room during these sessions was electric.

Now, several months later, as I look at the manuscript with a critical eye, I am struck by several things. The first is a personal dread at adding to the glut of channeled books. That's the last thing any of us need, I tell myself.

But the material is like nothing I have ever seen. As a student of internal alchemies for over three decades, I have been fascinated by the similarities as well as the differences between the world's alchemical traditions. And I have made it one of my personal quests to experience a vast array of alchemical methods for transforming and elevating consciousness. From this perspective, the techniques offered by the Magdalen are quite extraordinary. As a spiritual pragmatist I have always tried everything myself. If it works, I keep it. If it doesn't, I toss it out. I have personally used the techniques Magdalen describes, and they work. They work extraordinarily well. In fact, I can honestly say that practicing them has enhanced all of my other alchemical practices, regardless of the lineage from which they come.

All of this led me to one final logical conclusion. For those fellow students of alchemy, for those seeking deeper experiences of spiritual transformation, and for those who desire Sacred Relationship, this material may well prove invaluable. For this reason, I have decided to release the manuscript.

There are still some problems for me. I am a stickler for accuracy. And there is no way to verify if the story is true or not. There are so many versions of the Magdalen legend and it happened so long ago, I suspect we will never know for sure, at least from an objective point of view.

I found the story Magdalen painted during the sessions extremely evocative; parts of it I still do. However, the bulk of the story is, to me, just another story—could be true, could be false.

As a person firmly anchored (some would say marooned) on the shores of logic, I can't say whether the story is true or not. And this disturbs me. But I can say that the methods she shares and the insights she offers are extraordinary. And so, for me, as I sorted through the manuscript, I put the story back in the river and kept the methods. I ask you to do the same.

Read this with your own heart and mind. Keep what is of value for you, and leave the rest.

I realize that this book may very well be controversial in many circles. Still, I think it right to release this manuscript into the world. If it does nothing more than get us to question the various issues it brings up, then I think the book's existence will be justified. It is, after all, a time for all of Christendom to question its misappropriation of the feminine.

For those seeking a deeper understanding of internal alchemy as a means to transform consciousness, I believe the material unquestionably stands on its own.

During my re-reading of the manuscript, a funny thing happened. So get this: here I was looking at the material with a rational and critical mind. As I considered whether to publish it or not, Isis appears to me—yes, Isis. She asked me to finish the book as soon as possible.

What's a guy to do?

The Island of Paros,
The Cyclades, Greece
August, 2001

Judi's Introduction to
The Magdalen Manuscript

It was a chilly night, hung with heavy fog in Zurich, Switzerland. We'd had a splendid dinner at our favorite Thai Restaurant, next door to the Alstadt Hotel, and we had time on our hands. It was a rare window in our lives. It was Thursday, November 30, 2000.

I've had a growing passion for the Magdalen, both as an archetype and Magdalen the Being. Who was she really? So much we live with everyday in this civilization is based upon the church's branding of her and ergo, all of the feminine as whore, as shameful. Because of this branding—no less than holding down divinity and burning a hot iron into her flesh—the feminine has carried shame and been held as "less than" for over 2000 years.

There is absolutely no basis for the Church labeling her as whore; not one word from the original texts supports such accusations. It was, in fact, the Council of Nicea, under orders from Emperor Constantine that chose the prostitute "spin" to support the patriarchy, depose the authority of the feminine, shame all that is feminine, and unite the many diverse religions and the popular upstart religion called Christianity—all for the sake of Rome, for the sake of government.

Their grounds for branding Mary Magdalen a whore? Jealousy and fear of the power of the feminine, especially the kind of power that Magdalen had.

I have never believed that we were born in sin, and I have never believed that Mary Magdalen, hence all women in her stead, were whores. And I have never bought the image of Jesus Christ as a pious, celibate, holier-than-thou, fanatic evangelical.

I had followed the trail of the Magdalen through Southern France years before, and I wanted to take Tom on the same route my heart had found, to retrace my steps with my Beloved.

But I was afraid to trust my own heart and I desperately wanted more background. I wanted the story. I wanted more than the story. I wanted the truth. I remember telling Tom that I would only consider validity in the story he brought through, because I so value his integrity and his ability to contact true source. And so I asked him if he'd ever consider contacting her.

Now, I need to tell you that Tom Kenyon does not like to channel! The scientist and the mystic do frequent battle internally. And I love them both, equally. So I usually stand back and watch the scientist ultimately yield to the sweet light of truth that the mystic can evoke. And in the dance that prevails, in the end, the world is presented great teachings, cloaked in the veil of science the ignorant of this time demand. So be it.

But this night, for whatever reason, grace was standing by, and she was on my side. I asked if he would consider trying to contact Mary Magdalen.

And he said, "Yes."

"When?" I held my breath.

"How about now?"

He lay back on the bed and I grabbed the laptop. He quickly moved aside and the Hathors came to assist by adjusting his neurology, which they frequently do to quiet the scientist who protests too much.

And she entered. The room swelled with power and an intensity of electricity that I felt in my fingertips. My fingers trembled on the keys when she began to speak. It was as if all of eternity reached out and closed the gap of time. She was there. We were there. The hourglass cracked and time suspended.

I hope I never forget hearing her words. I swear I will

never forget to be grateful for her truth, for Tom's open heart, for Yeshua's honor, and for the trust that she extended to me, in telling me her story.

She continued over a period of weeks as we traveled through Switzerland, the Italian Alps, and down across Tuscany. She came through on a boat from Genoa, Italia to Palermo, Sicilia. And when Sicilia turned out not to be where we were meant to winter, she visited us on the boat from Livorno to Malta. She continued on Oudish (Gozo), the smaller island of Malta, oddly enough, within sight of where she landed to re-provision on her trip from Egypt to France. She uttered the words, "We are complete," just before Christmas, 2000.

Every night before she began, she made me read back what I had taken down from the previous visit. She corrected any word I hadn't gotten correctly and altered an occasional word, clarifying here and there. And before she left us each night, she asked me to read back what she'd given that night.

Many nights she waited, at a particularly poignant juncture in her story, while Tom emotionally experienced her story as she told it, emitting moans and little whimpers.

She would say to me, "This channel is feeling the emotion of what I am telling you."

My heart goes out to Tom that he felt, even for a moment, what it must have been like for her to love a man as she loved Yeshua and to lose him to death, for the sake of all humankind. And my heart goes out to Yeshua, only now after hearing and knowing her story is the truth. He loved her so, he almost didn't do what he came to do.

When we left Malta in the spring, the computers were safely packed and shipped home. I hand carried a disc with the manuscript on it with me everywhere, along with a hard copy. Thus Magdalen went with us into Russia, the Ukraine, back to Germany and Switzerland and Venezia, and then it landed, so to speak, back in St. Maries de la Mer, where she landed in Southern France. The disc and hard copy waited patiently in my suitcase while we toured Rennes le Chateau and imagined how the Pyrenees must have looked when she dared to brave the wilds of those majestic peaks.

And finally, at our tiny apartment overlooking the Mediterranean on the island of Paros in the Cyclades, she came back once more, to answer some questions about specific words in the manuscript. Until we received her permission, we did not change one single word, not even a simple and obvious change in tense, and she thanked us for our impeccability.

I figured if the ignorance we've had to live with for 2000 years was a result of someone editing Yeshua's words badly, I wanted to do my best to see that no one could possibly misunderstand what she was saying now, in setting the story straight.

I asked her several personal questions that I knew someone would ask us, when we presented this manuscript. I know the questions some of you hold in your hearts, and I asked her what to say to you when you asked us those questions.

Frequently she said, "Tell them Mary Magdalen has no comment."

The questions she did answer are in the last section at the back of the book.

We approached her one more time on Orcas Island. She spoke about the critical importance of this manuscript and its significance in the return of the Cosmic Mother. She said, "for the whole of the Earth, for the Galaxy, for the Universe and those contiguous." She said she would call people to this truth from all over the world and those who were ready would find the manuscript, one way or another.

She congratulates you for hearing the call and she thanks you, from the bottom of her heart, on her behalf and on behalf of the Cosmic Mother for being here. She says nothing will ever be the same.

Orcas Island
October, 2001

One

I was raised in the understanding of magic. My father was from Mesopotamia and my mother from Egypt. Before I was born she prayed to Isis to bless her with a child. I am that child. And I was known as Mary Magdalen.

When I was 12 years old I was sent to study with a secret sisterhood of Initiates, under the wings of Isis. I was trained in the secrets of Egypt, the Alchemies of Horus, and the Sexual Magic of the Isis Cult. When I met who you call Yeshua, I had passed all my Initiations. I had prepared for the meeting with him by the well.

The Gospels recount me as a prostitute, for all Initiates of my order wore a gold arm brace-let that was a serpent; and it was understood that we practiced sexual magic; and in the eyes of the Hebrews, we were whores.

When I saw Yeshua and our eyes met, I understood that we had been destined for each other.

What I am about to tell you has not been known, except by those who were with me. Many legends abound as to what happened. But for me it is a story of deepest love. That

Yeshua had a vision of the world does not touch me. My story is a love story.

Many people followed Yeshua. And the opportunities for us to be alone together were very few.

It is not written in the Gospels for no one knew, only the closest to us. Before Yeshua went to the Garden of Gethsemane, we conceived a child, and her name was to be Sar'h.

Two

The story I am about to tell sounds fantastical.

I remember the reeds of Maries de la Mer, although then, of course, it was not called that. It is a place where our boat came ashore. Sar'h was quite young. Not quite one year old. I was torn by grief and amazement.

I was there when Yeshua was crucified. I saw him in the tomb and wrapped him with his mother beside me. I will forever remember the smell of myrrh. That was one of the ointments we used.

Yeshua appeared to me in his luminous light. I could not believe my eyes, and so I touched his wounds. The disciples were jealous that he had come to me first.

It was strange to have my beloved transported to another realm, another world, while

I and our daughter crossed the Mediterranean alone. We were no longer safe and had to leave Egypt, for that is where we had gone.

When we crossed onto the shores of what was to become France, it was all wilderness. We were met by priestesses of the Isis Cult, and we headed north to the protection of the Druids, for Isis had spoken to them, and they had heard the call to protect her daughter, Sar'h. And so we headed North to another great body of water and crossed over into what was to become England.

And there we were secreted up into the most sacred heart of the Druids, to the Tor and the Glastonbury. Although we were safer than we had been in Israel or Egypt, the Roman influence extended up into England as well, and we were hidden.

We lived in this area for many years, and Sar'h wedded a man whose heirs would become the Templar Knights, and I went north into Wales and lived by the sea for the rest of my days.

I will say this, that in those years when I lived alone by the sea, Yeshua would often visit. Of course, it was not like before, for his body was more energy than flesh, more light; but still it was extraordinary to be with him again.

When I died he was there and took me into what some call heaven, but is just a place in the soul.

Three

I begin my story at the well, for in many ways that is when my life truly began. All the years previous were preparation for this meeting.

That morning I knew something was stirring, a kind of excitement—a trembling in the arms and legs—before I even met him. I was already at the well when he arrived. I had already sunk my jar into the shaft, and he helped me raise it. Some of the apostles saw my gold serpent bracelet and assuming me to be a whore, were aghast that the Master would help such a one.

But this did not touch me. I was in another world, transported by the eyes of Yeshua. When our eyes met it was as if I was looking into all of eternity, and I knew that he was the one that I had been prepared for—and so did he.

I continued at the fringes of those who followed him, and in the evenings we would go off together; not every evening for he was constantly sought after.

I, who was trained in the Alchemies of Horus and the Sex Magic of Isis, was considered to be highly advanced by my teachers, yet the first time in Yeshua's arms, I was a trembling woman, and I had to fight to find that central pathway through my desire to the highest throne, for that was my training.

Yeshua and I, using the techniques that I had been trained in, as well as the methods he had learned in Egypt, were able to charge his Ka, his energy body, with greater light and greater force, so that he could more easily work with those who came to him. And so it was.

And I still find it ironic that the Gospels report that I was at the well when Yeshua arrived; but those many nights when Yeshua and I were alone, he came to my well, to draw from me the powers of Isis, to build and strengthen himself.

I stand in time now, looking at all of this as if it were a dream and yet so—still, vividly clear. My heart trembles as I recount the story as if it were yesterday. That first night with Yeshua is sketched within my mind as clear as the skies over Jerusalem.

After I had been able to pass through the desires of myself as woman and ascend the path into spiritual alchemy in which I was trained, I could see Yeshua's spirit form— already luminous, already brilliant with light.

A dove was above his head, golden rays of light poured forth from it. The seals of Solomon, of Hator, of Isis, of Anubis, and Osiris were in his spirit form. They were signs that he had passed through these Initiations. There were other symbols I did not understand; for they were from cultures I had no knowledge of or training in; but of the Egyptian seals of which I knew he was on the path of the High God Horus.

But he had not yet passed through his death Initiation, and I knew in my trembling heart that that is why I had been drawn to him at this time—to fortify his soul with the powers of Isis and the Cosmic Mother, so that he could pass through the dark portal and attain the Horus.

That night, after we had made love and wielded and blended our spirit bodies together, the action of alchemy having begun between us, Yeshua drifted off to sleep. As I held him in my arms, I felt a turning within me, a desire to protect him, a desire to be always with him, and the knowledge, like the edge of a cold knife, that we would be parted by forces great-er than my desire.

Five

The Church would have you believe I was a whore, but I tell you now that the Church is the whore, for she would have you believe that woman is tainted and that the sexual passions between a man and a woman are evil. Yet it is here, in the magnetics of passion, that the womb of ascension is created.

This secret of secrets was known by all Initiates of Isis, and yet I had never imagined that I would be the one to bring it into fullest expression in union with such a one as Yeshua.

For me, this journey is of my spirit and heart.

But for those who wish to know the physical journey...after Yeshua's crucifixion, I, and his mother, Mary, Joseph of Arimathea, his twelve-year-old son, named Aaron, and two other young women set off from Northern Egypt.

Our course took us ironically east before we could turn westward, and we had to stop for provisions along the way, as our boat was very small. Our path took us to Malta and the tiny island of Oudish, from there to Sardinia and to the tip of what is now the Cinque Terra, finally landing at Saintes-Maries-de-la-Mer and making our trek Northward through Rennes-le-Chateau into Northern France, and across the channel into what is now England. We settled in Glastonbury for several years, until Sar'h was twelve.

Upon her twelfth birthday, we set off for the place among the reeds where we had landed. There, as close to Egypt as was safe for us to go, I initiated my daughter into the Cult of Isis and bathed her in the waters of the Mediterranean in accordance with the teachings I had been given.

We then returned to Glastonbury, until Yeshua's and my daughter, Sar'h, wedded at age sixteen. She married into a well-known family whose heirs became the Templars, although at that time the Templar Knights did not exist.

This family bloodline, through Sar'h, would be carried into the Templars themselves. When Sar'h was married and secure in her new life, I headed North for Wales and lived in a small stone cottage by the sea for the rest of my days.

Behind my cottage there was a stream that came out of the hill, and I would sit there many days. For there was a time when this stream split in two, and the two streams followed each other, and then one veered off to the left and one to the right. And I would sit there, in-between them, thinking about the stream of my life and the stream of Yeshua's—how, for a while, our lives flowed together and then parted.

Six

I will forever remember the first time Yeshua came to me after his resurrection.

It was a new moon and the sky was clear. A light fog hung over the heather and everything was silver from the light of the moon and stars. I saw a figure approaching me on the windy trail that led to my cottage.

Ironically, I had just gone outside to draw water from the well and there he was. He looked

the same, yet with a radiance—unmistakable!
My eyes filled with tears; my heart trembled.

I ran to him and stopping short, I remembered
his words to me right after the resurrection.

"Do not touch me yet," he had said then,
"for I am not ascended to the Father."

Oh, how I, an Initiate of Isis, have yearned
all these years to set the record straight!

What did he mean by these words? For the
Christians have inherited only a part of the truth.
The greater part of the truth is hidden within the
mysteries of the Great Mother; and because the
Church sought to disenfranchise women and all
that is feminine, it sealed away this truth.

And the truth has to do with the Ka body
itself—what we learned as Initiates to call
the Etheric Double or Spiritual Twin—for the
Ka body, when charged with enough energy
and vitality, looks like the physical body. But
unlike the physical body, the Ka body is not
made of flesh, but of energy itself—energy
and light.

And so when Yeshua came to me after his
resurrection, he was in his Ka, but it had not
been stabilized yet, for he had not gone to the
Father—meaning into the Great Spirit of his
own soul. So before he could do this, he had
to pass through the portal of death and travel
through the underworld of his own being.

He did this for two reasons, as I understand it. The first was, as a master soul, to do such a thing brings great power to the Ka. And the second reason was to cut a passage through death itself, so that others could follow and pass through the dark world more easily by following the trail of his light.

And so that first night when we were rejoined—I feel it now, still vividly clear and strong—my heart filled with joy at being with him again. He came to me that night just before midnight and left just before dawn. In those hours we lay together, our Ka bodies interconnecting yet again, no need for talk. Our communication was telepathic. And without the physical act of sex, the Serpent Power within him joined the serpent power within me and climbed upward along the sacred paths in our spines, to the throne of the crowns of our heads, sending me into sheer ecstasy and bliss. And this was how it was for many years. He would come to me this way several times each year. Sometimes we would speak. Most of the time was in union.

I asked him where he went in these times when we were not together. He said that he had gone to many sacred places throughout the earth—that he had met with many different peoples. He said that he was laying a path of light.

During one of his visits I asked him to explain to me this rather strange concept.

He drew a circle onto the dirt floor of my
cottage and then what I recognized as the
two triangles intersecting, to make the Seal of
Solomon, becoming the Star of David. He said
that there were many lands that we, in this part
of the world, did not have knowledge of. Many
of these lands had points corresponding to the
points of the Seal of Solomon. By going to these
areas, he was ensuring that his work would take
a deeper rooting into the soil of this world.

Seven

Of all the times that he visited, the time that
stands out the strongest is the time he came
when Sar'h had come to visit.

She had just become pregnant and wished
to see me for my blessing, and so I was
thrilled to see her and her traveling com-
panions. She had sent word of her coming
through the Druids, but their word got to me
only one day before her arrival. She stayed
with me for three days, and on the second
night, Yeshua appeared.

I don't know if you can appreciate how
odd it was. For Sar'h had never met her
Father, nor Yeshua, his daughter. And yet
here they met for the first time! And her
father's body had returned to the elements in
a flash of light in his resurrection, so now he
was in his Ka body, which emitted a kind of
unmistakable light.

Both of them were moved, Sar'h to tears and Yeshua to great pathos. They spent an hour together, just themselves, walking outside. I do not know what they talked about. But from the time they began, until the time that they ended, the sky was filled with falling stars.

Before Yeshua had left that evening, just before dawn, as was his way, he placed his hands over Sar'h's stomach and blessed the child. Sar'h left me the next day, filled with an unmistakable sense of peace.

And so I have told you what I wish to say about my life as a mother, and now I will turn my story to me as an Initiate, to the Alchemies of Horus, unto the secrets of Isis.

Eight

I turn now to my beloved sister, my sister in spirit, the Mother of Yeshua, also known as Mary.

Mary was a high Initiate in the Cult of Isis, having received her training in Egypt. That is why, when she and Joseph fled the king's wrath in Israel, they took flight into Egypt, for she had safety there, among the Priestesses and Priests of Isis.

Her training was different than mine, yet we served the same. In order for me to explain my understanding of Mary I must explain one of the deepest secrets of the Isis

Cult. For it was believed, and I hold this to be true, that under certain conditions the Goddess herself would Incarnate, either at birth or through spiritual Initiation.

Mary, the Mother of Yeshua, when she was quite young, was recognized for her purity of spirit by the great Priestesses of the Isis Temples. She was trained as an Initiate and reached the highest levels. But rather than becoming a Priestess, she was trained to become what is called an Incarnate.

To be an Incarnate is to be a very highly advanced soul and requires undergoing tremendous spiritual training and discipline. In a final Initiation, Mary became the holder of an energy stream directly from Isis herself. In this regard, she was an embodiment of the Cosmic Mother. It is as if there were two— Mary the human, pure of spirit and heart, holding within her a direct portal into the Great Mother, the Creatrix of all matter, of all time and space.

Thus the table was set, so to speak, for the conception of a being of remarkable qualities who would become her son, Yeshua.

When Mary underwent what the Church refers to as the Immaculate Conception, she was a witness to a Celestial and galactic insemination process, by which the Father Principle, or Spirit as we understood this in the Isis Cult, transferred his essence into Isis, the

Mother that receives the seed of the Father—
Matter receiving the impulse of Spirit. And this
highly refined and potent spiritual energy took
root in Mary's womb and gave birth to Yeshua.

Nine

Mary was with the apostles when they came
upon me at the well. She immediately recognized me as a fellow Initiate by the gold serpent
bracelet I wore on my arm and by the Seal of
Isis which glowed within my Ka body, for Mary
was quite clairvoyant and psychic.

The first person whose eyes I met were those
of Yeshua, and as I said, I felt transported into
other worlds in his immense presence. The second person whose eyes I met were those of his
mother. In her eyes was recognition and acknowledgement of my status as a fellow Initiate within
the Isis Cult, and although her training had not
been in Sex Magic, as mine had been, she understood that I had been prepared for Yeshua.

Between them, I felt lifted up on wings of
transcendent love. I felt my spirit soar.

Ironic then that the next eyes I would see
were those of Yeshua's disciples, who judged
me to be a whore, and countless generations
have held me this way.

But I say to you that in Yeshua's eyes and
those of his mother, I was not a whore, but a

clear vessel for the healing and nurturing powers of Isis herself.

There comes a time, in a man's life, whether human or divine, when his mother cannot give him the essence of what he needs. Her love continues, but what is required is sustenance from another woman. I was that woman.

Mary recognized me and my status, and passed her son to me in that moment by the well.

Mary and I spent much time together, time in which we discussed Yeshua's work, his needs and my place in his life. It was understood that I was a servant to a greater power. I had been trained for this, but I must tell you that the power of the recognition still shakes me. I still tremble at his recognition.

In those many nights and days together, Mary and I attended to the needs of Yeshua and his disciples, and in that period Mary and I became very close, for I loved her, and I love her still—for her physical beauty, the purity of her heart and spirit and the gentleness with which she dealt the world.

I can say, from my own clarity that Mary, having served as the vessel for Isis as an Incarnate, was a highly developed Master, but now having served in these ways, her mastery and perfection—her spiritual perfection—is staggering.

Ten

She exists within the heavenly realms, her compassion and love continually flowing to all humans. She is available to all, regardless of their beliefs. When someone calls upon her, know that they are heard.

I wish now to clarify my understandings. I wish to speak about the Sex Magic of the Isis Cult and The Alchemies of Horus. I wish to reveal secrets that an Initiate would never have revealed, even under threat of death. But the times are different now.

Time as you know it, is running out, and I have received permission from the Goddess herself—indeed, I have been asked by the Goddess herself—to reveal to you some of the most closely guarded secrets of all times. These are revealed to you in hopes that you will elevate yourselves in time.

Eleven

The Alchemies of Horus refer to a body of knowledge and methods for the alteration of the Ka body. In this understanding, as the Ka embodies, or acquires greater energy and light, there is an increase in one's magnetic field, and that which the Initiate desires becomes more quickly manifest.

However, in surrender to one's own Celestial Soul, or the Ba, the pursuit of personal desires,

Activate Djed through [handwritten margin note]

although not abandoned, is no longer the focus of one's entire existence. Instead, one looks upward, so to speak, to the higher capabilities of one's self, as perceived through the Ba, or the Celestial Soul.

Ba = Celestial So-l [handwritten margin note]
Khat = physical body [handwritten margin note]
Ka = Spiritual twin of Khat [handwritten margin note]

The Celestial Soul, or Ba, exists within a much higher level of vibration than the physical body (the Khat) or the Ka (the spiritual or etheric twin to the physical form). Within the Ka body there are pathways that can be stimulated and opened. The activation of these secret passages within the Ka brings it much greater power. The Alchemies of Horus are designed to strengthen these, to activate the latent powers and abilities of the Initiate through what is called the Djed, or the ascending seven seals, what the yogis and yoginis of India call the chakras.

Twelve

Within the School in which I was trained we learned how to activate the Serpent Power, moving it in specific paths in the spinal column, and opening up circuits within the brain. This created what is called the Uraeus.

The Uraeus is often a blue fire that extends up the spine both laterally and horizontally and into the brain, and it undulates with the changes in energy within these pathways. The activation of the Uraeus increases the brain's potential for intelligence, creativity, and most importantly—receptivity, for the task of the

Initiate is to change the quality of one's being, so that the attunement to the Ba or Celestial Soul is clear and unobstructed.

Thirteen

When I met Yeshua by the well for the first time, the mere proximity of his presence activated my internal Alchemies. A Serpent Power moved up my spine as if I had practiced the disciplines I had learned.

That first night when we were together alone, arm in arm, lying next to each other, we practiced the Sexual Magic of Isis. This specific form of magic charges the Ka body with tremendous magnetic force through the power of physical orgasm, for when one has a sexual orgasm there is a tremendous release of magnetic energy within the cells. As this energy spreads it releases a magnetic potential that can be used.

I wish to share the specifics of this, but in order to do so I must explain more of the basic understanding of sex and spiritual realization, for this secret was stolen by the Church.

Fourteen

When I, an Initiate of Isis, joined together with Yeshua, there were specific pathways I had to open within myself. I was stunned, however, to discover that many of these pathways

were spontaneously opening in his presence. I
mentioned at the beginning of this story how I
trembled as a woman, having to struggle with
my own passions and desires; for the path of
the Initiate is to use the energy of passion in a
highly specific way, and not to simply be carried off by it; for alchemy requires that energy
be contained so that it can be transformed.

Very quickly Yeshua and I achieved the
state—what is known as the Four Serpents.
This occurs when both have mastered the
internal Alchemies of Horus to the extent that
they can activate both the Solar and the Lunar
Serpents within their spines.

Clairvoyantly there is a central channel
that runs up through the spine, and to the
left there is a Lunar Circuit and to the right
a Solar Circuit, called the Ida and Pingala by
the yogis and yoginis.

In the Alchemies of Horus one causes these
two circuits to be activated by magnetic fields
that are snakelike.

The Lunar Snake on the left side is pitch
black, the color of the Void; so indeed, it is the
embodiment of the Void itself and holds the
potential as the Creatrix for all things.

The Solar Serpent is gold.

An Initiate causes these Two Serpents to
rise upward. As they rise upward they pierce

the chakras and cross over each other. In the Alchemy of Horus these Two Serpents cross each other through the fifth seal, or throat, and all seals beneath.

They then face each other, at an area approximately where the pineal gland is, or the center of the head. Here a chalice is envisioned with the pineal gland at the very bottom of the chalice itself.

These Two Serpents are living—in that they are not static but vibrate and scintillate and ripple with energy—and the writhing of their bodies within the Ka activates an increase of magnetic potential.

There are specific practices, which I will share at a later time, but what I wish to address in this moment is the practice of the Four Serpents.

When Yeshua and I made love, as you call it, we caused our Serpents to rise up our spines, up our Djed. We did this simultaneously, and at the moment of mutual orgasm the charge released from the first seals in the pelvic areas of our bodies was sent upward, into the Throne, which is in the upper part of the head—stimulating the higher brain centers.

At the same time during this moment of sexual ecstasy we placed our awareness fully

within our Ka bodies, for the Ka is strength-
ened by ecstasy. Ecstatic states are nourish-
ing and strengthening to the Ka body, and as
I said earlier, with each strengthening of the
Ka it becomes more magnetic, drawing to the
Initiate that which he or she desires.

The Sexual Magic of Isis has to do with the
innate ability of the feminine being to utilize
magnetic energies to open deeper levels of consciousness through the act of surrendering to the
sexual energies and pathways that are opened.

When a woman is deeply loved and appreciated, as was I by Yeshua, something lets go at
the deepest levels of herself, and at the moment
of orgasm there is an uncontrollable shuddering
that takes place. If she feels safe and allows this
shaking, this quivering, to overtake her, there is
a tremendous magnetic vortex that opens, the
center of which is in her womb.

Two Initiates engaged in the Sexual Magic
of Isis can strengthen themselves and rapidly
expand their consciousness through the power
of this magnetic field.

In the advanced practices of the Sexual
Magic of Isis the male Initiate causes both of
his Serpents to rise through the Ka body of
the female and the female causes her Two
Serpents to rise through the Ka body of the
male. The explosive power of this practice is
like the energy released by an atomic bomb.
The massive tidal waves of magnetics can

strengthen the Ka beyond imagination—or destroy it, if not handled properly.

It was this advanced practice of the Ka that Yeshua engaged that night before the Garden of Gethsemane. For him this tremendous increase of magnetic potential within his Ka strengthened him for his hardships and for the task that faced him in his final Initiation through the portal of death; so that when his physical body dissolved into it's constituate elements it was done so in a flash of light and heat—that the church calls the Resurrection. But this was simply an effect of something that was occurring much deeper within him. It was caused by the magnetics of his Ka body, for it was through his potentized Ka that he journeyed through his underworld, through death itself.

As Yeshua and I engaged the Sexual Practices of Isis in our relationship we both understood that this was the purpose.

For him each union with me was a means to strengthen his Ka. This is why I said earlier that he came to my well, for the well that the woman Initiate offers to the male is an endless well of magnetic potential. But it is only opened when the female feels safe and loved. Only then will the practices work. For the practices without the nurturance of love become just techniques and will not give the result required or desired.

For me, I was both woman and Initiate. I had been trained for years and knew what to do with the pathways, but I was surprised to find myself swept away as a woman.

I found myself waiting in deepest anticipation for a look or a touch by Yeshua, and our times together alone were the most precious times I had ever experienced. Something about his touch and his eyes—the feel of him—caused something within me to open, and I found myself sometimes almost laughing at myself.

I, who had been trained in the most secret practices of the Sex Magic of Isis and had been judged by my Priestesses to be very advanced—this Initiate—found herself, a mere beginner in the presence of the woman.

For I tell you now that within the heart and the mind and the body wisdom of the feminine lie some of the greatest secrets and greatest powers—and they await to be revealed.

And all of it is laid open by the touch of another!

And so whenever I speak of Yeshua I am overcome by my love and the feelings that I hold for him throughout all time.

Sixteen

The Sex Magic of Isis is based upon the realization that the feminine principal holds within her nature, specifically her sexual nature, an alchemical key. This alchemical key is revealed in the act of what you call love—sexual love. When this is activated strongly enough, the Alchemies of Horus spontaneously present themselves.

Within my training it was understood that there were two paths, alchemically speaking, to the same goal.

The Alchemies of Horus were the foundation of both alchemies, or practices, since the same fundamental pathways were used. For those who did not wish to engage in partnership, the Alchemies of Horus would provide a means to strengthen and activate the Ka body to the levels of High Initiateship.

For those in partnership, the Sexual Magic of Isis would provide the wings by which they would ascend the Djed and enter the Throne of Highest Consciousness.

From my vantage point I see a great tragedy in that the secrets and the holiness of our sexual natures was made evil by the Church— by the Church Fathers. And for nearly two thousand years now the most dynamic and one of the most rapid ways to God Realization has been made wrong.

And I find it indeed ironic that the Church

has made it a sin—and therefore terrified those who might have stumbled upon it.

Seventeen
    While the miracles of Yeshua are considered extraordinary by many, they are from the standpoint of the Initiate, simply the expressions—the natural expressions—of the potential of consciousness. They are a sign. There are reasons for miracles, and I wish to discuss these from the standpoint of the Initiatory knowledge that Yeshua and I possessed.

By the time I met Yeshua, he was already demonstrating the signs. His level of creation was very high.

My task was to assist him to strengthen his Ka body for his final Initiation through the death portal to the High God Horus. This was accomplished, as I have said, through the Sex Magic of Isis and the Alchemies of Horus.

Of all the miracles that I witnessed Yeshua perform, the one that is most dear to me is that of the loaves and the fishes.

It was a very long hot day. The disciples, Mary and myself were following the Master as usual. A very large crowd formed, listening intently upon every word from Yeshua's mouth. We were all enraptured by his vision and his means of expressing.

It was as if, for several hours, we were transported into heaven itself, and I noticed that Yeshua's Ka had expanded to include everyone—another sign.

When he had completed his speaking it was late in the afternoon and filled with compassion for them, realizing that their walk home would take some of them several days, he called upon food to be gathered and shared.

So the disciples, Mary and I, and a few others who joined us from the crowd began to collect food.

But when it was all gathered, there were only a few fishes and a few small loaves of bread. Hardly enough.

It was then that I witnessed a most remarkable event.

Yeshua went inside and closed his eyes. I could feel the intent of his prayer, although I did not hear the words. Running the full course of his Djed from the base of his spine to the top of his head, I clairvoyantly saw a burst of light flowing upwards through his crown, into his Ba, his Celestial Soul. And then an energy descended, as if in answer to his request; and he placed his hands over the two small baskets and began to hand out the loaves and fishes, breaking them into pieces and handing one to each person himself.

It was most remarkable; over a thousand people were fed and the loaves and fishes never exhausted themselves. After the crowd had been fed, Yeshua gave pieces to his Disciples and to Mary and myself, and the bread had the most sweet taste and the fish a wonderful flavor I have never experienced again.

Such miracles are natural to a Master of Yeshua's caliber, and from the Initiatory standpoint, such miracles are the potential of anyone if they practice what is required.

Eighteen

Yeshua often used the phrase, "I and the Father are One." This has led to great misinterpretation. For from the Initiatory standpoint, it is simply another word for Spirit. And in these words Yeshua was indicating that he merged with his Spirit, and that is how the miracles were accomplished.

passing between bodies or ♀-♂ ⚥

And so he would go back and forth between two ideas, which the gospels report in their own limited way.

On the one hand, Yeshua would sometimes say, "I and the Father are One." At other times he would say, "Without my Father, I can do nothing." This is the oscillation that occurs with the Initiatory process in which the Initiate oscillates between the strength and conviction of his/her connection to the Spirit Source and then to the other state of mind, in which they realize that they are nothing and can do nothing without Spirit.

So the one state of mind has a feeling of omnipotence. And the other state of mind has the feeling of impotence. And the Initiate must pass between these two. That Yeshua used these phrases several times indicated to me, as a fellow Initiate, that he was in the middle of this paradox.

And he lived with this paradox in consciousness until the Garden of Gethsemane. For it was before his time in the Garden, as reported by his Disciples, that he came to me and we practiced the Four Serpents for the last time. There was an intensity in our time together, for we both knew that the time was near at hand.

With the explosive force released with the practice, Yeshua's Ka body scintillated with power and conviction, which he took with him into the final hours of his life, fortifying him for his journey through death. But the times before were often spent—I search for the right words—in a kind of self-questioning.

Those who followed Yeshua, who call themselves Christians, like to think that he was surefooted and always clear about his purpose and mission and that he never wavered. But I, who spent the nights with him, tell you otherwise.

Just because a being has attained a level of mastery does not mean that they are able to pass through uncertainty—untouched.

Yeshua felt the pressure of his Celestial Soul, but it is an odd thing being an Initiate. For one is human with all that goes with it—and one is increasingly connected to, and a part of, one's Celestial Soul.

It is the Ba, the Celestial Soul, that is the voice of God speaking. The high Initiate acts like a reflex from the mouth of God, but just because the Celestial Soul is clear does not mean that the human is necessarily so.

Yeshua saw in others the potential for God-Realization, and he spoke to this several times. One of these was mentioned in the Gospels when he said, "you shall do greater things than me." For he understood that miracles are a natural expression of consciousness, and that as the consciousness of mankind expanded, miracles would be commonplace.

And yet at the same time he was very aware of the limitations of those around him—of their addiction to hatred, ignorance and bigotry—and this troubled him deeply. We spent many evenings talking about this. And until a few days before Gethsemane, he was not sure if he could attain what was required to pass through the final Initiation.

I do not know the reason for the change in him, but a few days before the Garden and our final Initiatory act together through the Four Serpents, a deep sense of peace came over him, and he was sure in a way I had never seen him.

Nineteen

I stand in time nearly two thousand years after Yeshua's crucifixion, and still I shake at the thought of that. It was very strange to be both the Initiate and the Woman.

As the Initiate, I stood by Yeshua through the crucifixion holding my Ka in fervent prayer—which is another way of saying I held steadfast in my intention to be there for him as he passed into death. This was an Initiatory action on my part that required detachment.

As a trained Initiate such a task was easy, but as the Woman in love with Yeshua, the Man, my heart was ripped apart. And so I stood at Golgotha, wavering in my strength as an Initiate, and my grief as the Woman in love whose beloved was suffering.

In that moment I did not care for the Initiation. I did not care that Yeshua was laying a trail of light through the death realms for all those who would follow him.

I even yelled at Isis.

"How dare you," I said!

In the greatest moment of my torment,
Mary reached out and touched my hand. I had
been alone in my grief and had not noticed
hers. Our eyes met, filled with tears, and we
sobbed in each other's arms. She for her son,
and I for my beloved.

The Gospels report that an earthquake
struck right after Yeshua's passing, and I
say to you that this is true. It was as if all of
nature went into travail, and the earth shook
with anger and rage, that such a Master,
such a being, could suffer at the hands of his
fellow men.

But such is the paradox of life on earth.

A great storm came across the city as
well—winds like I had not seen. The sky filled
with dark clouds and bolts of lightning—the
sound of thunder shaking everything. This
horrific display lasted it seemed, forever, but I
suspect it was only for an hour or so.

At the tomb, Mary and I washed his body
in accordance with Jewish ritual and tradition,
wrapped him and left the tomb. We did this
in silence. The only sound the sound of our
muffled tears.

I thought it odd that he had been able to
raise Lazurus from the dead, but had not been
able to help himself.

I did not understand what he was doing.

But after his resurrection, and I saw him in his Ka, radiant and beautiful as ever, I understood.

From the Initiatory standpoint, to become the High God Horus means that one has activated the highest potentials of consciousness within the human form. But this was traditionally done for one's self only. But Yeshua had done it on behalf of all mankind. This is his legacy.

But I say to you it has nothing to do with religion! It has to do with physics and alchemy.

The simple teaching of Yeshua was that we are all Gods—that we all have within us the power to love and to heal—and he demonstrated this as best he could.

In the early days of the Church—meaning the community of those who formed around Yeshua's teachings—a most beautiful ritual emerged.

Those who wished to continue to be in his energy or presence would share bread and wine. Sometimes the men would share the ritual and sometimes the women. This simple act of sharing among each other was in keeping with Yeshua's intent, and yet as the years progressed the simplicity of this got lost, and only those ordained by the Church could give Communion, something which Yeshua would find most distasteful. (Having known him as well as I did, I can tell you this.)

The truth and power of Yeshua's teaching have been perverted by the Church.

And the secrets of the elevation of consciousness through Sacred Sex, as was practiced by I and Yeshua, have been stolen by the Church.

I realize in the sharing of my story that only a handful will understand—but that is enough.

 Twenty   I wish now to reveal some of the secrets of the Sex Magic of Isis.

As I said earlier, it is possible to scale the heights of consciousness alone, without partnership; and in this, the Alchemies of Horus were designed to assist the Initiate.

However, for those in partnership—Sacred Relationship—the Sex Magic of Isis was revealed. There are several aspects to this I wish to discuss.

The first of these is the understanding that at the moment of orgasm, magnetic fields are generated. In truth, these fields are created through what you would call foreplay—the stimulation of the senses through touch. This sensory stimulation begins the process of building the magnetic fields and is crucial to the alchemical practice of Sex Magic.

There are several methods available to Initiates, and I will discuss some of these—but essential to the practice is the understanding of the nature of the interaction of the two alchemical elements within the man and the woman.

On a mundane level the semen of the man carries the information of his genetic lineage, which is passed on to the child. When the sperm within his semen joins with the egg of the woman life is created, and life is a complex interconnecting of magnetic fields. The growing child within the womb develops organs and systems, but at the magnetic level these can be viewed as interconnecting, complex vibrational and magnetic fields. And so at the mundane level, the act of sex creates new patterns of magnetics.

Initiates trained in alchemy use the sexual energy to also create complex magnetic fields—but these fields do not become a new being, a child; they become incorporated into the Ka bodies of the two Initiates themselves, strengthening and elevating their Ka bodies. This is the first essential point to understand. Everything revolves around this.

The task of the Initiate within this system that Yeshua and I were trained in is to strengthen the Ka body beyond the confines of the physical form, or Khat.

The next level to understand has to do with the emotional tuning of the female Initiate—for the female Initiate's receptivity is dependent upon her emotional state. This is part of her nature and cannot be sidestepped if these techniques are to work.

Essential to the female Initiate is the authentic feeling of safety and love, or appreciation at the very least. When these are in place, something within her being lets go and allows the alchemy to occur.

The alchemy is created by the joining of the male Initiate's Ka and the female Initiate's Ka. As they make love, the Ka bodies interconnect, and this causes the female to open her *Magnetic Floor*. This is a strange term. It comes from the language used in the Temples of Isis.

The floor is the foundation upon which one stands. When we set something to be secure, we place it on the floor. So the floor was used as a type of slang within the Temples, referring to the very basic piece that is required. So when I say "the female's Magnetic Floor," I am saying that this is the fundamental piece that has to occur.

As the two Initiates continue in their lovemaking, and as the passion of their connecting increases, powerful chemicals are released in the brain and in the body. These transport the Initiates into another space than their normal ways of being. This further opens the magnetic fields and generates an increase in magnetics.

There are two options to the male Initiate at the moment of orgasm. He can ejaculate, or hold his seed. If he ejaculates, and the previous conditions have been met, there is an instantaneous reaction that occurs within the womb of the female. As the energetic essence of his sperm strikes the walls of her inner sanctum there is an explosion of magnetic energy—worlds within worlds, spinning. And to the extent that the male Initiate has attained a high status as well as the female, the magnetics released from such contact between such sexual fluids can be enormous. So it is important to understand that this creates complex magnetics that both the male and female can draw into their bodies.

A second phenomenon occurs in which the female Initiate may begin to shake uncontrollably. As she shakes, the center of it is usually the womb itself, which sets off a cascade, a rocking effect in the pelvis. This action also creates very complex magnetic fields, again, which the male and female Initiates can draw into their Ka bodies. This is the fundamental or basic understanding.

As Initiates, it is possible to also cause the Serpent Powers to rise within the spine during the sex act and wherever the Two Serpents meet, will tend to magnetize that chakra and its attendant abilities or powers.

More than this I am not permitted to say, since the attainment of this practice can lead to a significant increase in one's powers. I leave it to those who read this to see between the lines. If you are ready for this practice, you will know how it is done.

Twenty-One

In the training of both the Sex Magic of Isis and the Alchemies of Horus, Initiates would be trained in the basic exercises of the Two Serpents.

In this practice, the Initiate alone generates energy through the power of RA, or the internal fire, to create an elevation in awareness—to create complex magnetic fields within his or her own body—and then to bring these into the Ka.

Ra = internal fire

I wish to share this method. It is the core practice for both those who wish to do this work alone, and for those who wish to do this work in partnership.

The fundamental practice requires that the Initiate sit upright, breathing in a rhythmic, calm manner.

Then the Initiate becomes aware of the base of the spine, and on the breaths draws the Black Serpent rising from the left and the Gold Serpent rising from the right, up the spine.

As the Two Serpents enter each chakra, they cross over, making their way up to the

crown. But in this practice, the Two Serpents
are brought up to the center of the head, to the
vicinity of the pineal gland.

The Initiate then, using the power of the
breath, sends the energy of the inhales into
the Serpents and then with the exhales sends
the energy of the breath deeper into the serpentine bodies, causing them to become
"alive," so to speak.

Eventually they will writhe, or move, from
the power of the breath and the intention of
the Initiate.

At this point, a Chalice is imagined inside
the head with the Two Serpents facing off each
other at the lip, the pineal gland resting at the
bottom of the Chalice.

The next phase draws the energy of RA
upward. The Initiate images a living ball of fire,
like the sun, at the solar plexus, and with each
exhale the Initiate silently repeats or intones
the sound RA. This causes the light, the fire of
the internal RA, to be activated, and it spontaneously begins to move up.

As this light and heat moves upward it passes
through the center of the Chalice between the
Two Serpents, up to the crown of the head. From
here, a most remarkable phenomenon occurs.

From the left side of the crown an energy
descends that is liquid-like in its nature. This

liquid is called the Red Serpentine Drops. From
the right side of the crown another liquid-like
energy moves down into the Chalice, called the
White Serpentine Drops. It is the heat and light
of the internal RA that causes the crown to
secrete these substances.

The Red Serpentine Drops are related to
the biological mother of the Initiate. The White
Serpentine Drops are related to the father of
the Initiate. As the two mix together several
things can occur. There can be the sensation
of a sweet taste in the back of the throat—
what the yogis and yoginis call Amrita—but
which we in the Isis Cult refer to as the Spring
Waters, for they seem to come from the spring
within the head.

Sometimes this is the first presentation;
and if an Initiate focuses upon the sensation
of the Spring Waters, a kind of ecstasy arises.
Sometimes the Initiate senses light in their
head. Again, if they focus upon this light, a
kind of ecstasy arises.

Sometimes as the Red and White Serpentine
Drops mix, there is a spontaneous arising of
ecstasy. This ecstasy, no matter what caused it,
is crucial to this alchemy. For ecstasy is food
and nourishment to the Ka body.

There is a tendency for this ecstasy to
remain in the higher centers, since this is where
they were birthed in this practice. But in this
method, upon the first arising of ecstasy, the

Initiate must shift his or her awareness to the entire Ka body itself. This causes the ecstasy to spread throughout the entire physical body, Khat, and is then absorbed by the Ka, strengthening and revitalizing it.

This is the basic, fundamental practice.

For those in partnership practicing the Sex Magic of Isis, the ecstatic states naturally arise. For those in the solitary practice, the ecstasy must be self-generated.

Both practices, however, require that the Initiate become aware of the Ka during moments of ecstasy, so that the Ka body can partake of the rich, magnetic fields created by such bliss.

Twenty-Two

In a very real sense, the male Initiate faces the greatest challenges in the practice of the Sex Magic of Isis, for it requires that he seemingly go against his own nature. By nature the male is electric from an alchemical standpoint, while the female is magnetic.

It is the nature of electricity to move and to act, while it is the nature of magnetics to nest—enfold.

In the practice, the focus becomes the strengthening of the Ka body through the incorporation of magnetic fields released by the sex

act. Right after orgasm, the magnetic fields generated by the female Initiate continue to unspiral
and circulate. This is a time to rest and be with
the magnetics, but by nature males tend to
either get up and do something, or go to sleep.

So the male Initiate must train himself to
nest, to allow the magnetics that have been
created to spiral into his Ka and his body.

This is different from what occurs normally,
for in the male, orgasm is confined to the pelvic area, and in some cases it spreads. But
for the female Initiate, especially one who has
been able to relax into the experience, the
orgasm spreads through the entire body and
can continue in various levels of intensity for
several hours.

Some male Initiates might be concerned
that by changing themselves, by nesting,
they will become less masculine—but I can
assure you that nothing could be further from
the truth.

For the truth is, that as the male Initiate
nests in the magnetics, his Ka body becomes
stronger, and his sexual energy becomes more
potent. One of the tasks for the male Initiate
is to sensitize himself to new levels of feeling,
so that he can incorporate the magnetic fields
released through sex into his own body and Ka.

To clarify the term nesting, it does not mean
that the male's member remains inside the

female, necessarily. It does mean that the male remains close to the female—touching, stroking, being with the physical sensations and the emotions after orgasm. It is through the portal of nesting that the male Initiate is able to enter the feminine mysteries of creation.

Another aspect that the male Initiate needs to be aware of is what is called Adoration of the Beloved.

As the alchemy of the Sex Magic becomes stronger there are certain signs that occur. One of these is that the Beloved becomes adored or cherished.

This happens both for the male and female Initiate. When Adoration of the Beloved occurs from both partners, the alchemy and Sex Magic greatly intensifies, for the harmonics and magnetics created by such emotion are very beneficial to the magic.

Twenty-Three

I would like to speak to the term magic at this time.

The reason the term magic is used refers to the transformation of the individual human into a God. This is indeed magic. It is symbolized by the God Horus, part man, part hawk, and through the practices of alchemy, is raised to the status of the High God Horus, meaning that one has attained the most elevated states of consciousness.

So the Sex Magic of Isis is precisely a method for the elevation of consciousness, which is, in itself, magic—and this is done through the energies and ecstasy created through sex.

The other reason the term magic is used is that there are methods, once the Ka body is potentized, that one can use to affect one's reality in very direct ways in methods that seem magical. Take, for instance, the basic core practices of the Alchemies of Horus—the raising of the Black and Gold Serpents up the spine, the creation of the Chalice, the activation of the internal fire of RA, and the meeting of the Red and White Serpentine Drops—are all acts of magic, acts of intent and both personal and spiritual will. This is why it is referred to as magic.

Returning to the paradox facing the male Initiate, we find that his nature works against him to a certain extent in these practices, specifically the Sex Magic. For once a male Initiate's Ka is charged, he, by nature, wants to act, to do something. Yet if he can discipline himself, train himself to continue lying with his Beloved, he can nest himself in the rich magnetics created through their love, their sex, and strengthen the Ka to a greater extent.

Twenty-Four

There is another aspect facing the male Initiate in this process, and it has to do with what we in the temples refer to as Obstacles To Flight, but which in your language is best stated as "psychological issues." The term Obstacles To Flight refers to hindrances to the unfolding of one's Horus nature, the aspect specifically that can fly upward into elevated states of consciousness.

There are attitudes, beliefs and emotional habits that are counter-productive to flight, or the elevation to consciousness, which is what we refer to when we say Obstacles To Flight. It is here for the male Initiate that one of the most intricate passages, requiring great skill, occurs.

As a child, the male was carried by his mother in her womb and protected and nurtured by his mother in his infancy, until a point where he had autonomy and could act for himself. At this point the male child pushes the mother away, so to speak, in order to face the world.

It is at this juncture in his development that he may feel confined or limited by his mother, and a battle of wills can ensue. As a man, as a male Initiate, he may still carry these emotional habits within him. If this is the case, he will find it difficult to relax into the nesting of the magnetic fields, since at a psychological level, it is experienced as surrendering to the feminine.

If the male Initiate has issues with his mother of childhood, he may engage these consciously or unconsciously with his partner.

Twenty-Five   It is important for both Initiates undertaking the Sex Magic of Isis to realize that they are embarking on a long journey and that the process is essentially one of alchemy. The purpose of alchemy is to transform one substance into another. It does this by burning off the dross, or the negativity of a substance, so that the pure substance remains or is created.

In the process of the Sex Magic of Isis the substances transformed are literally the sexual fluids, hormones, neurotransmitters and other substances not yet discovered by your science. But it also involves a transformation of one's psychology.

By nature, the Sex Magic of Isis steps up the alchemical process. The heat gets turned up, so to speak, the dross becomes clear, that which needs to be purified comes painfully into focus.

If one does not understand that this is one of the byproducts of alchemy, one might be disturbed by the arising of difficult psychological material. But actually this is one of the results, for the internal pressure created through the intense alchemy generated through the Sex Magic of Isis causes the Ka body to extrude, or press out of itself all impurities and to clear itself of all Obstacles To Flight.

In those practicing alone, without a partner, the Alchemies of Horus also create internal pressure, extruding impurities, but the task is more difficult in that the energy required comes from one's own personal efforts, and there is not the benefit of reflection from another. However, it can be done.

Twenty-Six

This is the basic understanding required for the practice of the Sex Magic of Isis. In the previous pages I have revealed to you the secrets of the ages, one of the most closely guarded secrets of the Temples of Isis.

Understanding of these practices was reserved for the most advanced students.

Whether one practices the solitary path through the Alchemies of Horus or the path of Sacred Relationship through the Sex Magic of Isis, one is stepping upon the road to Godhood.

The central key in this journey is the strengthening of the Ka through ecstatic states of consciousness. Whether self-generated or created through the ecstasy of sex does not inherently matter; the Ka is nurtured and potentized by ecstatic states, regardless of their source.

On the contrary, shame is a poison to the Ka body, a toxic element that decreases its vitality and potency.

I, an Initiate of Isis, find it tragic that the Church has shamed women and men around their sexual natures and closed a door on one of the most direct paths to God-Realization. Whatever you do along this path, my advice is to free yourself of all shame.

Search out the catacombs of your own mind and heart, seek out the dark places in yourself where shame resides and remove it.

Find every opportunity to create ecstasy, for it strengthens you and potentizes the Ka.

May the obstacles to your flight be few and the blessings along your journey be many.

Twenty-Seven

I wish to turn my attention now to some loose threads concerning the practice of Alchemy and the Sex Magic of Isis.

For the male Initiate, it is essential to understand that it is the magnetic fields created first by the touching and stroking of the female Initiate, his beloved, that starts the cascade of magnetic fields, building an intensity to the point of orgasm.

It is important that the male Initiate train himself to be able to nest in the magnetic fields.

It is extremely important to both Initiates to

place their attention on the Ka body during the ecstatic states of consciousness that are generated by their lovemaking, for this strengthens and potentizes the Ka body, and this is essential for this type of alchemy as was practiced by I and Yeshua.

At the moment of physical orgasm, there is a tendency for the magnetic surge to move either up through the top of the head or down through the feet—but in either case, this magnetic field exits the body and dissipates. It is important during the moment of orgasm to contain the magnetic field or surge. Ideally the Initiate would place his awareness in the upper Throne or the upper brain centers. This would cause the surge of orgasm to rise up into the head, sending its energy into the brain itself and into the Ka body.

Twenty-Eight

There are times when the male Initiate may wish to hold back his seed. Within the Sex Magic of Isis male Initiates were taught a specific practice called Stopping the Lower Nile.

From the Initiatory knowledge of ancient Egypt, the Nile existed both externally and internally, the external Nile being the physical river and the internal Nile being the Djed and its flow through the seven seals or chakras. At the moment of physical orgasm, when a man ejaculates, the creative powers that have descended from the upper Nile into the lower Nile are released.

This semen carries great potential for creating magnetic fields in the form of new life or an alchemical reaction in the womb of the female Initiate, as we discussed earlier.

At times, however, a male Initiate may wish to hold his seed, primarily because, depending upon his vitality, ejaculation may actually decrease his energy, and it was for these times that the technique for Stopping the Lower Nile was developed.

The male places a finger over the prostate, just in front, so that at the moment of ejaculation the semen goes back instead of forward, and the magnetic fields of his sexual essence re-circulate through his body and his Ka. But even in these moments there are magnetic fields generated by his Ka which interact with those of the female Initiate and they can both nest within these interactions.

Twenty-Nine

And now I wish to address a relatively rare form of partnership but which sometimes occurred within the Initiates of Isis. You would call this same sex partners.

While the building of magnetic fields and the nesting in these fields and the arising of ecstatic states can be created through same sex partners, the interaction of semen and the womb does not occur, and so this aspect of the alchemy is not present.

However all other aspects of the Alchemy and the Sex Magic are relevant.

Finally, I wish to turn my attention to the term Initiate, for I have used this term extensively throughout this material. The term Initiate refers to one who has decided to live upward in consciousness, one who has decided to leave behind the mundane life and to enter into an adventure of consciousness.

Generally speaking, the crossing of the threshold from mundane to sacred life is marked by a ritual of Initiation. In the ancient practices a candidate would be Initiated by a Priest or Priestess, and this Priest or Priestess would have the power to confer upon that individual the relative power of the lineage to which they belong.

In certain types of transitions an external Initiator is needed or required.

However for the beginning phases it is possible for a person to Initiate themselves, for the true essence of Initiation means to mark a threshold, the crossing from mundane life into sacred life.

For those who feel drawn to practice the Alchemies of Horus and who wish to mark their commitment to living the sacred life, I offer this simple ritual. I give this instruction because there is such a scarcity of qualified persons to conduct Initiations into the ancient lineages of Egypt.

For this ritual one would need a candle and two glasses or cups.

One cup is filled with water and the other is empty. If you wish, you could add flowers and incense, making the ritual as aesthetically pleasing as you desire, but fundamentally Self-Initiation is an act of intention and personal and spiritual will.

The ritual is simply an external reflection of something that is occurring deep within oneself. And indeed, this internal choice can be made without the need for an external ritual at all, for the ritual without internal choice is worthless.

For this ritual you would light the candle and then speak these words...

"Spirit of all life, be my witness here. For the sake of my own elevation and the elevation of all life, I shall strive to be harmless to myself and all others."

Then holding the glass or container of water in the right hand, you would pour the water into the container or glass in the left hand, and by these words you would seal this action...

*"By the pouring of this water, I signify the
transfer of my sacred waters of life
From the mundane to the sacred. Spirit of all
life, by my witness here.
Amen. Amen. Amen."*

**Thirty-
One**

I wish to end my story with thoughts about
my beloved, Yeshua. As an Initiate of Isis, I
had been trained for the moment when I met
him. And from the moment our eyes met, I was
transported into other worlds.

I understood the teachings that had been
obscure. I understood the deepest secrets of
Isis, as she revealed them to me not through
the sacred writings, but through the living presence of my love for Yeshua.

As the Alchemy between us intensified, I
came to adore him and he me. It was a great
difficulty for him to part from me.

There were stirrings within him that longed
to be with me rather than to face the death
Initiation of Horus; yet as a master soul he
had come to lay a trail of light through the
dark realms of death. He did this for his own
sake and for the sake of all mankind.

There are many who misunderstand what he
did and why he did it.

There are those who believe that all they need to do is believe in him and no effort on their part is required. This was never Yeshua's belief or understanding. He came as a *shower of light*, a beacon of love at a time when the world was still in the shadow of a jealous god. Yeshua, as a master soul, demonstrated immense courage and strength, to teach love at such a time.

It was odd for me, being both the Initiate and the woman in love, for I understood that my task was to assist him to build his Ka, in order that he could face the realms of death with greater power.

As an Initiate, I understood my task; and to some extent I understood what Yeshua's vision was. But as the woman in love, I was swept away by my feelings for my Beloved.

And so I stand in time, looking back, as it were, upon our life together; and it is a bitter-sweet taste.

The sweetness of Yeshua's presence will, for always, fill and sustain me, yet the bitterness of our parting will always be there as well.

In my last days upon this earth, Yeshua came to me again in his Ka body, as he had done for so many years. He was with me as I took my last breath and took my Ka through the realms of death, through the trail of light that he had laid through the power of his intention, and took me into what you would call heaven, but is a place in the soul.

I rest in this place with his presence through all time and space.

I was content to remain here with his essence that I carry in my heart and mind, but Isis, herself, came to me and said that now I must tell my story...that the lies of the last two thousand years must come to an end...that the feminine is returning in balance to the male...that the Cosmic Mother is revealing herself at the beginning of the ending of time.

And so it is that I reveal one of the lost secrets of the ages—that Spirit, the male principle, in order to return to itself through it's journey into Matter, requires the assistance of the feminine principle, the Intelligence of Matter itself.

But from the solar light-filled perspective of the masculine principle, the feminine principle carries within her a dark, moist and dangerous abyss. The solar principle feels threatened by the darkness of the lunar aspect. But it is in the joining of the Sun and the Moon, the joining of the masculine and feminine principles, in equilibrium, in energetic balance, that true illumination is attained.

When Yeshua prepared himself with me for his ordeal before the Garden at Gethsemane, I was the embodiment of Isis. I was she. There was no difference between her and myself. I had been trained in the practices that would ensure this. And so, Yeshua as the Sun, the solar principle manifest in the realms of matter, joined with me, the Moon; and he was joined with Isis herself and his elevation could not have occurred without her. She is the Cosmic Mother. Other cultures call her by other names, but she is the same.

To the extent that the male Initiate is able to nest into the magnetic fields with his Beloved and draw into himself the vibrational energies of these magnetics—to this extent he is making contact with Isis herself, the Cosmic Mother, the Creatrix of all time and space.

To the extent that the female Initiate is able to surrender to the magnetics and the letting go into her own nature, she becomes Isis herself. When these two events occur at the cosmological level, the male Initiate becomes energetically attuned to Osiris and the female Initiate becomes attuned to Isis, and out of the co-mingling of their magnetic fields, Horus is born—except that Horus in this case does not take form as a child. Horus takes form and Horus takes flight within the Ka bodies of the Initiates themselves. They are raised up in a very real manner. They can take flight within the celestial realms of their own being.

The truth is that Osiris cannot rise without Isis, nor Isis without Osiris. The High God Horus is birthed from the magnetics of their joining.

The male Initiate, being electric by nature, thinks that he can make it happen by himself, but he cannot.

Isis waits for him to recognize this, but he does not.

For centuries she has waited, and now we are at the beginning of the ending of time, and the pressure is strong. This is one of the reasons I have come forward.

To those male Initiates able to find the pathways in themselves to surrender to the Isis powers carried within the natures of their Beloved, or carried within their own natures if practicing the solitary path, know that you do this not just for yourselves, but for all mankind.

When one undertakes the Sex Magic of Isis, it is not possible to do this just for oneself, for the practices quickly elevate the Initiate into the level of the living myth, for in its highest expressions, as we have indicated before, the male Initiate becomes Osiris himself, and the female Initiate becomes Isis...and the Horus is birthed out of their magnetics.

For those engaged in the solitary practice of alchemy, this is accomplished through the magnetics of the Lunar and Solar Circuits. As the

basic practice shared earlier is mastered, the
Black Serpent of the Moon, holding the essence
of the Void, quivers and shakes within the
Ka body of the Initiate, much like the female
Initiate quivers and shakes within the arms of
the male when practicing the Sex Magic.

Within the Initiate practicing the solitary
way the Gold Serpent of the Sun meets the
Black Serpent of the Moon in the center of the
head, and the magnetic fields created by their
co-mingling and the energetic reactions created
by their intersections through the chakras or
seals, creates the Horus.

So whether it is done alone or with another
does not intrinsically matter, but what must
occur in both is the same. The Sun and
the Moon must be in balance, and then the
Illumination, what we call Horus, occurs.

Thirty-Three

I have offered you my story and the teachings I have been given in deepest hopes that
you will find a passage into your own great-
ness, for that is what this world needs now
more than ever.

It is my hope that you will be uplifted by my
insights, and that you will be inspired, as was I,
by the magnificent being you call Yeshua, but
that I call my Beloved.

To those who have the courage to practice the Alchemies of Horus, and for those who choose to live in Sacred Relationship with themselves or with another, I give my blessing.

May the blessings of the Cosmic Mother follow you upon your journey to yourself. May the path between the Sun and the Moon be revealed.

Spirit of all life, bear witness. Amen.

—Mary Magdalen

Training Protocols
in the
Alchemies of Horus

This section is for those who wish to explore a basic practice within the Alchemies of Horus. Magdalen gave an advanced form of the individual practice in the *Manuscript*, but this may be too complex for many readers. I therefore asked her if she might offer a simpler form of preparatory exercise, and this is the result.

The *Manuscript* was not meant as a teaching manual, but to convey a message. And so the protocols below serve as the teaching function. They will give you the basic experience needed to enter into the advanced *Practice of the Two Serpents,* mentioned in the *Manuscript.*

According to the Magdalen, the Alchemies of Horus were the foundation for both those on the solitary path and for those in partnership. The main difference between these two paths is that the person on the solitary path must generate the extra energy and ecstasies from his or her own efforts. Those in sacred Tantric relationship acquire the needed energy and ecstasies spontaneously from the sex act.

The *djed* or sacred pathway of the chakras begins at the base of the spine and goes up through the spine and into the head. There is a secondary djed pathway that moves from the perineum directly up to the crown called the *Central Column* or *Central Pillar.* In some esoteric schools it is referred to as the *pranic tube.* The training exercises, below, use both of these pathways.

The fundamental alchemical task in relation to the djed is to accumulate enough energy so that it can be sent up through the pathway and into the head centers.

The training exercises below generate the needed energy from the power of the breath. Their purpose is to familiarize you with the feeling, the physical sensation, if you will, of subtle energy moving up the djed.

The first section of the training protocol consists of three different exercises. The first one deals with the secondary djed (the Central Column or Pillar) that runs directly from the perineum up to the crown. The second exercise deals with the primary djed that runs up the spine. And the third exercise works with the energy after it is brought up into the head.

The second section of the training protocol familiarizes you with how to transform the energy moving through the djed into a serpent-like form. And finally, the last exercise familiarizes you with activating the pathway of the Two Serpents by experiencing energy moving simultaneously through both the lunar and solar pathways.

Cautions to the Reader:

Due to the fact that these exercises bring energy into the brain and upper head centers, they are con-traindicated for some individuals. If you have suffered a head injury or experienced a stroke, speak with your physician before proceeding. Those who suffer from seizures such as epilepsy should also seek the advice of their physicians before undertaking these training meditations. Finally, for those who are manic-depressive, these exercises are contraindicated, especially during manic phases. For all other persons, the meditations are quite harmless and very beneficial. If you experience headaches at any time during the meditations, stop and rest.

First Section

The First Exercise

Sit comfortably and close your eyes. Place the focus of your attention, in other words, the *alchemical container of your awareness*, on your pelvic floor. This is the area of your body at the lowest part of your abdomen in the cradle of your pelvis. Find a rhythm that is pleasurable for you and breathe deeply (yet comfortably) drawing the breath into your belly. As you inhale, let the lower abdomen expand, and as you exhale pull in the lower abdomen. This form of breathing is called abdominal breathing and may feel odd to you at first. After awhile, however, it will feel natural and comfortable. Throughout all of these exercises it is very important that all breaths be gentle and comfortable. Nothing should ever be forced in these practices.

As you inhale, imagine the energy of your breath reaching down into every nook and cranny of your pelvis. The reason for this is that you are causing *sekhem* to stir, and sekhem, or your life-force, is cradled in the pelvic area. As you exhale, keep your focus in the pelvis. This will cause the energy of sekhem to build or intensify in the pelvic area. Continue this for a couple of minutes or so.

Then imagine a subtle energy pathway or channel that runs from your perineum up to the top of your head (the crown). The perineum is located at the lowest point of your torso, midway between your genitals and the anus. Next, there is a slight but significant shifting of your attention.

As you inhale keep your focus in the pelvis as before. But when you exhale, shift your attention, the alchemical container of your awareness, into the channel. This will cause the energy of sekhem to enter the channel and begin to move upward. As you continue to exhale, move your attention all the way up the channel and into your head. Then repeat the breathing pattern all over again. In other words, each time you inhale, shift your attention to the pelvis, and hold it there throughout the entire inhale. As you exhale, shift your attention to the channel, and begin to move your focus up the channel towards the head. Repeat as many times as needed to clearly sense a movement of energy up the secondary djed and into the head.

These exercises are built upon each other so it is important to master each one before proceeding to the next. Make sure that you feel a definite movement of subtle energy up the secondary djed and into the head. If you don't have a clear sense of this, repeat the exercise over and over again until you do.

A note about uncomfortable physical sensations:

Occasionally a person might experience tension or headache from these exercises. This may occur if there is habitual tension in the muscles of the jaw, face, and/ or neck since this type of muscle tension tends to constrict the movement of sekhem or life-force as it moves up into the head. If you experience discomfort at any time during these exercises, you should stop, put them aside and return to them later.

If you find that this type of tension arises whenever you do the exercises you might try yawning since yawning helps to lessen muscle tension in the face, jaws, and shoulders. Simply yawn as you inhale and exhale. It can be quite effective and besides that, it's fun.

If tension persists, I suggest you shift your attention to the area of tension and imagine that the tension dissolves and leaves with each exhale. Try it for a few minutes. It often dissolves this type of muscular tension quite nicely.

The Second Exercise

In this exercise you basically do the same thing you did in the first, except that the movement of sekhem is up the spine (or the primary djed).

Sit comfortably and close your eyes. Place the focus of your attention, in other words, the alchemical contain-er of your awareness, on your pelvic floor. Find a rhythm that is pleasurable for you and breathe deeply (though comfortably) drawing the breath into your belly. As you inhale, let the lower abdomen expand, and as you exhale pull in the lower abdomen.

As you inhale, imagine the energy of your breath reaching down into every nook and cranny of your pel-vis. The reason for this is that you are, as in the first exercise, causing sekhem to stir and sekhem, or your life-force, is cradled in the pelvic area. As you exhale, keep your focus in the pelvis. This will cause the ener-gy of sekhem to build or intensify in the pelvic area. Continue this for a couple of minutes or so.

Then your attention changes somewhat. On the inhales, attention is still in the pelvis, but on the exhales shift your attention into the spine (the djed), and move your attention up the spine from the base to the top of your head with each exhale.

Continue this for a few minutes until you sense a clear sensation of energy moving up the spine and to the top of the head.

After you clearly sense this flow of subtle energy, proceed on to the next exercise. If you do not sense this flow of energy then repeat the exercise until you do.

The Third Exercise

In this exercise, you follow the same procedure as you did in exercise number two with one difference. When you exhale and the energy of sekhem or life-force moves up the spine, you bring it into the center of the head instead of to the top. As the energy is brought into the center of the head you allow it to circulate through the brain sensing the movement of energy.

Sit comfortably and close your eyes. Place the focus of your attention, in other words, the alchemical container of your awareness, on your pelvic floor. Find a rhythm that is pleasurable for you and breathe deeply (though comfortably) drawing the breath into your belly. As you inhale, let the lower abdomen expand, and as you exhale pull in the lower abdomen.

As you inhale, imagine the energy of your breath reaching down into every nook and cranny of your pelvis. The reason for this is that you are, as in the first exercise, causing sekhem to stir, and sekhem, or your life-force, is cradled in the pelvic area. As you exhale, keep your focus in the pelvis. This will cause the energy of sekhem to build or intensify in the pelvic area. Continue this for a couple of minutes or so.

After a few minutes of building the energy in the pelvis, you are ready for the next phase. On the inhales, attention is still in the pelvis, but on the exhales shift your attention into the spine (the djed), and move your attention up the spine from the base to the center of your head with each exhale. The energy of sekhem will follow the circuit of your attention and flow upwards into the central area of the brain. Then pause for a moment and sense the flow of energy as it moves on its own through different areas of the brain.

Continue this for a few minutes until you sense a clear sensation of energy moving up the spine and into the center of the brain.

Second Section

First Exercise: Rising of the Single Serpent

In this exercise, you repeat what you did in the last exercise of the previous section. However, instead of taking the energy into the center of your head, you bring the energy up and over the two hemispheres just under the top of the skull. This movement of the energy is cobra-like, in that the tail of the serpent extends down the full length of the spine to the base while the hood of the cobra is extended over the two hemispheres of the brain. Holding the energy in the image of a cobra in this way causes a distinct type of brain stimulation and is a precursor for the *uraeus*.

Sit comfortably and close your eyes. Place the focus of your attention, in other words, the alchemical container of your awareness, on your pelvic floor. Find a rhythm that is pleasurable for you and breathe deeply (though comfortably) drawing the breath into your belly. As you inhale, let the lower abdomen expand, and as you exhale pull in the lower abdomen.

As you inhale, imagine the energy of your breath reaching down into every nook and cranny of your pelvis. The reason for this is that you are causing sekhem to stir and sekhem, or your life-force, is cradled in the pelvic area. As you exhale, keep your focus in the pelvis. This will cause the energy of sekhem to build or intensify in the pelvic area. Continue this for a couple of minutes or so.

After a few minutes of building the energy in the pelvis, you are ready for the next phase. On the inhales attention is still in the pelvis, but on the exhales shift your attention into the spine (the djed), and move your attention up the spine from the base to a space above the two hemispheres of the brain and directly under the top of the skull.

As you sense this space above the brain, allow yourself to feel the movement of the energy. Imagine the form of this energy as a cobra with its hood extended over the brain itself. Then repeat the procedure until you have a clear sense of the serpent-like form of this energy over the brain.

The Second Exercise: The Two Serpents

In this exercise, it is assumed that you have successfully experienced the single serpent in the previous exercise. If you haven't clearly experienced the single serpent, return to the previous exercises before continuing.

In the *Manuscript*, you will find a description of the Black and Gold Serpents. The Black Serpent rises through the lunar pathway on the left side of the djed and is connected with the Darkness of the Void or the creatrix of all creation. The Gold Serpent rises through the solar pathway on the right side of the djed and is connected with light. In a sense the Two Serpents are alchemically opposites and when you bring two opposites together within an alchemical container there is the possibility of immense energy.

In this preliminary training you will be causing the energy of sekhem to split into two different streams of energy. As the life-force rises up the djed it takes two different yet parallel paths. The Black Serpent rises from the left side at the base of the djed while the Gold Serpent rises from the right side of the djed, also from the base. However, as they continue to rise up the djed toward the head, they cross over each other as they enter the chakras.

Thus the Gold Serpent crosses over to the left side of the djed as it enters the sexual chakra and the Black crosses over to the right. As they climb further up the djed, the Gold Serpent crosses back over to the right side as it enters the solar plexus and the Black Serpent crosses back over to the left.

Next, the Gold Serpent crosses to the left side as it enters the heart and the Black crosses over to the right

side. As they enter the throat chakra, the Gold Serpent
returns to the right side of the djed and the Black
Serpent returns to the left side.

Finally, they meet at the center of the head with the
Gold Serpent hovering on the right side while the Black
Serpent hovers on the left side. Both of them face each
other with the pineal gland sitting between them.

The *Manuscript* gives further instruction on how to
do the practice. The purpose of this exercise, however,
is just to familiarize you with the phenomenon of raising
both serpents up the djed and into the head.

To do the exercise, sit comfortably and close your
eyes. Place the focus of your attention, in other words,
the alchemical container of your awareness, on your pelvic floor. Find a rhythm that is pleasurable for you and
breathe deeply (though comfortably) drawing the breath
into your belly. As you inhale, let the lower abdomen
expand, and as you exhale pull in the lower abdomen.

As you inhale, imagine the energy of your breath
reaching down into every nook and cranny of your pelvis.
The reason for this is that you are causing sekhem to stir,
and sekhem, or your life-force, is cradled in the pelvic
area. As you exhale, keep your focus in the pelvis. This
will cause the energy of sekhem to build or intensify in the
pelvic area. Continue this for a couple of minutes or so.

After a few minutes of building the energy in the pelvis, you are ready for the next phase. On the inhales,
attention is still in the pelvis but on the exhales shift your
attention into the base of the djed. Through the power of
intention (will) imagine the Two Serpents being charged
with the energy of the breath. As you continue to exhale,
send the energy up through the two pathways of the serpents. Imagine them as clearly in your mind as possible
sensing them crossing each other at each of the chakras
and finally ending in the center of the head.

Continue the practice until you have a clear sense
of the two serpent-like energies running up the spine
and into the head. Allow yourself to sense the movement

of life-force up these two pathways as the serpents "writhe" in response to your breath. Sense the subtle energies that are generated within the brain as a result of this practice.

The Pathway of the Two Serpents

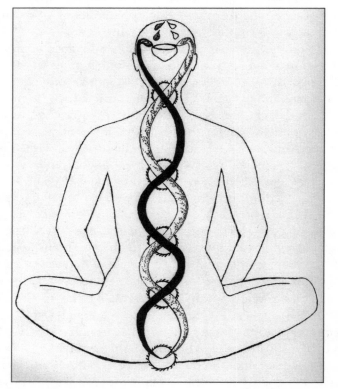

Left Side:
Black Lunar Serpent
Red Serpentine Drops

Right Side:
Gold Solar Serpent
White Serpentine Drops

Internal Alchemy

Tom Kenyon

Introduction
to the Fundamentals of
Internal Alchemy

Without an understanding of the alchemical terms used in the Manuscript, *it will be rather difficult to understand its essential concepts. In addition, some of the central ideas at the heart of internal alchemy may not be familiar to many readers. For this reason, I have included a brief overview of internal alchemy in general and a larger overview of Egyptian alchemy in particular. It is my hope that these introductory sections will provide the reader with a deeper understanding and appreciation of the* Manuscript.

—A Personal Note from Tom

I decided to make tea this morning. Rumbling through the cupboard, half-awake, I found a small kettle hiding in the corner. I poured some water in and sat it on the stove. Lighting the burner, I went off to do other things, like cleaning the counter from last night's dinner.

Soon I heard the familiar rumbling of boiling water. Sure enough, small clouds of hot mist were hovering over the stove. I turned off the gas and poured the hot water into an empty cup. The water hissed as it slid over the hot metal surface of the pot into the waiting container. I plopped in a tea bag and finished cleaning the counter. While attending to the task at hand, invisibly, imperceptibly, the hot water found its way into the tea leaves. What had been just a cup of hot water was now a cup of tea.

What, you may ask, does making tea have to do with alchemy? Plenty.

The art of alchemy is simply changing one form into another. Most people think of alchemy as a medieval obsession for changing lead into gold. And while this is one form of alchemy, anything that causes a change in form is alchemy as well. Turning water into steam is alchemy. Changing a dry tea bag into tea is also alchemy.

While external alchemy, like changing lead into gold, is a fascinating enterprise, I am more intrigued by internal alchemy, like the type discussed by Magdalen in the *Manuscript*. But whether one is attempting to create enhanced abilities in oneself or to brew a cup of tea, some of the principles are the same.

All successful alchemies must have three elements: 1) a substance to be transformed; 2) a container to hold the alchemical reaction; and 3) energy. Had I, for instance, stumbled into the kitchen this morning and poured water onto the burner instead of into a kettle, I would not have created alchemy. I would have created a mess.

In external alchemies, like making tea or nuclear fission (yes, atomic power is alchemy as well), the containers are pretty obvious. Different containers are required for different tasks. A teacup, for instance, will do quite well for making tea, but is a very poor container for a nuclear reactor. For that you will need massive amounts of concrete, lead, and a tremendous quantity of water.

With internal alchemies, the containers are more abstract, as are the goals. The purpose of internal alchemy is to change consciousness, to accelerate one's own personal evolution. I do not, by the way, mean evolution in the usual sense. I doubt that anyone will physically sprout wings and fly as a result of practicing internal alchemy. However, the changes wrought by such practice can be so profound that one feels as if one is flying above life and viewing it from a greatly expanded perspective. This is why many of the alchemical symbols from around the world involve flying beings—like the garudas of Balinese Hinduism, the dragons of Taoism, or Horus, the hawk-headed god of Egyptian alchemy, to name a few.

In all systems of internal alchemy, the container for the alchemical reaction is awareness itself—in other words, mental focus. As you read these words, you are holding them in the container of your awareness, and they are, hopefully, making sense to you. But if your awareness were to wander, say to a conversation in the next room, the container would shift and my words would not register. Even though you might be going through the motion of reading, the words would not be impacting you because they were *outside* the container of your awareness.

There is a basic concept in all forms of internal alchemy which can be stated quite simply: *energy follows awareness*. In the reading example above, for instance, the energy of your attention follows where you put your awareness. If you pay attention to what you are reading, the words will make an impression in your mind. If, however, you pay attention to that conversation we were talking about, the words of this book won't impress your mind, but the words in the conversation will.

The alchemical container of inner alchemy is awareness itself.

The substances transformed through the processes of inner alchemy vary according to the stream or lineage. Some of these substances include such things as physical neurotransmitters, hormones, saliva, and sexual fluids. There are also, however, whole classes of *subtle substances* that include such ephemeral things as *chi* in the Taoist stream, *prana* in the Yogic stream, the *winds (lhung)* in the Tibetan stream, and *neters* in the Egyptian.

It is this class of subtle substances that inner alchemy is most concerned with. And for the average person this is one of the most difficult concepts to understand. The reason, I think, has to do with our conditioning to the Newtonian world of everyday reality. We are not trained, generally speaking, to attend to the subtle energies behind the shadow play of physical reality. Let me give you an example of what I am talking about.

Remember that cup of tea I made this morning? Well, I never finished it, and it now sits cold on the counter. I got caught up in other things and forgot about it. For some reason, I didn't rinse out the old cup, but instead got a clean one from the cabinet. I put it next to the old one, filled it with hot water and plopped in another tea bag. There were small billows of steam rising from the new cup of tea, but nothing was rising from the old cup except the smell of cold tea. How odd, I thought. I picked up both cups of tea, one cold and one hot. I felt like Goldilocks and the three bears. This one's too cold. This one's too hot. I put down the hot one to let it cool off so that it might get to be "just right."

I was in the two side-by-side worlds of Newtonian and quantum reality. I could hold the tea cups in my hands. One was cold and one was hot. But the reason for this difference was from a realm much subtler than the two teacups or the watery tea they contained. It had to do with the individual molecules of water. Although I could not see it, the molecules in the hot water were running about helter-skelter like a mob at a shopping mall, bumping into each other and in the process heating up things. In fact, when I had brought the water to a boil on the stove, they were at their most riotous, a molecular Mardi Gras of extreme proportions.

The cold cup of tea, on the other hand, held a group of lethargic molecules. The energy that had heated them up had long ago passed out of the cup in the form of radiant heat, and the once riotous molecules were now slow like dowagers in a nursing home. The only difference between the party animals in the hot cup of tea and the sleepy ones in the cold cup was energy.

I could not, with my physical senses, see the difference between the molecules of water, since they were too small for me to see. All I could sense were the after-effects of their energy or lack of it, namely heat or cold. In point of fact, that is all any of us experience in the physical world: the after-effects of something happening in the subtle or quantum world. The task of the alchemist is to become aware of and sensitive to the subtle realms that escape most people. The reason for this is that the subtle realm or quantum world holds the best types of substances for alchemical transformation. For the most part, the substances in the Newtonian or dense physical world are too gross, too dense to be transformed through the power of alchemical attention. But the subtle realm, the quantum world, is very receptive to the focus of such attention.

In my example of the two teacups, the common element was energy or lack of it. In this case, the energy was applied from an external source. In most internal alchemies, however, the source of energy is usually the energy of consciousness itself. What do I mean by this?

Become aware of one of your hands for a moment. Just shift your attention to it. Be aware of its position, its weight, and the physical sensations in the hand. After a moment of this become aware of your other hand. Which hand has more sensation in it? In other words, which one has more *energy?*

For most people, the hand that has been focused on will have more sensation. This is because energy follows awareness. The alchemical container of awareness was focused on a particular hand and this resulted in an increase of perceived energy in the hand. The neurological reasons for this are quite complex, but the practice of holding attention is quite simple. We do it everyday.

Sometimes the energy of the breath is used to power an alchemical reaction. At times, an external energy source might be used, such as the sun or a ceremonial fire. In some rare forms of alchemy, other elements such as water or air are used.

In the use of external energies to *drive* an alchemical reaction, the alchemist might focus on a flame while holding (within the container of awareness) the substance to be transformed. Or the energy of the sun might be used to power an internal alchemical reaction in the same way.

To give you an example, I am writing this part of the book in the month of August on the island of Paros in the Cyclades of Greece. Every afternoon around six, when the sun is not blazing hot, I sit on the deck for about an hour and do an alchemical practice within the ancient Egyptian stream.

To explain how I do this practice, I need to define a term from Egyptian alchemy: the Ka. The Ka body is sometimes called the *etheric double* or *spiritual twin*. It is the same shape and size as the physical body (the khat), but it is made of energy and has very little mass (or density). As I hold this subtle body in the container of my awareness, I sense the sun. And I draw the subtle energies available to me through the sunlight into my Ka. Some of these energies from the sun have been scientifically documented such as ultraviolet radiation and the primary colors of full-spectrum light. Studies have shown that full-spectrum light has a very positive effect on health. But there are whole classes of more subtle energies that science has not yet verified. These extremely subtle energies are presumably too subtle for our current methods of measurement.

Taoists might refer to this type of subtle energy as *solarized yang chi*. A yogi might refer to it as the *prana of sureya* (the sun). And an alchemist within the Egyptian stream might simply say that it is the *neter of RA* (the power of the sun god).

But whatever you call it, there is another type of subtle energy in sunlight. In my practice of this technique, I have discovered what I call the *armchair method*. I used to use an elaborate system of standing movements to draw the sun's energy into my Ka. I still sometimes do this when I am feeling particularly energetic. But I have also found that the method works just as well if I am sitting on my butt.

In this case, at around six in the afternoon I sit in a canvas lounge chair provided by our benevolent landlord, Stephanos. I take off my shirt and lean back. Holding my Ka body in the container of my awareness... I simply become aware of my Ka, or you might say I imagine it, as a body of luminous light. Then I breathe in a relaxed manner and on the inhales I draw the subtle energy of the sun into my Ka.

Sometimes I draw the energy in through my navel and circulate it through the Ka. At other times I draw the energy of the sun into my solar plexus, which is, from the viewpoint of Egyptian alchemy, an aspect of RA. As I charge this miniature sun within my Ka, the excess energy spontaneously flows outward into my body. Sometimes I prefer to imagine my Ka as some kind of magnet (which it is), and draw the energies from the sun directly into the entire Ka at once.

While this method may seem odd or lackadaisical, it has all three elements of substance, container, and awareness, and so it is, in fact, a form of alchemy. As I focus on my Ka, I am holding it in the alchemical container of my awareness. The substance to be transformed is the Ka itself. In this case I am engaging something called an *energy building practice*. Why I would do such a thing will become clear in the next section when I talk about Egyptian Alchemy.

So there we have it, two of the essential elements: a substance to be transformed (my Ka) and a container to hold the alchemical reaction (my own awareness). The third element, energy, is of course provided by the sun itself (RA). When I do this practice correctly (i.e., hold all three elements together), there is a tremendous increase of energy and vibration within my Ka body. At times, however, my mind will wander into thoughts or fantasies, and at these moments the building of energy in the Ka decreases. If I don't bring my mind back to an awareness of the Ka, the building of energy will completely stop. This is, of course, because I have lost the container for the reaction when my mind wanders. To use our tea analogy, whenever my mind wanders, it's like taking the kettle off the stove.

The art, if you will, of internal alchemy is to hold all three elements of substance, energy, and container together long enough for an alchemical reaction to occur. And the discipline required of an alchemist to accomplish such a feat can be considerable.

All alchemists, regardless of their lineage, must attend to these three elements: container, substance, and energy. Each stream offers its own particular ways to strengthen the alchemical container. And by practicing the methods for strengthening the container of awareness, the alchemist can hold together ever-increasingly intense alchemical reactions.

The alchemical practitioner must also become keenly sensitive to the subtleties of substance. As awareness becomes refined, the alchemist is able to distinguish the most subtle characteristics of energetic substances. And a sense begins to unfold of how best to use these substances in an alchemical reaction and to what end. These substances range from actual physical materials such as saliva, sexual fluids, etc., to very subtle substances that are purely in the quantum realm of existence. As I mentioned earlier, it is these quantum substances that are most easily transmuted during the process of inner alchemy.

Finally, the alchemist must collect energy, since it is needed to drive alchemical reactions. There is a virtually unlimited field of possible energy sources for such inner work, and each alchemical tradition or stream offers its own suggestions on how to collect these types of energy. Indeed, the various streams of internal alchemy throughout the world offer a wide variety of clever, ingenious and, sometimes remarkable methods for the cultivation of energy.

In the *Manuscript*, Magdalen states that her task, as an Initiate, was to assist Yeshua in the building of his subtle body (the Ka) through specific *energy-building practices*. This was accomplished, according to the Magdalen, through the masterful use of sexual energy. As an Initiate of Isis, she was using methods from one of the oldest alchemical streams on the planet, and it is to this that we now turn our attention.

Egyptian Alchemy

According to the alchemists of ancient Egypt, we possess two bodies. The first, called the khat, is our physical body of flesh and blood. It is the body we normally identify with, the body we eat and drink with. The body that lives and dies.

The second body is called the Ka, and is sometimes referred to as the etheric double or spiritual twin. It is a duplicate of the physical body (khat) but is made of pure energy, not flesh and blood. This Ka body interpenetrates the khat (physical body) and there is no part of the khat or physical body that is not enclosed by the Ka.

Transformation of the Ka body is a fundamental focus of Egyptian alchemy. But before we discuss how this is done, I think it would be good to take a look at these two bodies (the Ka and the khat) from the standpoint of physics. I believe this modern context will give us a foundation to better understand the strange world of the Ka body and its non-ordinary potentials.

Quantum Physics

We can describe the khat (the dense physical body) quite well in terms of Newtonian physics. It obeys, for instance, the laws of gravity. And you can predict with a good deal of certainty where it will be physically, if you know the direction it is heading and the speed at which it is moving.

Not so with the Ka. The Ka body is outside the realms of Newtonian physics, and is best described using the laws of quantum physics. And what, you might ask, determines if something is bound by Newtonian laws or the laws of quantum mechanics? Size.

Objects larger than one thousandth of an inch obey the laws of Newtonian mechanics. This is because they have enough mass (i.e., density or weight) to have gravitational fields.

However, objects less than one thousandth of an inch follow a different drummer. This is because their density or mass is too small to create a gravitational field of any consequence. The Ka *body* exists within this realm (the quantum world) since the Ka is primarily light/energy and has very little mass.

The quantum world that the Ka body dwells in is very strange indeed. So is the fact that you and I live in both the Newtonian and quantum universes simultaneously. Our bodies are squarely in the Newtonian world. If we jump off a cliff, for instance, we will fall until we hit the ground, victims of gravity. (Unless of course, we are bungee jumping, in which case, an equal and opposite force pulls us back.)

But if we enter the atomic and subatomic levels of our bodies, we are in a different world altogether. The minuscule particles that comprise our bodies are not bound by the laws of Newtonian physics. They are, instead, bound by quantum mechanics.

The quantum world is very bizarre by our standards. Perhaps one way to describe this is to discuss experiments with light. Now, light can take two very different forms, with very different properties. It can, for instance, take the form of particles (photons), or it can take the form of waves.

As absurd as it sounds, if a researcher is looking for light in the form of waves, that is how light will present itself in the experiment. If, however, the researcher is looking for light in the form of particles, that is what he or she will see. This early discovery in quantum physics eventually became formalized as Bell's Theorem which states that at the quantum level, there is no objective observer, since the intention of the experimenter affects the outcome.

Somehow the *intention* of the researcher mysteriously affects the behavior of subatomic particles. How this happens has not yet been explained by science, but it is generally accepted that Bell's Theorem is true.

Physicists are reluctant to ascribe Bell's Theorem to phenomena outside the minuscule world of subatomic particles. The reason for this is, of course, because everyday objects, like billiard balls and rockets, are too large to be affected by intention. Intention is known to have an effect at the quantum level, but not so much in the Newtonian world.

But there is a weird place where the quantum world and the Newtonian world meet, and it is, of all places, inside our minds.

Tucked away inside our brains are teeny tiny gaps between nerve cells. These spaces between neurons are called synapses, and the average distance of these gaps: you may have already guessed it, is approximately one thousandth of an inch, the entry point into the strange world of quantum events.

A nerve impulse has to travel the length of a neuron and jump across the tiny synaptic gap if it is to get to the next neuron. Nerve impulses are much like relay races in which they run the length of a neuron and jump a hurdle. What actually jumps the hurdle is a little molecule called a neurotransmitter.

At any one moment, there are thousands upon thousands of these neurotransmitters jumping hurdles. And each moment is a *quantum event* since these molecules are approximately less than one thousandth of an inch. This is one reason why our thoughts can be so novel and unpredictable. Some of the neurotransmitters jumping the synaptic hurdle "make it" while others do not. Those that make the leap create a response within the next nerve cell. If these hurdles take place in the thinking part of the brain (neocortex) then we will have the experience of thought.

The concept of intention is crucial to both quantum physics and internal alchemy. Indeed, we will find that it is through the agency of both mental attention and personal will (intention) that the alchemist is able to affect specific quantum events within his or her body/mind.

We will see this very clearly later on. But for the moment, let me just say that internal alchemies, such as the Egyptian system, are primarily methods to alter certain aspects of the quantum universe. The Ka body is, itself, in the quantum realm and as such is easily affected by the *intentionality* of the alchemist.

There are other oddities in the quantum world. You can't, for instance, predict things. In the Newtonian world, if you throw something, you can predict where it will land, but not so in the quantum. Here there are only probabilities, possibilities. Objects flying around in the quantum world might land where you'd expect them to, or they might just spin around in circles or dissolve into light. The possibilities are virtually endless.

There are other strangenesses tucked away in the quantum realm. A very bizarre phenomenon develops when two particles meet in the quantum world. Now get this: after their chance meeting, the two particles spin off into space, each of them going along its merry way. But if one of them changes the direction of its spin, the other one instantaneously changes the direction of its spin as well. There is simply no current plausible explanation for this weird behavior. And although we need not concern ourselves with such shenanigans in the Newtonian world, they are part and parcel of the quantum.

I already mentioned how our thoughts exist within the weird twilight zone of quantum reality. What I mean by this is that the neurological events responsible for thought (i.e., the jumping of neurotransmitters across the synaptic gap) are clearly in the quantum world. And it is this strange quirk in our neurology that affords us the possibility of affecting quantum events within our own bodies and minds.

So what do I mean by this statement? Am I implying that you and I can have an effect on our own physiology through mere mental attention? Yes, I am, and this is one of the reasons internal alchemies are so effective.

Our bodies and minds are intimately connected. They are, in a very real way, two sides of the same coin, and research verifying the interconnectedness of body and mind is flooding scientific journals all over the world.

A relatively new field in medicine is an area called psychoneuroimmunology. It's a big word, but it basically means how our thoughts and emotions affect our physiology and specifically our immune systems.

I could quote numerous studies in this regard, but I think a story might serve our purposes more effectively. Although the situation involved pain management and not internal alchemy, some of the principles are the same.

Several years ago, a client was referred to me for the treatment of immense physical pain. She was in the advanced stages of cancer, and it had metastasized into her spine. She was, in her own words, in constant and unrelenting pain.

As Joan (I have changed her name) described her situation, I asked her to rate her current level of pain and discomfort, ten being the worst she had experienced and zero being the least. She self-assessed her pain level at around eight.

I then asked her to describe the most relaxing and refreshing experience she had ever had. She went into a long detailed account of her visit to Sedona, Arizona, and how she loved the red rocks and canyons of the area.

Reaching over to a stereo that I had in my office, I played some music that had been specifically written to lower brain wave activity into the more relaxed states of increased alpha activity. I then asked her to imagine being in Sedona again. I asked her to make it as vividly real as possible, seeing it, hearing the sounds, sensing the physical sensations, perhaps even smelling the aromas.

Her face muscles, which had been quite taut, relaxed a bit as she recalled the scene. I then suggested she find a place that she found particularly beautiful and soothing. She chose a large boulder overlooking a canyon. I then suggested that this boulder had powerful healing energies and that with each breath she was effortlessly drawing these healing energies into her body.

After a few minutes of this, Joan opened her eyes suddenly and reached for her purse. Opening it, she pulled out a tissue and deftly patted the area around her eyes.

"What happened?" I asked.

"It's gone," she said.

"What's gone?" I asked.

"The pain," she said. "The pain is gone!"

The release from pain had been quite emotional. And after giving her a moment to compose herself, I asked her to rate her level of pain for me. Zero.

Over several sessions, I showed Joan how to control her own pain through both mental attention and intention. She reported that although the cancer was still spreading, she was able to greatly reduce her pain without the need for medication.

The neurological events responsible for ending Joan's pain were quite complex and they were birthed— spawned if you will, from the quantum world.

Had someone stumbled into my office, they would have seen a woman with her eyes closed, sitting in a chair listening to some music. But this was the Newtonian realm, the world of objects and people.

The quantum realm would have remained unseen, but it was this world that was responsible for the change in Joan's condition. It was in this realm, tucked between the synaptic gaps within her brain, that neurotransmitters battled for supremacy. Some of these neurological messengers carried messages of pain. The dying cells in her spine were, after all, sending their constant death cries to her brain. But at the same time, other messengers were carrying feelings of peace, relaxation, and comfort. For a moment, the messengers of comfort won out over the messengers of pain and death. And, if I may be so poetic, all this took place in the froth and foam of the quantum sea.

This ocean, though hidden from our eyes, is the birthplace of everything that exists both inside and outside our minds. It is the *mother-spring* of all creation and it is this that is ultimately the focus of all internal alchemies, regardless of their methods.

The means to alter quantum events within the body and mind of an alchemist is similar in many regards to what happened with Joan. The primary difference is that the alchemist is not seeking to alter pain, but rather to alter consciousness itself.

The agency responsible for this momentous alteration is nothing less than *thought joined with awareness.* Thought and awareness are ephemeral *things,* as anyone who has tried to hold either for a long period of time knows.

It is also in thought that we can experience things we could never do in *the real* world. By the real world I mean the Newtonian reality of everyday life. We are used to the force of gravity, for instance. We expect things to fall if we drop them. We do not expect things to float in air, perhaps in our dreams but not in *reality.*

What I would like to propose to the reader is the idea that we live in two realities simultaneously. One of these realities we are quite familiar with. It is our everyday world, the world where things fall if you drop them.

There is another reality, however, just as real as this one. It is the reality of the quantum world, and although you are not aware of the zillions of neurotransmitters leaping across space to create your experience of thought at this moment, it is happening nonetheless. And this reality is not Newtonian; it is quantum, with all of its attendant unpredictability and paradox.

The closest most of us come to an experience like the quantum world is when we dream. Things have a weird logic here. In the Newtonian world, the alarm clock you set on your bed stand will stay there the whole night. It will not budge, a captive of gravity and entropy. Unless someone or something knocks it off, it isn't going to move. But in one of your dreams, the clock could very well float in the air, and its hands might move backwards propelling you into your past, or the hands might move forward and rocket you into some distant version of your future. Our *quantum-like dreams* are not inhibited by the logic of the Newtonian world. These phantoms from the subconscious realms are anarchists when it comes to logic and predictability.

Now in the Western consensus view of reality (Newtonian that is) such things as dream experiences are viewed as imaginary and summarily dismissed. What I wish to suggest to you is that not all of them are imaginary—certainly not any more imaginary than your current view of yourself.

I suggest you think of some of these weird dream-like events as alternate perceived realities, not more or less real than your Newtonian version of reality, just different. After all, scientific studies have demonstrated beyond a shadow of a doubt that you and I do not experience *reality* (whatever that is) directly. Our perceptions of reality are filtered through the limitations of our physical senses as well as our beliefs and expectations.

You are, for instance, inverting the pages of this book inside your brain. Your retina actually receives the image of these pages upside down. But your brain creatively turns them right side up! Your brain also tends to perceive what it thinks should be there, even when it isn't! And anyone who has tried to proofread a document knows what I am talking about. The brain tends to see what it expects to see. A misplaced comma often slides past the attention of a copy editor just because the brain doesn't expect one to be there.

All of this mumbo-jumbo is just to point out that we do not directly experience reality, our perception of it being a co-creation of both our body and our mind.

Dreams, in this context, are just another form of created perceptual reality.

I do not, by the way, believe that all dreams are alternate realities bearing significance, only some of them. Most dreams are just the brain unraveling stress and some, quite frankly, are the result of bad food combining at dinner. But some dreams are deeply significant from a psychological standpoint and can even be portentous. These types of dreams, I believe, are of a different order than the others, and anyone who has had such a dream knows what I am talking about.

Indeed, in the actual practice of internal alchemy, the alchemist enters a state of mind that is quite dream-like. This is, I believe, a result of specific brain changes that are created through alchemical meditations. Many internal alchemical practices increase alpha and/or theta wave activity in the neocortex. And the deeper states of theta are experienced very much like dream states. These waking-dreams allow the practitioner to enter worlds of experience that are not possible in normal waking states.

As I said earlier, the methods of internal alchemy can be viewed as a means to directly affect certain aspects of the quantum universe. We will also find that manipulations of quantum reality (through the actions of internal alchemy) take place, most effectively, in dream-like states of mind. And every alchemical tradition has developed its own methods for generating dream-like states of awareness.

Operational Reality

It is really simply a matter of what world you are identifying with and what behaviors best operate in that world.

You have learned, no doubt, how to operate in the everyday world of Newtonian reality. You know that if you drop something, it will continue to the floor. You know how to pick up this book and turn the pages. When you are done, you know how to put the book down again. These are learned neuromuscular behaviors. You did not know how to do this when you were six months old, but now you do. You have learned this skill over the course of interacting with the everyday world of Newtonian-bound things.

I suggest you think of internal alchemies (including the Egyptian system) as simply a means to operate in another reality, namely the quantum. Just as you learned how to pick up a book and put it down, you can learn how to do things in the quantum world as well. You just need a reliable "teaching method." And internal alchemical systems are just that: teaching methods.

Alchemical mastery brings with it an amazing array of non-ordinary abilities or powers of consciousness which are called *siddhis* in yoga. These abilities may seem very strange to Western minds, as weird as the quantum world from which they are derived. But they are simply the natural expression of an evolving consciousness.

Siddhis and the Powers of Consciousness

The siddhis or powers of consciousness naturally unfold as one progresses along the path of spiritual development. There are many well-documented cases of Buddhist, Christian, Islamic, Jewish, and Taoists saints and mystics who have attained these states. In addition, it is well known among indigenous cultures that shamans often exhibit such powers as well.

I have personally made a study of siddhis for the last few decades. To the Western materialistic consciousness some of these powers seem outlandish, but they have been well documented in numerous cultures. Several years ago, I had an experience with the siddhis of a mystic in one of the most unlikely places on earth—Kodiak, Alaska.

I had been invited to teach a workshop in Anchorage, and the following weekend I taught a workshop on Kodiak Island. After the final session on the island, I had a few days off. My organizer gave me a few options, and I chose the boat ride to a small island inhabited by Russian Orthodox monks where an Orthodox saint had lived. I was told that visitors more often than not had to turn back due to rough seas. In fact, I was told, the prelates of the Church in charge of the monastery had never been able to see it, as every time they went for a visit, high seas forced them back.

This was a source of immense humor among the native peoples.

We took a small airplane ride to a nearby island and landed on a spit of land that ended abruptly into turbulent and frigid waters. We were greeted by a local fisherman's wife driving a pickup truck, and I hopped in the back. My organizer got in the front.

It was summer, but there was a light snowfall as we headed for her house by the sea. I remember feeling quite cold and wondering how in the hell people survived here in the winter. We pulled up to a small house surrounded by cedar trees and went inside. Sitting by a large wooden table, we sipped tea. Now anyone who has been to northern Alaska knows that time is a strange bird in these parts. We just sat and sat, talking a little here and there, waiting, it seemed, for some opportune time to leave. Finally, our host announced that it was time to go and we piled back into the pickup and headed for the dock where her husband was waiting with a fishing trawler.

We took off across an amazingly placid sea. Our host sat next to a boom, knitting, and commented how unusual it was to have such a calm passing. I sat looking out at the rich, unbelievably beautiful landscape of the neighboring islands as our boat chugged along at a fairly crisp pace. Seals followed us partway.

Passing an outcropping of boulders, we came into a small natural harbor. The water was too shallow for the trawler, so we got into a dinghy and headed to shore. The scene was like something out of the Middle Ages. A group of men were on the beach burning brush, the air thick with billows of white smoke which swirled in eddies against a stark blue sky. The monks wore long beards, typical of Russian and Greek Orthodox clerics, and they were wearing long grey robes with thin ropes tied about the waist. Each one of them also wore a crucifix.

Stepping out of the boat onto the sand, we were greeted by someone who appeared to be in his early thirties and had the air of authority about him. Our host explained that I had come from Washington State to visit. The abbot smiled approvingly and proceeded to take us on a tour of the small monastery, which consisted of perhaps a dozen men or so. As we headed up a path into the shade of cedars, he noted that the monastery did not often get to host pilgrims.

He took us to several spots, including the small hut where the Saint had lived. I recall the air being musty from the old manuscripts and icons that had been in the Saint's possession. But there was also an unmistakable sense of serenity. The abbot also took us to a sacred spring reputed to have healing powers. Finally he took us to the small chapel where the Saint had been previously buried. His body had since been removed but the site was still considered holy.

The abbot caught me staring at a corner of the cha-pel. He asked me what I was seeing, and I said I was seeing a column of white light coming out of the floor and going up through the roof. The abbot seemed to smile a bit and said that the Saint had been buried in that corner of the church. Then he said something in a somewhat dreamy voice as if he were partway into another world; I remember his words because they sounded so odd to me at the time: "Would that we were all so sensitive."

Seeming to rouse himself from his reveries, the abbot said, "There is one more thing I would like to show you."

He guided us back down the hill to a very small chapel that had obviously just recently been built. It was quite unusual in that it was perhaps nine feet square and some twenty feet tall. The inside of the building glowed from the gold pigments of recently painted icons. They depicted the lives of saints along with other prominent figures of the Russian Orthodox Church. In the back of the tiny chapel there was a very small altar with a bible in Russian.

The abbot pointed out the various icons and their meanings, and then he said that the tour had come to an end. He motioned us out of the chapel and closed the door behind us. I remember suddenly having a question about mysticism I thought the abbot might be able to clarify. I knocked at the door, but there was no answer. I knocked again; still no sign of anyone inside.

Gingerly, I opened the door to find the chapel completely empty. For a moment I stood in shock. Then my ever-skeptical mind came in and I began to search for trap doors or other entrances. I even picked up the small frayed rug on the floor to see if there was a secret exit. Nothing.

Still in a kind of shock, I wandered out the door and out to the beach where our party was waiting. There, clearly in view, was the abbot. He was talking to my host and as I stepped up he nodded his head with a distinct twinkle in his eyes. We boarded the dinghy and headed back to the trawler. The sun was low in the sky and I stood on the deck looking over the stern as we headed back to sea. I was very quiet.

As I write these words, I find myself caught up in the feelings of awe and wonder I felt then. I had known the siddhis existed, had studied the physics of them, and had made it a hobby of mine to collect stories and documentations. But here on a small island off Kodiak, a humble contemplative had shown me the mystery of yogic powers firsthand.

Halfway through the ride back, the fisherman's wife

turned from her knitting and said, "You know, they do things like that all the time!"

"Things like what?" I asked.

"Oh, you know. Teleporting, bi-locating. Things like that."

"Really," I said.

"Yes", she replied, not taking her eyes off her knitting. "That island is a remote place. There is no mail service. We see them sometimes in town picking up their mail and buying things. And," she said in a most conspiratorial tone, "they don't have any way of getting there!"

The powers of consciousness or siddhis range from what are called the lesser siddhis to what are termed the greater siddhis. The lesser siddhis include such psychic abilities as *clairvoyance* (inner seeing), *clairaudience* (inner hearing), *clairsentience* (inner feeling), as well as *clairgnosis* (inner knowing), as in knowing something but not knowing how you know it. The first three powers—clairvoyance, clairaudience, and clairsentience—are refinements of the physical senses.

As psychic powers unfold, they often first present themselves in one of these three forms, or in combination. Thus one might begin to see images in the mind that can't be physically seen—in other words, mental visual impressions. In scientific studies involving remote viewing this siddhi is most often used.

Studies show that some people can, under the right conditions, (i.e., mental relaxation) accurately report visual impressions of objects or locations hundreds of miles away without any previous knowledge of them. The reception of such visual information must presumably come from some other source than that of physical sight, since the *viewers* were nowhere near the locations they described.

Many yogis/yoginis, saints, and mystics have reported that they could see their disciples in distant locations when it was called for. In one account, the yogi Neem Karoli Baba suddenly asked for large amounts of food to be brought to him. Those present report that he consumed a mind-boggling amount of food before going into samadhi (a form of deep yogic trance). When the yogi came out of meditation, his disciples asked him what had happened. He reported that he had suddenly seen one of his disciples dying in the desert. The last desire of the dying man was to eat. Baba said that the chela (disciple) had reached a level of attainment where there was no further need to reincarnate. But with the desire for food on his mind at the moment of death, he would have been brought back into the wheel of reincarnation just through the power of this one unfulfilled desire! Baba had taken upon himself the task of fulfilling the man's last wish for food, and using his yogic powers, he transmuted the desire.

When psychic information is received auditorially, the person is called clairaudient. Such persons have subtle impressions of hearing sound and/or voices. The inner realms of consciousness are filled with sound and music that can be incredibly beautiful. It has been suggested by some that many of the great composers actually heard the music of these realms and this *music of the spheres* greatly influenced their compositions.

Some individuals feel things at a very subtle level; these persons are called clairsentients. There is often a fine line between a clairsentient and an empath. Empaths have highly developed sensitivities and often feel other persons' feelings, especially those immediately around them. Clairsentients may also be empathic, but in addition, they receive psychic impressions in the form of subtle physical sensations.

Clairgnosis is one of the more fascinating siddhis. When you have a hunch about something, but have no idea how you might know such a thing, this is clairgnosis. (That is if your hunch turns out to be true. If it turns out to be false, we call that delusion.) Some have suggested that clairgnosis is an attribute of pure consciousness which is, by nature, omniscient and omnipresent. As one rises up the ladder of consciousness, one's own personal awareness takes on some of these qualities of pure consciousness and episodes of clairgnosis increase.

The lesser siddhis also include such things as healing abilities and limited powers of prophecy. This class of yogic powers also includes the ability for awareness to become very small or very large—in other words, not confined by the limitations of the body.

The greater siddhis include such things as *levitation* (in which the body floats or hovers in air). Again this siddhi is not confined to Indian yogis or yoginis as some believe. There are well-documented sightings of St. Francis of Assisi, for one, hovering in the air. St. Francis exhibited other siddhis as well. In fact, his physical remains still have spiritual powers even after his death. While visiting his shrine in Assisi, I was transported into the spiritual realms through the emanations from his crypt! I heard a sound like wind blowing through aspen trees when I stood near his body, and when I returned to my hotel room my skin was red as if I had a light sunburn.

By the way, if you are ever at Assisi, here's a little tip. As you enter the main entrance into the basilica where St. Francis's remains are kept, turn to your left. Off to both sides, there are stairs that lead down to the crypt and it is certainly worth visiting. The problem is that there are usually throngs of people milling about, and it is difficult to find a quiet space. If you proceed further, past the stairs, you will see a large altar in the distance, the only one in this part of the church. On the floor, in front of the altar, there is a geometric figure. It sits directly above St. Francis's tomb and the emanations from this area are very strong. No one seems to know about it, so you can stand directly on the spot and receive the emanations in relative peace.

The greater siddhis also include such remarkable abilities such as *teleportation* (like the abbot I mentioned earlier) and *bi-location* (being in two places at once). There are other abilities that fall under this category as well, but the purpose of this chapter is not to discuss the siddhis in depth.

It is important to realize that the siddhis or yogic powers are attained as a natural consequence of spiritual development. There is, however, a very real danger with the siddhis. They have a glamour and a seduction for many people. The advice often given is to avoid the pursuit of yogic powers. And when they do arise, to not pay them much attention.

A short story about the dilemma of siddhis will help to make this clear. This concerns a living yogi who is quite well known, so I will avoid using his name. And although he teaches kundalini yoga there are very strong parallels with the system of Egyptian alchemy.

He is quite a powerful being, and I had the wonderful experience of studying with him at a weeklong retreat many years ago. According to a close disciple of his, who I came to know, the yogi had gone to India for a spiritual retreat in his early twenties after having attained some of the Siddhis. He was resting against a tree, listening to the beautiful music of a master musician who was caught up in the fervor of *bhakti* (divine love), and due to the intensity of devotion within the music, our yogi was transported into a deep state of samadhi and experienced great ecstasies and bliss.

The concert ended abruptly when it started to rain and the musician rushed indoors. Using his siddhic powers, the yogi caused the rain to stop, and the musician returned to his *kirtans* (sacred singing). Very quickly our yogi was transported back into samadhi, but his bliss was rudely ended by an old man kicking him in the side. The man was also a yogi, and in a furor he continued to kick the younger yogi, yelling obscenities at him.

"What are you doing?" he asked. "Don't you realize this area has been suffering from a drought? And you, you stopped the rains for your own selfish desires." The ancient yogi raised his staff in the air and pointed it at his younger peer. "Mark my words, if you don't stop this, you will pay a great karmic debt. You will spend a thousand lifetimes as a sea creature!" The old yogi then kicked some dust in the direction of the young man and left before he could respond.

Immediately the younger yogi went into meditation and through his siddhic powers returned the rains. He fervently prayed to God to take away his siddhis, and miraculously they left him. But over the years they slowly returned to a much wiser and less flamboyant man.

I believe that the siddhis are a natural expression of evolution. They are perhaps, one of our next evolutionary benchmarks. And anyone practicing internal alchemy long enough will eventually have to contend with them.

The siddhis are to us, like apples are to apple trees. Apples are intrinsic to the nature of apple trees. But it is only when the apple tree reaches a certain stage of development that the fruits appear. Until then, they are only a potential.

When an individual human consciousness reaches certain stages of development, the siddhis spontaneously appear.

Every alchemical lineage deals with the non-ordinary powers that are attained as a result of spiritual practice. And every alchemical tradition has its own methods for developing and handling these spiritual powers. In the Egyptian stream, these powers were developed as a byproduct of strengthening the Etheric Double or Ka.

Strengthening the Ka

So let us return to the Ka for it holds such a prominent place in Egyptian alchemy. Unlike the khat (dense physical body), the Ka body can seemingly walk through walls, float in air, and cover vast distances in a moment. In yogic literature, there are many reliable accounts of saints and mystics bi-locating (being in two places at once). One explanation often given for this phenomenon has to do with the Ka body. When the Ka is sufficiently charged it can have a kind of density that can be seen by others. Because the Ka is an etheric double of the person, it looks exactly like him or her.

In the *Manuscript*, Magdalen talks about Yeshua appearing to her after the crucifixion before his ascent into heaven (spirit). This was, from the perspective of Egyptian alchemy, a form of his Ka, highly charged as a result of the alchemical practices they had engaged in.

According to the *Manuscript*, Magdalen had been assisting Yeshua in one of the primary tasks of Egyptian Alchemy: to charge his Ka body with an increase of energy. Anyone wishing to experience the fruits of the Egyptian alchemical system must engage in *power building practices* for the Ka. There are many methods used to accomplish this, but it is not in the scope of this chapter to discuss them. A couple of methods are discussed by Magdalen in the *Manuscript* itself, and I would refer the reader to them. (Note: the method of drawing in solar energy I described in the first chapter is one example of a very simple *energy building practice).*

By whatever methods used, as the Ka accumulates more energy, its magnetics become stronger. The use of these magnetic fields for the elevation of consciousness was one of the great discoveries of Egyptian alchemy.

While strengthening the Ka is a fundamental focus in this system of alchemy, it is only the first task. The second task is to successfully shift identification from the khat (the dense physical body) into the Ka—shifting, if you will, identification from the Newtonian world into the quantum. In identifying with the Ka, the practitioner does *not* disregard the physical body (khat), but in the practices of alchemical meditation, one's identity is shifted from the physical to the luminous body (Ka). This shifting of attention and the growing awareness of the Ka as an autonomous body usually takes place within a spiritual context. This is crucial; since without a mental understanding regarding the Ka, it is unlikely that one would be able to utilize its extraordinary abilities.

The Shifting of Identification

When I teach *the shifting of identification* in workshops, I use many different methods, some of them involving movement and some of them involving inner attention. After an unusually long training session at an Egyptian Alchemical Retreat a few years ago, someone shared his startling experience. He had just finished the last inner practice and had opened his eyes. He felt someone beside him, though no one had been there when he started. He turned to his right to see himself looking back at himself, smiling. He literally jumped out of his seat. The exercises in the workshop had managed to energize his Ka to such an extent that he could see his own subtle form with open eyes!

But sometimes a person can possess a strong Ka body even if he or she has not practiced alchemy.

A Modern Experience with the Ka

I had an unusual experience with a client's Ka several years ago. At the time, I was a practicing psychotherapist and was referred a man in his late twenties suffering from depression. In the course of our therapy together, it became clear that he had suffered extreme physical and sexual abuse as a child. I always had a strange impression whenever we met. Although he was deeply depressed, he seemed to emanate a very intense energy, as if somewhere behind those electric blue eyes there was an inferno of unbelievable power.

Now, I always make it a policy with potential suicide risks to enter into a contract. They must agree to contact me physically or at least by phone if they plan to take their own lives. And I agree not to talk them out of it, but to make sure that that is what they really want to do. In the course of trying to get me and actually speak, they usually come to their senses and the crisis is averted.

In the case of this man, I had to leave town for a professional seminar about six weeks into our work together. I gave him the phone number in Washington, D.C. where I would be staying.

Now, here is where it really gets weird. The seminar had just moved into the section on death and dying when an attendant handed the speaker a piece of paper. She asked if Tom Kenyon was present. I raised my hand and was given a piece of paper with a name and phone number. It simply identified the person as the sister of my client.

I went to the nearest pay phone and called the number. She answered and informed me that her brother, my client, had committed suicide. I was extremely grieved and pissed. He had violated our contract agreement, which had been put in place to be a safety net. Had he contacted me I could have gotten him to see that he really did not want to take his own life, but he had taken the coward's way out. He killed himself while I was out of town.

I steamed about this for several days. Then one night, I had this strange dream in which he came to me and asked for my forgiveness. In the dream, I forgave him and he went on his way.

Now, it gets very, very strange. My office happened to be next to my house, and I usually saw clients in the afternoons and evenings, never in the morning. That day, after the strange dream, I was in town and was approached by an acquaintance. He said that he was thinking about seeing me. I asked him why, since he didn't seem to be the type interested in personal growth.

He told me that he had driven by my office/house at around 5 a.m. that morning and had seen a very sad-looking person going inside. Mind you, I wasn't even awake at 5 a.m., much less seeing anyone. He said he came back around the house about a half hour later and saw the same person coming out with a smile on his face and skipping down the block. I asked him to describe this mystery person, and his description matched my client perfectly. I was stunned.

I had not yet stumbled upon Egyptian Alchemy and its ideas regarding the Ka body, and so I had no way of explaining this to myself for several years.

Effects of Strengthening the Ka

As the Ka body becomes stronger (due to energy building practices) the powers of mind and will also become stronger. Thus, the practitioner can draw to himself or herself objects of desire much more quickly. The ability to accomplish this feat of magnetizing desires occurs as an interface between the actual strength of the Ka and one's degree of spiritual understanding regarding the possibilities. If one possesses a strong Ka without a spiritual understanding of its significance, then the Ka cannot be fully utilized. Conversely, if someone has a high degree of understanding, but has not taken up the task of strengthening the Ka, then likewise the Ka cannot be fully utilized. In this case however, the deficit is due to a lack of energy, not a lack of understanding.

One of the side-effects of a strengthened Ka is an increased potential for spiritual illumination. In such instances, the luminous body of the Ka literally radiates more light. This *inner light* is usually not visible except in the rarest of instances. But those who are psychic can see this type of light quite clearly.

There is also an interesting benefit gained from building the Ka. Once the Ka has autonomy, it can do all kinds of things, like travel in other dimensions of consciousness to gain insight and knowledge. This activity can be quite rewarding to the alchemist. I remember my own first encounters with a master alchemist in the other realms. He continues to this day to be a great source of insight and encouragement.

The Djed

As the Ka builds in strength there is an alchemical task that the alchemist can undertake. However, this cannot be accomplished until there is enough energy in the Ka since this act takes tremendous energy and intent. The task to which I refer involves the *djed*.

The djed is the central pathway of the chakras up the spine. As energy is progressively moved upward, there is an accompanying expansion of awareness. This movement of energy up the djed is sometimes referred to as the act of *raising the djed*. And the power that drives this energy up the djed is nothing less than sekhem or life-force. The term literally means "that which makes things erect."

To better understand the profound effects of raising the djed, it might be helpful to take a look at how the chakras filter perception since they are radically affected by this action.

The Chakras

In terms of spiritual evolution and the relativity of perception, the chakras are very significant. Let's say that there are seven people at a picnic. It is a balmy day and the park is full. Each of these seven people will have a very different experience of the world based upon the activity of his or her chakras. This is a hypothetical example, since rarely are the chakras activated sequentially. Most of us have a mixture of open and closed. But for illustration purposes, our seven imaginary people will help us to better understand the filtering of perception that occurs through the chakra system.

Let's say that the first person is living primarily through the first chakra, which is located in an area near the base of the spine. This individual will be most concerned with security and survival. Forget that it is a beautiful day. This person will be anxious. All those people roaming around are possible threats, and this person would be very guarded around strangers.

Our second imaginary person lives mostly in the second chakra, located about two inches (four centimeters) above the base of the spine. This person is driven to constantly search for new sexual experiences. If he or she is not actively engaged in trying to find someone to have sex with, he or she will be besieged by constant sexual fantasies. This person may even find it difficult to have a conversation with anyone else in our group, because he or she cannot help cruising the crowd.

The third person in our group is stuck in the solar plexus, which is located back behind the pit of the stomach. His or her only real concerns are status and power. If this person engages someone in a conversation, it will only be for what that person might offer (i.e., those corporate power lunches and cocktail parties).

Moving our attention to the fourth person, we note that he or she is in the heart chakra, located behind the sternum in the center of the chest. For this individual, the world will be full of love. This love is not romantic, but is more akin to what the ancient Greeks called *agape*, or divine love. For this person, the world is love. This love can range from a soft feeling of interconnectedness to an intense experience of universal love. In some cases, such persons spontaneously enter samadhi due to the intensity of their bhakti (experience of divine love). When the heart opens, such persons often assume that those around them are experiencing the world in the same ways they are. This can be quite a disconcerting experience when he or she realizes that this is not the case.

The fifth person in our little gathering is centered in the throat chakra, located in the area of the vocal cords. This person will be highly creative, and depending upon the strength of his or her will, creations might come into reality very quickly. It is said in many alchemical traditions, that when an individual enters highly advanced evolutionary states, his or her words instantly move into manifestation.

Our sixth person is psychic and possesses the gifts of the inner senses due to the fact that the third eye is open. The third eye is an oddity in that the energy-point for this chakra is located in the forehead area just above the eyes. However, according to some yogic systems, the chakra is actually located between the eyes and back behind the bridge of the nose about an inch (two centimeters). Interestingly, this is an area of the brain where the pituitary gland (master regulator of the endocrine system) and the hypothalamus sit. The hypothalamus, the brain's information processing center, allows the brain to communicate with the rest of the body through what are called the hypothalamic pathways. The coincidental juxtaposition of this subtle energy center and such a major nerve plexus in the brain is most interesting.

The person with an opened third eye sees the world through the filter of psychic vision. He or she might easily see the auras or energy fields of those around them. He or she might even sense their desires or hear their thoughts. In some cases, he or she might even have prophetic vision in that he or she can sense the probable futures of those around them. Note that I say *probable* futures. I do not believe that the future is pre-determined. There are possibilities or choice points, and a psychic individual can sometimes sense these.

But no one can predict one's future with certainty because we all have the power of choice. And choice affects our destiny.

Finally, the seventh person in our group is centered in the crown chakra, which is located at the top of the head. For this person the world is seen as the play of Maya, illusion. Though in the world, he or she is detached from it. He or she senses the world in a way that is very difficult to imagine, for consciousness has become aware of itself. The mirror of awareness has been directed inward and the yogi or yogini has seen *the Self*, the one great being living and expressing through innumerable forms. While such a person may have compassion for the sufferings of others, he or she is not caught up in them. This person sees the world much like a shadow play. No longer affected by the dramas of life, he or she has become aware of the puppeteer and the light that casts the shadows. What was taken as reality is no longer perceived in this way. The yogi or yogini has attained enlightenment.

In reality, the situation is much more complex than this, since rarely are the chakras balanced sequentially. Thus it is possible for a person to have one or more chakras highly activated while residing in another in terms of their psychological motivations.

Many an unsuspecting disciple *(chela)* of a spiritual master has been disillusioned by this phenomenon. One is drawn by the obvious spiritual power and perhaps psychic abilities of a teacher, only to find out that he or she is power-hungry and manipulative. Or he or she might be promiscuous and not honoring of sexual boundaries. The conflict for a student caught in the unwanted sexual advances of a spiritual teacher can be psychologically quite difficult.

The problem is that the attainment of spiritual powers is not necessarily connected with psychological maturity. Just because a yogi or yogini has attained high states of samadhi and bliss does not mean that they have addressed their psychological issues. Thus someone who has unresolved issues in the lower three centers may misuse their spiritual powers.

You might, for instance, have a person who is a great teacher, but has not resolved his or her inherent psychological hostility; God help the student of such a teacher. Or you might encounter someone with extremely developed psychic abilities but with an unresolved need to manipulate others. Such a person might show all the signs of spirituality, but he or she will subtly, and perhaps not so subtly, use his or her psychic powers to sway you.

In many of these cases, the person is unconscious of his or her own psychological motivations. But just because something is unconscious does not mean it cannot do harm. In point of fact, our unconscious motivations often do more harm than those of which we are conscious. This is one reason I believe that persons undertaking the path of alchemy need to become cognizant of their own psychological history and motivations.

Sekhem

As I mentioned earlier, the raising of the djed and the activation of the chakras takes tremendous energy. The energy that propels itself up the djed is nothing less than one's own life-force, called sekhem, or literally, "the power that makes things erect."

Sekhem is the hidden meaning behind obelisks. Obelisks are free-standing kinds of pillars except that they don't support anything, and they are pointed at the tip. They were erected all over Egypt, usually in honor of an important personage. However, they are essentially monuments to the vital power of sekhem. One of the primary tasks of the alchemist within the Egyptian system is to raise his or her excess life-force, or sekhem, up the djed. The net result of moving sekhem up the djed is that the seals or chakras become activated and strengthened. As each chakra is stimulated, latent areas of consciousness and awareness are opened.

It is important to understand that sekhem is intimately related to both one's life-force and one's sexuality. This power can be used to create a new being, as through the act of sex, or it can be used to create higher states of consciousness, as through the act of raising the djed. The primary power to accomplish both of these feats is the same. It is simply a matter of what is done with the energy that determines what is accomplished. To put this in its most simplistic terms: a major source of spiritual illumination within the Egyptian system of alchemy is transmuted sexuality.

The Uraeus

When the energy of sekhem or transmuted life force pours into the head through the raising of the djed, there is a tremendous stimulation of the higher brain centers. This activation of these centers eventually generates what is called the Uraeus.

In sacred Egyptian art, one often sees important personages with a snake coming out of their foreheads. This serpent symbolically signifies that the person has attained the uraeus or has the authority granted by the uraeus. It often appears on the headdresses of gods and goddesses as well as royalty. I suspect the artistic use of the Uraeus eventually degenerated into a stylistic statement and the original spiritual intent was lost. However, its primary symbolic meaning is that of having attained an activation or *anointing* of the higher brain centers. This implied that such a person could see beyond the duality of the world, symbolized by another serpent form, that of Apophis. Unlike the serpent of the Uraeus, which is related to enlightenment,

Apophis represents the sine wave of all form, the dualistic play of opposite forces in creation. The gift of the
Uraeus is a type of psychic vision (clairvoyance) that
allows one to see beyond the veils of illusion (the play
of dualistic opposites).

Activation of the Uraeus brings with it a whole host
of non-ordinary awarenesses and abilities. From my
own personal research I believe that, for one, it increases creativity and intelligence. For another, it stimulates
some of the powers of consciousness or siddhis I mentioned earlier.

Once again, the changes created by alchemy can be
tracked to changes in brain function. As yet, there are
no studies on the specific brain changes created by the
uraeus phenomenon but I suspect, based on personal
observation, that they involve changes in neurotransmitters and increases in endorphin levels. Since the
Uraeus is sensed in dream-like states of awareness, I
also suspect increases in alpha and/or theta activity.
Finally, I believe that there is a radical increase in non-
dominant hemispheric functioning in those who experience this phenomenon. My reason for this is that in
my own experiments with precursors to the Uraeus my
sense of space became highly altered and there was
a cessation of internal dialogue which would indicate
a decrease of activity within the dominant (or talking)
hemisphere.

It is not in the scope of this introduction to discuss
the many interesting points regarding alchemy and brain
physiology, but I will say this: the practices of internal
alchemies, such as the Egyptian stream, create definite changes in brain function which, in turn, directly
affect perception. By masterfully controlling these brain
states through meditative practices, the alchemist is able
to enter non-ordinary realms of awareness. And it is
through these unusual states of inner attention that the
practitioner is able to affect the quantum realm (i.e., the
Ka body and the Uraeus).

Raising the Djed and the Myth of Horus

Through the power of intention (will), the alchemist eventually causes sekhem to move up the spine (the djed) and into the head centers creating, over time, the uraeus. As the electromagnetic force of sekhem moves upward through the chakras (seals) these centers are stimulated. This rising of sekhem up the djed is called raising the djed as I mentioned earlier. As the seven main seals (chakras) are activated through this process, the consciousness of the alchemist is radically transformed.

Symbolically, this movement of consciousness is mirrored in the story of Horus. There are two views of Horus. The first view holds Horus as an actual physical being who lived at the dawn of Egyptian history. The second view does not supplant the first view, but is more symbolic in nature. Whether Horus physically existed, we cannot say for sure. Legends and stories abound, as do the theories regarding the origins of his mother (Isis) and his father (Osiris). Some view these figures as aliens from another world, starseed, if you will. In this view, Isis and Osiris were geneticists and we are the descendants of this ancient science. Some starseed theorists even relate these figures to the early Sumerians. The most common view (and one that is generally accepted by academic Egyptologists) is that Isis and Osiris were divinities that existed within the living mythos of the time. They were, to use Jungian terms, archetypal realities within the collective unconscious of the ancient Egyptians.

From a purely practical standpoint in regards to alchemical practice, it does not matter if Horus physically existed or not. The story holds alchemical keys, which if understood, open up a wealth of understanding.

Horus is depicted as a hawk-headed man. As the son of Isis and Osiris, he symbolically represents the fusion of spirit and matter. In many ancient cultures, the feminine principle (Mother) was viewed as matter. Interestingly enough, our word matter derives from the Latin word mater, which means mother. In these early cultures, the male principle (Father) was viewed as spirit. Thus, at a symbolic level, Horus is a result of joining together spirit and matter.

Horus' journey to the High God Horus is allegorical to our own journey up the djed. In one form of the story, Horus must overcome evil by killing his uncle, Set, who murdered his father. The myth is very complex and has many versions. But for our purposes here, we will focus on one stage of the battle—the moment when Horus becomes the god Min.

The God Min

In order to overcome Set, Horus must accumulate vast amounts of energy. At the alchemically symbolic level, the alchemist must rise above the lower three chakras, and this takes energy, a tremendous amount of energy. As anyone who has ever tried to rise above their own conditioning knows, the power of entropy is very strong. Entropy is the force that keeps things from moving. Psychologically it shows up as lethargy, a reluctance to make the efforts required to change a situation (evolve). Whether one is trying to stop a bad habit or activate the higher powers of consciousness does not matter. Entropy and lethargy become one's nemesis. To overcome this limiting factor in our psychological makeup requires a level of energy stronger than the force of entropy itself. This energy is in the form of sekhem, or "that which makes things erect."

In other words, Horus harnesses his procreative powers. This is symbolized by the god Min, who is shown with a large erection while holding a flail in one hand. The flail is often a piece of wood with leather strips tied to one end, and it is used to discipline a horse especially when riding a chariot. The *flail of Min* is never actually used. It is a symbol of intent, of purpose. This may be an unfortunate symbol for the modern mind since the flail carries intimations of self-abuse or harm. Nothing could be further from the intent of this symbol.

A charioteer managing a spirited horse needs to direct its attention in the direction desired. If he or she does not direct the steed, the horse will take off on its own. This can be both wasteful and dangerous. The flail allows the charioteer to get the horse's attention by whacking it on the rump. Now a sensitive equestrian knows that he or she does not need to hit the horse hard to get its attention. If rapport has been established between horse and man/woman, a slight movement of the flail is all that is needed. Thus the flail, in this sense, is a symbolic reminder to harness the procreative energies of sex.

Instead of sending his "seed" out into the world through the sexual act, Horus (as the god Min) harnesses this energy and sends it up the djed. As the energy makes its ascent into the higher brain centers, Horus is transformed by the power of the Uraeus into the High God Horus. He is no longer a god in potential; he has become a creator god in his own right. Then and only then is he able to defeat Set.

This depiction, to set things straight, is not a call to celibacy. The holding of the god Min's "seed" is symbolic and refers to the holding and transformation of subtle forces within the sexual fluids. It is these subtle forces that are cultivated and sent up the djed whether male or female.

In actuality, there is no need to refrain from the sex act in order to practice this form of alchemy. Indeed, as Magdalen discusses in the *Manuscript*, there are ways that the sex act can greatly empower the ascent of sekhem up the spine. For various historical reasons, too complex to go into here, the Church separated sex from spirit, but in the ancient Egyptian understanding, they were intimately connected.

Misunderstandings Regarding
the God Min

In the Middle Ages the flail was adopted by over-zealous monks in attempts to purge themselves of sin. The essential teaching behind the flail and the god Min had been lost. Instead of being viewed as a symbol for the attainment of god-like powers, the flail was used to inflict self-torture in sadomasochistic rituals of flagellation.

Mendicants would sit in their cells and lash themselves with flails to atone for their imagined sin. Perhaps they entered altered states of mind as a result of exhaustion and blood loss, but these macabre rituals had nothing to do with alchemy or the secrets of the great god Min.

But foolishness in regards to Min was not confined to the Middle Ages. At the turn of the last century, there was a tremendous interest among the Victorians in the lost secrets of Egypt. Egyptology was in its infancy, and many an adventurer trekked off for the deserts to discover the secrets of the Golden Age. To their horror, these stiff anal retentives discovered large statues of Min all over the place. And every one of them had a big, you-know-what. So distressed by these discoveries were they, some of the more shocked zealots cut off the offending organs. And reliefs of Min taken off to museums were, I am told, often mutilated. At the very least, a judiciously placed plaque would serve to hide the offending member from their more civilized countrymen.

The Victorians had missed the point, as had their predecessors in the Dark Ages. The ancient Egyptians were not glorifying sex. They were acknowledging it as a sacred act. It had its place, not just in the bedroom or in the bordellos and whorehouses, but in the temples, at the very center of their quest for the divine.

Immortality

Ultimately the goal of Egyptian alchemy is immortality or, at the very least, an extension of the self after death. In this regard, there are two means available to the alchemist, one of them temporary and the other permanent.

In the first method, the energy-building practices are pursued until the Ka is virtually scintillating with energy and light. When death of the physical body (the khat) ensues, the alchemist shifts his or her attention into the Ka. Much previous experience in the *shifting of identification* insures that this process is accomplished with little effort. With the sense of self fully in the Ka, the alchemist, now an *energy-being*, is unaffected by death of the physical body. To him or her, it is like taking off an old suit of clothes.

The duration of the alchemist's existence as an energy-being depends upon how much energy was collected while alive. If the alchemist has learned to collect and conserve energy as an energy-being then the length of existence could be quite long. For whatever it is worth, I have met energy-beings who claimed to be thousands of years old.

In the second method, the energy building practices are pursued just as in the first way since charging of the Ka is vital to both methods. However, there are significant differences.

In this second path to immortality, the alchemist must align himself or herself with his or her Celestial Soul (the BA). This aspect of self is transcendent, outside of space and time. Some might refer to it as the Soul or High Self. But whatever one calls it, there is an alignment that takes place with the BA (the Celestial Soul) and the Ka through the djed, or sacred pathway of the chakras.

When this pathway is aligned with the BA, there is a great influx of spiritual energy into the Ka body. When this reaches a critical mass, the Ka ignites, as it were, with an *etheric fire*. This is sometimes called the *Golden Raiment* but was referred to by the ancient Egyptians as the *Sahu*. This body is immortal.

Just how an alignment with the BA or Celestial Soul creates such a metamorphosis of the Ka is a closely guarded secret. It involves the highest aspects of alchemy and is revealed to the Initiate when he or she is ready. This revelation may come directly from an embodied teacher, but more often it comes from an *Akul*, one who has attained the light body and who now lives in the realm of spirit. Sometimes this information is revealed directly from the BA to the alchemist.

In regards to survival after death, I should point out that many spiritual traditions say that there is a spark of consciousness that always survives death, regardless of the level of attainment. However, this spark does not hold the sense of personal identity in the ways of the Ka or Sahu. Thus, at death, one's personal sense of self, as well as the memory of personal history dissolves unless one of these subtle bodies has been stabilized.

The Ammit

In addition to energy-building practices for the attainment of immortality (the Sahu), there must be a moral or ethical attitude toward one's life. One must learn the right use of energy (righteousness), and how to conduct oneself in relation to others. There is a real danger in the attainment of powers brought about through the practice of Egyptian alchemy. As one's consciousness becomes stronger, so does the ability to create manifestation of one's intentions. If an alchemist purposefully harms others in the course of his or her actions, he or she is in danger of being devoured. The sacred texts warn the alchemist of this dangerous passage through a very strange creature called the *ammit*—part crocodile, part lion, and part hippopotamus. The ammit is usually shown with a representation of the djed, that depiction of the seven chakras or seals in ascending order, and sits with its reptilian snout resting ominously between the third and fourth chakra (the solar plexus and heart). This position symbolically refers to the place between power and love.

The ammit is sometimes referred to as the Great Devourer since those persons stuck in the lower three chakras will be devoured by their experiences. For instance, persons centered only in the first chakra will seek security above anything else. Those centered in the second seal will be obsessed with sex, and those in the third will be driven for power. If a person remains motivated solely by these energies without moving upward along the djed, he or she will eventually be consumed by them.

Persons engaged in the practice of alchemy can fall victim to their own misguided lusts for security, sex, and/or power. The seduction can be very strong, since the practices of alchemy build the magnetics of the Ka and desires are more quickly attained.

It is important to understand this clearly. The practices of Egyptian alchemy build the magnetic fields of the practitioner. By magnetic I do not mean the force of magnetics as in physics, though there is some relationship. Rather I mean a psycho-dynamic force that is magnetic-like in its properties. Persons with strong psycho-magnetic fields tend to draw to themselves the objects of their desires more easily than those with weak psycho-magnetic fields. Because the Ka-building practices greatly increase the psycho-magnetic force of the practitioner, he or she must be careful.

The ammit stands as a reminder of the passage from the lower three seals (chakras) into the heart. Those persons insisting on experiencing life from the lower chakras without passing into love will eventually be devoured by their desires in the lower three realms (the quest for security, sex, and power).

When someone passes through the initiatory gate of the fourth seal (chakra), he or she will experience a spontaneous arising of agape (unconditional divine love). When one experiences the world from this place in consciousness, it is not possible to knowingly harm another person. Agape is all-inclusive. By nature it generates feelings of connectedness. Because the egoic-sense of *self* is expanded to include *others,* harming another person would be unthinkable.

But this sense of *harmlessness* is only present at the level of the heart. Persons coming solely from the lower three centers can easily manipulate and harm others in order to get their own selfish desires met. The ammit stands as a sobering reminder to those on the alchemical path. Those who insist upon living their lives without love will be devoured by their desires.

As if the scary prospect of being devoured by the ammit is not enough to temper the desires of an alchemist, there is another figure. This one stands on the other side of death.

Maat

Maat is an important deity in the Egyptian pantheon having to do with the dead. Maat is often depicted with a scale. On one side is the heart of a person seeking entrance into the abode of heaven. On the other side of the scale is a feather. If the dead person's heart is as *light as a feather,* he or she is given entrance into spiritual paradise. If, however, the heart is weighted by regrets, guilt, and shame, the person is not given entrance and must wander through the underworld.

Symbolically, I think the figure of Maat is, as a friend of mine says, *a call to presence,* a reminder that what we do in this life will follow us into the next.

Final Thoughts

The ancient Egyptian mentality is so far from our own, it is difficult to imagine what they really thought and felt. We have fragments of writings, a few sacred texts, and the myths of their gods and goddesses. Fortunately, we have also inherited some of their alchemical secrets, but much of that glorious civilization is lost to us. The chasm in time is too large.

By the time Magdalen had trained in the temples of Isis, Egypt had fallen, its Golden Age a long-lost glimmer. But enough of the ancient alchemical knowledge had survived along with an understanding of how to use it. By the last century B.C., the Isis cult and the secrets of sexual alchemy had spread throughout much of the ancient world.

Undoubtedly, as with all things, each culture introduced its own understandings and interpretations into the Isis mythos. Over time, churches were built upon the ruins of temples and the spiritual practices of that earliest time were often modified or forgotten. But anyone seriously looking beneath the surface of the alchemical traditions of the world can often find the mark of Isis and the alchemy of ancient Egypt.

We stand now, two thousand years more distant than did the Magdalen from the alchemists of that ancient time. For those of us working with this alchemical system, the task is clear. We cannot relive the past. For one thing, we can never truly know it. We must learn what we can from the fragments that have been left behind. We must practice the ancient alchemy of transformation as we understand it, to see where it will take us. And we must forge a new alchemical way for this time.

May the Akul, the ancient ones who have attained the Sahu, help us in our quest.

May the light of illumination guide us through our own darkness.

A Brief
Comparative of Internal
Alchemies

A primary task of Egyptian Alchemy as taught by the Magdalen is to strengthen the Ka body. This is done through states of high ecstasy since ecstasy and bliss strengthen the Ka. There are two primary paths that can be taken in this regard. For those in sacred relationship explor- ing the Sex Magic of Isis, the ecstasy naturally arises dur- ing love making. But for those engaged in the solitary path and the Alchemies of Horus, the ecstasy is self-generated.

For those on both the solitary and dyadic path, I believe this section will prove invaluable by placing the Manuscript *within the context of other alchemical sys- tems. I also feel that those working with other systems of internal alchemy may find the information below helpful in placing their own practices in relation to the* Manuscript.

—A Personal Note from Tom

This section explores comparisons between three of the four major alchemical systems: *Tantric Yoga, Taoism,* and *Tibetan Buddhist Tantra.* Egyptian alchemy was presented in the previous chap- ter, and readers will undoubtedly recognize some com- mon elements between the Egyptian system and the other three lineages discussed in this section. Those already familiar with these systems of alchemy have, no doubt, recognized the unusual position taken by the *Manuscript* in regards to the sex act. As a student

of comparative alchemies and mystical traditions, this
was one of the first things that struck me about the
Magdalen's material.

If I may summarize these differences, I would say that
the system introduced by the Magdalen is archetypally
female-based. According to the Magdalen, the female
holds within her nature the secrets of creation.

Magdalen goes on to mention how she was trained
in the Alchemies of Horus and how to raise the serpents through meditative powers. But in the presence
of Yeshua and especially during their love-making, the
Alchemies naturally presented themselves. In other
words, they engaged without her having to do anything.

She speaks at great length about how the female
must feel safe and appreciated in relationship with her
Beloved. Then and only then can the alchemy of transformation she calls the Sex Magic of Isis occur. If these
elements (safety and appreciation) are in place within
the relationship, the female can *let go* and allow the feminine mysteries to express themselves through her. When
this occurs during love-making there is often a shuddering in the female. If she allows this shaking to proceed, it
will take her deeper into the mysteries.

If the male has trained himself to *nest* within the vibrational energies released by his partner then both he and
his Beloved can strengthen their Ka bodies (one of the
primary goals of this system).

The central place of the female in this alchemical system is strikingly different from many other
alchemical streams.

In many regards the main alchemical systems of the
world are male-biased. For instance, in Taoist literature
there are fewer written instructions for females than for
males. Even though Taoism is considered by some to be
matrilineal, in practice (at least in the last few hundred
years) most of the emphasis was upon male practitioners. There were, no doubt, very developed female sages
in China, but their presence is not generally represented

in Taoist alchemical treatises (with some notable excep-
tions). In fact, some Taoists practicing *Dual Cultivation*
(the sex practices of Taoism), in previous centuries,
viewed women as mere containers of *chi*. These unscru-
pulous practitioners would engage in the sex act solely
for the purpose of extracting the female's excess chi with
little regard for her comfort or safety.

In Tibetan Buddhism, although the feminine principle is deeply honored, in practice women are often
relegated to lesser places of power and importance.
One of the great Bodhisattvas of Tibetan Buddhism
is Tara, a woman who historically lived in the general
area of Tibet. When she attained illumination, legend
has it that a group of lamas set out to find the new
light, noting that an enlightened being had entered the
world. Upon tracking the light to her village they were
dismayed to discover that she was a woman. They
reputedly said to her, "Now that you have attained
illumination, you can be reborn as a man." To which
she replied, "I will remain forever in the form of a
female." To this day she resides as a feminine presence in a subtle realm of being the Tibetans call the
Samboghaya, the realm of pure light and sound. She
is known as the Swift Protectoress and is a powerful
and beneficent being. Yet that attitude of inherent male
superiority shows up again and again in not only certain aspects of Tibetan Buddhism but through much of
Buddhism in general.

A cursory look at the history of Christianity reveals
patriarchal attempts at the disenfranchisement of
women within the Church and within its historical
documents. In the Dark Ages, the Church formulated
the Nicene Council in an attempt to edit the numerous Gospels and sacred writings of the early Church.
Under the orders of the Roman ruler Constantine, the
Council was charged with choosing which of the many
scriptures would become part of the New Testament.
The result was that the Council threw out many of the

sacred texts of the time, choosing only those that fur-
thered their own ends.

The early mystical vision of the Christians had been
shaped into the territorial and political desires of the
Church and State. And in the process, many of the
writings honoring the feminine were declared a heresy
and the Holy Church of Rome began its long campaign
to disempower women. During the Middle Ages and
especially during the Holy Inquisition, the Church rou-
tinely burned women suspected of being witches. Often
these women were just herbalists and healers. Indeed,
any woman standing up to the patriarchal power of the
Church risked a terrible death.

The disenfranchisement of women by the Church
continues to this day, although it is certainly more subtle
than during the Middle Ages.

I believe that religion and culture are an intimately
woven tapestry. The threads of religious belief pass
into the culture and the attitudes of a culture get sewn
into the fabric of its religion. They are in many ways,
inseparable.

So too, the mystical traditions and alchemical practices born out of religious insight, which are supposed to
be above earthly issues, are invariably affected by cultural assumptions as well. Thus, one can see the threads
of male dominance in the very fabric of mystical and
alchemical systems throughout the world.

As a document purporting to impart an alchemical
system, the *Manuscript* is unique in that its methods are
steeped in the feminine mysteries. Perhaps this is because
it shares roots with the Isis cults of ancient Egypt.

Some of the alchemical presuppositions of the
Manuscript are in alignment with the major alchemical
schools or lineages of the world. However, some of its
views differ quite radically from other alchemical systems.

For example, the *Manuscript* holds the relationship
between sexual partners in high regard. The sex act is
used to activate certain alchemies within the initiates, but

the emotional relationship between the male and female is viewed as the sacred foundation for these alchemies.

For another, the female is seen as holding, within her nature, certain alchemical keys for transformation. These keys cannot be forced, but are accessed only when there is safety and love in a relationship. This approach makes the *Manuscript* unique within other alchemical systems.

Believing as I do in the power of synergy, I feel that those undertaking personal experiments with the Magdalen material would do well to become aware of the other major alchemical schools accessible at this time. In other words, place the *Manuscript* in context to other internally based alchemical systems.

For this reason, I have presented a brief survey of three other major alchemical streams in regards to the sexual practices of internal alchemy. I present this in hopes that it will provide interested readers with a broader context to understand the implications of the *Manuscript* and to better utilize the practices to their benefit.

Tantric Yoga

Tantric yoga is an ancient system of personal transformation that uses sexual energies to develop spiritual illumination. Its roots reach back thousands of years into India's past, and its goals are nothing short of divine transformation. Under the spell of Tantra, a man becomes transformed into a god while his consort is likewise transformed into a goddess. Tantra calls the divine into this world through temporary embodiment in its *tantrikas* (those who practice Tantra). And it is this potent joining of the divine and the human worlds that make this type of yoga so powerful.

This kind of yoga demands arduous training and is fraught with danger. Unless the energies of sex are mastered appropriately, one will not attain the promised liberation of consciousness. One will, instead, be deluded by the heat of one's own passions. Indeed, there are ancient cautions regarding this path of yoga. It is not suitable for everyone. Only those who can enter the fires of sexual passion with sobriety and detachment should attempt it. This type of Tantra is a far cry from the weekend Tantric workshops so popular in the West.

Tantra is a term that means energy practices, and it can be applied either to sexual practices or, as we will see in the section on Buddhist alchemy, it can refer to the energy practices of consciousness itself, as in meditation.

Samadhi

The central piece critical to most alchemical yogas, like Tantra, is the attainment of samadhi. By alchemical yogas I mean those yogic systems that work with the transformation of consciousness through alchemical means. Not all yogas do this. For instance, Tantric Yoga is an alchemical system in that the subtle energies of sex are transformed through alchemical meditation. Raja Yoga, on the other hand, is a philosophical pursuit that may lead to a type of enlightenment but does not impart alchemical methods along the way.

The attainment of samadhi, or *inner attention,* allows the yogi or yogini to explore his or her inner worlds. During successful meditation practice, the mind turns away from the physical senses. One focuses, instead, upon consciousness (*chitta*) itself.

There are innumerable ways to attain samadhi, some of them involving concentration, *mantras* (words of power), *yantras* (visual geometries), and pranayama (breath control), to name a few.

There are varying degrees of samadhi, depending upon the depth and the phenomena that arise within the mind. In some states of samadhi, for instance, there is simply a deep sense of calm and inner peace. The yogi or yogini in such meditative states might also see lights in his or her inner mind, or experience other sensory displays, seemingly without stimulation, in other words, arising spontaneously from the mind.

In deeper states of samadhi, the sense of a separate self may altogether disappear and be replaced by an awareness of pure being (*sat*) without thought. As the yogi or yogini enters these deeper states of samadhi there is often an arising of bliss or ecstasy since the nature of consciousness is bliss (*ananda*).

Kumbhaka and the Suspension of Breathing

As the yogi or yogini enters these deeper samadhis, there is a spontaneous retention of breath, called *kumbhaka*. In this fascinating interplay between body and mind, the breath is suspended. And as long as the yogi or yogini stays in the deeper states of samadhi, there is no need to breathe. When the awareness of the yogi or yogini shifts out of samadhi, however, into an awareness of the physical senses, the body spontaneously takes a breath. There are well-documented cases of samadhis lasting several hours or days with its attendant suspension of breath.

The phenomenon of kumbhaka is remarkably similar to the effects of Taoist *stillness-practices* in which the practitioner enters a timeless state of mind and the breath becomes very shallow or stops altogether. When we get to the section on Taoism, I will talk about a personally striking experience with a stillness-practice, so I won't go into it here. But I will say that every one of the alchemical streams has its own methods for entering stillness of mind. This is due to the simple fact that without stillness of mind, many inner alchemical reactions simply will not take place.

The practice of meditation and the entering into samadhi bring with them many developments of the psyche.

One of these is a greater sensitivity to and awareness of subtle energies. This development of sensitivity is crucial for the alchemist to develop, since one cannot contain (in the alchemical container of awareness) what one is unaware of.

Alterations in Time and Space

Next, we come to a common element experienced by all alchemists, regardless of the stream in which they are practicing—*the alteration of perceived time and space.*

While in samadhi, yogis and yoginis experience a powerful alteration in their sense of both time and space. I believe this is due to radical shifts in brain function (meditative states greatly increase alpha and/or theta activity). In these relaxed brain states, time seems more fluid and space often takes on strange attributes.

What might last an hour in linear time may be experienced as lasting for eons or for just a moment. Yogis and yoginis also report space being affected. They might experience themselves as very large, like the size of a galaxy, or very small, like the size of an atom. They might feel as if they are spinning or floating. These types of phenomena are, by the way, reported by practitioners of all the alchemical streams.

The Three Gunas

There is another reason meditation and the attainment of samadhi is crucial to the practice of alchemical yogas (including Tantra). I call them the three stooges, but the sacred writings of India call them the three *gunas.*

The three gunas are sub-atomic forces responsible, according to yogic philosophy, for everything that exists in creation. They are symbolically represented by the Hindu trinity of Brahma, Vishnu, and Shiva. The first of these forces is called *raja* (meaning king) and is responsible for starting an action. It is associated with the god *Brahma,* who created the universe by uttering the sound Om. His consort is the goddess *Saraswati,* who is associated with the arts and with science.

The second of these forces is called *sattva* and sustains an action. It is associated with the god *Vishnu,* who is responsible for sustaining creation. His consort, or female counterpart, is *Lakshami,* who bestows wealth and beauty.

The last of the gunas is *tamas.* This rather unfashionable guna is responsible for ending an action. It is associated with *Shiva,* the Lord of Death. Shiva is also the Lord and Protector of yogis and yoginis. His consort is *Parvati,* the Cosmic Mother and mother of *Ganesha,* the Destroyer of Obstacles.

When I talk about tamas in workshops, I mention that people are sometimes afraid of Shiva, frightened by endings. But without destruction there can be no creation. I point out that the three gunas operate at all levels of creation, including our breath. The impulse to take a breath is raja or Brahma. The act of inhaling is sattva or Vishnu, and the act of exhaling is tamas or Shiva. I then tell them to be Brahma by starting to take an inhale, and then I tell them to be Vishnu as they continue the inhale. But then I tell them to avoid becoming Shiva. Whatever they do, don't destroy the breath. Well, everyone usually starts laughing at the ludicrousness of my suggestion. Our body wisdom understands the need for endings, even if our minds do not.

According to one of the earliest sacred texts of India, the *Bhagavad-Gita,* the three gunas are responsible for *maya* (illusion). Yogic philosophy states that you and I are deluded. We believe ourselves to be separate beings, but in point of fact, there is only one fundamental Consciousness expressing itself through innumerable forms. Your form is only one of them, as is mine. We tend to take ourselves seriously and get upset if someone or something impinges on our little island of self. But all of this is the play of maya. There is no *you* and there is no *me*; there is only the play (*lila*) of cosmic forces.

The yogi or yogini who has attained this detached state of being is said to have attained God Realization or Unity Consciousness. But this is not just a mental attainment. It is a perceptual attainment as well. One who has attained this unified state of consciousness is no longer deluded by the illusion of maya. He or she sees through the smoke and mirrors of maya to the Self behind all things. And how is this done, you might ask? Well... we do this by getting the three stooges to go to sleep. To be more yogically correct, we might say by getting the gunas to settle into a state of quiescence.

If we enter into samadhi deeply enough, the activity of the gunas within our minds calms down. Discursive self-talk slows down and then stops altogether. Fantasies stop being generated from the deeper layers of mind, and we enter a state of deep quiescence. The three stooges have gone to sleep. Then and only then, can we catch a glimpse of our deepest innate consciousness—the *Self.*

By entering and re-entering meditation, over a long period of time, we can attain varying states of samadhi. If we enter the deepest states enough, our minds will be trained to see past the smoke screen of creation. But until we reach this lofty state of mind we will continue to experience ourselves as separate from each other, victims to the play of maya.

To bring us back full circle, the task of yogic meditation is to enter into deeper and deeper states of samadhi. As we re-experience this liberating awareness over and over again, we slip through the knot of our desires and are freed from the power of maya.

It takes a certain kind of spiritual development to even consider the need for such a radical action. Most people are quite content to pursue their own desires and are simply not interested in seeing behind the illusion.

It is crucial to understand that all perception is relative—relative to the state of the perceiver. The state of mind of a yogi or yogini who has successfully attained an awareness of the Self is very different from the state of mind of someone caught up in the everyday drama of his or her life. Maya is like a television playing a soap opera. Deluded, we continue to watch the show, convinced that it is our lives being played out. The successful yogi or yogini is one who has seen that it is just a show, enters the room, and turns off the TV.

In Tantric yoga the yogi or yogini harnesses the power of sexuality to leap through the illusion of maya, to turn off the TV of limited-mind, if you will.

But without the detached awareness of samadhi, a tantrika (someone who practices Tantric Yoga) can easily be overtaken by passions that arise through sexual contact. The goal of Tantra is a type of meditation, not hedonism. The tantrika uses sensations that arise during ritualistic sex as objects of meditation. Without being able to control their passions, tantrikas will not be able to hold the alchemical container of their awareness.

Another reason for training in samadhi is that the tantrikas must be able to still the mind enough during the sexual act to directly experience their sensory pleasures as the play or interaction of the three gunas. This takes a very sophisticated level of sensitivity, to say the least. And this level of subtle perception can only be attained through experience with samadhic states of awareness, as in meditation.

Sexual Bliss

Let me be specific here. In the experience of sex the sensations of pleasure naturally arise. For most of us this is enough, but not so for the tantrika. He or she is not only entering the sexual experience for pleasure, but also as a means to achieve greater spiritual insight and awareness. A side-effect of Tantra is that pleasure states far exceed normal kinds of sex, but this is not the goal.

For the tantrika, the sensations of foreplay are experienced on many levels. First of all, the actual physical sensations and the release of endorphins occur as they do with most of us. But in addition, due to the mental training of a yogi or yogini, the sense of pleasure is experienced against a backdrop of mental stillness or quiescence. Discursive thought has stopped. Fantasies cease to be generated by the subconscious, and the practitioner experiences the arising of pleasure in its most subtle aspects. At its subtlest level, the practitioner senses the interaction of the three gunas as the creators of his or her sensory delight. At these very subtle levels of awareness, the slightest touch to a Tantric yogi or yogini can set off extraordinary cascades of pleasure and bliss.

As the brain secretes pleasure hormones such as endorphins and other brain chemicals induced through Tantric practice, the tantrikas become highly altered. They become intoxicated with bliss, but this bliss is not just from the sex act. It comes from making contact with *the Self,* the one behind the one who is experiencing the moment. It is the joining of these two blisses that makes Tantra so powerful. And what are these two blisses? They are the bliss of sexual touch and sexual union joined with the bliss of the Self, which is, by its nature, blissful without the need for another.

The methods of Tantric union are quite varied, but most of them require the yogi to hold his seed (avoiding ejaculation) as long as possible. This is because the cycles of arousal, sexual tension, and the dissolving of sexual tension without ejaculation propel both the yogi and yogini into powerful altered states of consciousness. It is thus not unusual for a yogi to make love with his yogini for several hours at a time. The goal of Tantra, unlike the act of sex

itself, is not to have an orgasm, per se, but to experience
the vast multidimensionality of consciousness itself.

Ojas

There is another aspect to Tantra that I should
explain. It has to do with the transformation of sexual
essence into enlightenment. This goal of turning sexual
energy into illumination has some very strong correla-
tions to elements of both ancient Egyptian and Taoist
alchemies. In order to explain this, however, I need to
discuss yogic anatomy.

According to Tantra, there is an energy point near the
top and somewhat to the back of the head. It is generally in the area where the hair grows out from its whorl
and some males of certain Hindu lineages shave their
heads except for a small circle of hair around this area. It
is called the *bindu* and it is a kind of energy transformer
that collects the higher frequencies available to the practitioner. Yogis would say that it is where spirit begins its
descent into matter.

This energy then steps down in frequency (slows its
speed of vibration) as it moves down towards the mulad-
hara (first chakra). Here it reaches its densest state and
becomes the sexual fluids of the individual. According to
this view, a man's semen and a woman's eggs carry not
only their genetic information but also hold the essence
of their spirituality as well.

As the male yogi practices alchemical yoga, especially in Tantra, the energetic essence of his semen,
as opposed to the semen itself, moves upward into
the higher brain centers. This spiritual process is, in
many regards, the opposite of the bindu phenomenon
in which the spiritual energy of the yogi condenses into
his sexual fluids. In this case, the energetic essences of
the male's sperm are transmuted into higher vibrational

energies, called *ojas*. The female yogini has a similar process that arises in herself.

Ojas has very potent effects of consciousness. Yogis and yoginis who successfully accomplish this alchemical distillation universally report radical changes in perception. Their sense of *inner light* is dramatically increased, and there is an increase in spiritual insight. These changes are due, no doubt, to complex alterations in brain chemistry.

Entering the Mythic Realm: Becoming Divinity

Tantric yogis and yoginis go through elaborate preparation for tantric union, including ritualistic bathing, fasting and meditation. The space for the actual Tantra is adorned with things of beauty—flowers, fruit, and assorted foods as well as beverages believed to have aphrodisiac properties.

A crucial part of advanced tantric union is the transformation of the yogini into an embodiment of a goddess and the transformation of the male into an embodiment of a god. The deities used for this transformation vary according to the lineage that is being practiced. And the methods of metamorphosis are closely guarded. Many of them involve the use of specific mantras (words of power) that hold the vibratory essence of the deity being called upon as well as yantras (geometric patterns) also related to the deity.

In addition, the transformation is aided by complex visualizations and occasionally, though not always, through the use of psychoactive plants. Some lineages of Tantra forbid the use of such drugs, since their use during Tantric rituals can be dangerous.

Finally, before making love, both tantrikas envision themselves to be divine beings. Nothing less than full embodiment of the chosen deities will suffice. At some point, a successful tantric ritual demands that the yogi and yogini be transformed. The change is not imaginary, but is real, as real as the mythic entering this realm can be. Thus as the two tantrikas enter into the inner mysteries of Tantra they are, for all intents and purposes, making love, not with a mortal but with a divine being.

This mythic aspect has immense consequences in terms of its transformational effects. It is a key component in advanced Tantric ritual. And those who practice Tantra without this component have missed the kernel of the mystery.

Taoism

There were two primary streams of philosophical thought in ancient China—those of Confuscianism and Taoism. Confuscianism was pragmatic and focused upon one's position in, and one's responsibilities to family and state. Taoism, on the other hand, was largely mystical, and was concerned with such things as one's relationship to the cosmos and the means to extend one's life for the purpose of spiritual illumination.

The foundation of Taoism is based upon an abstract concept known as the *Tao*. This ephemeral field of intelligence is said to be responsible for the entire universe. It continually emanates energy but is untouched by its creations. According to Taoism, mankind is blessed due to the fact that his/her deepest nature allows him/her to make direct contact with *the source of all things*. Taoist alchemy is fundamentally a means to make contact with one's deeper nature, thereby giving access to the Tao itself. Such contact is highly transformational. Those sages who accomplished this feat attained almost mythical stature, due, no doubt, to their exhibiting the powers of consciousness (siddhis) mentioned in the last chapter.

In order to comprehend Taoist alchemy, we must come to an understanding of a subtle force called chi. From the immense mystery of the Tao, which creates all worlds but is untouched by them, there is an eternal flow of this vital force (chi).

There are many types of chi. There is, for instance, a vital force flowing out of quasars and stars, though this is quite different in quality from the chi created by a stream. When most people think about chi, they usually think about the subtle life force in air. This type of chi is most concentrated in natural areas, away from cities. This kind of vital force is strongest in large areas of tree growth, by lakes, rivers, and streams as well as by larger bodies of water like oceans. Some individuals have speculated that this type of chi is related to negative ions and there is some evidence that this is so. But there are other types of chi as well—more subtle, more refined types of chi, and this is one of the focuses of advanced Taoist alchemy.

Traditionally, Taoist sages spent much of their time as hermits in nature. In later periods, groups of men or women would form communities to pursue their alchemical search with others. But almost always, these Taoist abodes were far from cities. They were usually located in places where the chi was especially strong, often in areas designated as *Dragon Points.*

Dragon Points are places of convergence where one form of chi meets another. They are most dramatically seen in mountain ranges. When two ridges meet, there is often a trench or a gorge that flows down the sides of the mountains. As *celestial chi* (the type of chi generated in the sky), flows downward, it meets the *terrestrial chi* of the mountain at the point between the ridges. This is called a Dragon Point.

Where two streams or rivers converge, there is a detectable increase of chi, and this too, is called a Dragon Point. Taoist sages would search for these places and put their abodes either in the Dragon Point itself, or nearby. This made their alchemical work easier since there was a ready abundance of chi that they could draw upon in their practices.

Thought, Time, and Breath

As with Tantric yoga, the Taoist alchemist must train the mind to enter prolonged states of stillness. This quiescence of mind is crucial, since the Tao can only be experienced in mental silence. Furthermore many of the alchemical transformations in Taoist alchemy require a silent mind as well.

There are many classes of stillness practices, some of them involving movement, such as T'ai chi and others involving sitting meditation, such as the *Celestial Gate,* which I will discuss to some extent in a moment.

In these stillness practices, the mind is eventually led to a state of deep quietude. In actual practice, especially at the beginning, there may be a flurry of mental activity. Thoughts come and go, sometimes in a torrent, sometimes in a trickle. Eventually the practitioner notices that the speed of his or her thought seems to be slowing down. There seems to be more space between thoughts, and at some point they stop altogether, if only briefly.

The practitioner also notices that the breath changes during these states. There is a tendency for the breath to slow down as thought slows down. And when there is no thought there is often no breath, or it is very shallow. This is significant for several reasons.

From a neurological standpoint, we could say that this is because the brain waves of the practitioner are in the lower states of alpha and/or theta where the breath naturally gets slower. Research on meditation has noted, by the way, that these states also produce a decrease in muscle tension, heart rate, blood pressure, and respiration, all of which are quite positive in their stress-reducing effects. In fact, studies have shown that those who practice forms of meditation that produce these effects, as in the Taoist stillness practices, are generally less stressed than their counterparts who do not meditate.

Several years ago, about an hour before twilight, I chose to do a stillness practice known as the Celestial Gate (sometimes referred to as Heaven's Gate) in a park. As twilight descended around me I was still doing the practice, and noticed that my breathing had stopped. Not only this, but thought seemed to be arrested. My mind was clear and as calm as the surface of a tranquil lake. But most impressive to me, in the moment, was that time also seemed to have stopped, and I was suspended in a timeless dimension of mind.

I decided to walk back to my car as it was getting dark, and the trip took me twenty minutes or so. I noted that the impulse to go back to the car came as a sensation, as if it had come from deep within my body, and not as a thought. I did not think—"Now I need to get back to the car." This non-speaking state of mind seemed oddly amusing to me at the time. During my saunter, I noticed that my breath was very shallow even though the trail back to the car was over hilly terrain. That timeless feeling was still very strong and I seemed to move over the hills with little effort.

Ironically, when I saw my car in the parking lot I remembered an appointment later that evening, and I spontaneously took a deep breath. My breath had returned to normal and that feeling of timelessness vanished. I was firmly rooted back in time.

There is a fascinating relationship between the perception of timelessness and the cessation of breath. In yoga, you may recall, the cessation of breath is called kumbhaka. In Taoist meditation practice, this suspension of the breath is often encountered as well, especially when entering the deeper states of mental quiescence.

Interestingly, the idea of breath suspension can be found within Egyptian alchemy in the concept of *ankh*.

The ankh, sometimes called the Egyptian Cross, consists of three main parts—the *cross* itself, representing matter, the *shen* loop representing spirit, and the *shen knot* which represents the breath. As long as we are breathing, our spirit is bound to the matter of our bodies, our embodiments. However, when the shen knot loosens, the breath stops or gets very shallow, and we can, in that moment, enter timelessness. Once again, we see a central concept in one alchemical system repeated in other alchemical traditions. I do think it fascinating that the Taoist word for spirit (shen) is the same as the Egyptian (shen). I do not know if it is simply a coincidence of translation or if the terms really were the same. Nevertheless, it is quite interesting.

But back to the paradoxes of time, thought, and breath. As a psychotherapist who often worked in the area of psychoneuroimmunology (how our thoughts and feelings affect immunity), I find the time paradox also intriguing from the vantage point of health.

A study of patients admitted to an emergency room due to cardiac arrest reveals some fascinating information about the interplay between body and mind. During recovery, these patients were asked some questions about their perception of time. Based on their responses, researchers could predict who would recover and who would die from another heart attack. Those patients who said that they were letting things go to take care of themselves and who reported feeling that there would be more than enough time to do what needed to be done were more likely to recover and avoid a second heart attack. Those patients, however, who stated that they were under tremendous pressure to do what had been left undone and who felt that they were running out of time invariably suffered a higher incidence of death due to a second cardiac arrest.

None of this would come as a surprise to a Taoist sage. From the standpoint of Taoism, our modern time-crunch world is disturbing to both health and spiritual attainment.

We need to bring our time-bound minds back to tranquility on a regular basis or suffer the ill effects of our modern age.

I have taught a simple form of a Taoist stillness practice to hundreds if not thousands of people by now. Everyone has expressed a deep appreciation for a method of meditation that is so quick and easy to enter into. Those who have never been able to meditate due to continual thought (inner dialogue) are especially appreciative of this method since thought is not a hindrance to the practice.

I think this meditation is so effective I have included a brief description of how to do it below. If you aren't interested in experiencing this for yourself, just skip it and go to the next part.

The Celestial Gate Meditation

The Celestial Gate Meditation practice is based on Dragon Points. Dragon Points, as I mentioned earlier, are places of convergence where one form of chi meets another.

There are several Dragon Points within the human body. The Celestial Gate is just one of these, and happens to be a place where *heavenly chi* (a very subtle form of chi) flows into the body and meets the *terrestrial (or earth) chi* of the body itself. Thus this place is an energetically *charged area,* and Taoist sages discovered a long time ago how to take advantage of it.

Sit comfortably and close your eyes. You can lie down if you wish, but this makes some people go to sleep. For a moment, just notice your breath. Don't change it in any way; just watch it. Notice the rhythm and the depth of your breath. Then after a moment become aware of the space about an inch behind the bridge of the nose. Imagine that there is an opening about one inch square in this area. This is the Celestial Gate. All you do is focus on it.

Do not concentrate on it. Just be aware of it. If you are having thoughts or fantasies, this is not a problem. Let them continue on their merry way. Just let some part of your attention be on the opening. You can think all you want about anything you want and the practice will still work, so long as some part of your attention is on the Celestial Gate (the opening).

As you continue to focus at the gate, you will notice that thoughts seem to slow down. There will seem to be more spaces between the thoughts or fantasies. And eventually they will stop altogether, if only temporarily. It is during these moments that you might find that your breath has stopped or has become very shallow. This is natural and is, in fact, a sign that you are entering the deeper states of stillness. It is in these deepest states of quiescence, where there is no-breath and no-thought that contact with the Tao takes place.

Doing it for about five minutes will usually give you a clear sense of how this practice alters awareness. Eventually you can extend the period of time for deeper experiences.

Don't let the simplicity of this meditation fool you. It is a profound stillness practice that will lead you directly to the Tao itself. Gently extend the periods of stillness so that you become acquainted with and comfortable with these deep places of quiet. As you explore your own inner worlds, you might eventually encounter celestial beings who may grace you with their guidance and instruction.

In Taoism, the deepest secrets are revealed only by the Tao itself. You cannot find these truths written in books, for it is forbidden to write about them. Thus, meditations like the Celestial Gate are like cosmic keys. Like keys, however, you must turn them to open the lock. If you wish to experience the mysteries of the Tao for yourself and not just read about them, you must turn the key.

Cultivation of Chi

As with the Tantric yogi or yogini who attains samadhi, a Taoist practitioner will become aware of ever more
subtle levels of perception. This subtlety of perception
allows the Taoist to sense the flow of chi directly and to
draw it into the body (called *collecting)* for the purpose
of alchemical transformation (called *cultivation*).

With a heightened sensitivity to chi, a Taoist alchemist undertakes several things. First of all, he or she
collects chi throughout the day, drawing this vital force
into the body to strengthen organs and systems. There
are many forms by which this is done. Chi Gong masters
from China have recently started teaching in the West,
and this is one form of chi collecting and cultivation. But
there are other forms as well.

Depending upon the school and methods used, most
Taoists eventually turn their attention to the *chi body*.
This is the same as the etheric body of the yogis or the
Ka body of the Egyptians. And like the aforementioned
bodies, the chi body is the same shape as the physical
body. It interpenetrates the physical body and there is no
part of the physical body that is not within the chi body.

The development of the chi body is a crucial element
in many forms of Taoist alchemy. Part of the reason for
this is that it (a potent chi body) lays the foundation for
more advanced practices. If either the physical body or
the chi body is depleted, certain alchemical processes
cannot be undertaken. And strengthening of the chi body
is crucial for the attainment of Immortality.

One of the more interesting ways of cultivating chi,
and thereby strengthening the chi body, involves what
the Taoists call the *elixir fields*. These energetic res-
ervoirs of chi are in three areas of the chi body itself.
When they are fully charged with chi, they emit an energy that is called an *elixir* due to its strengthening effects.

The *first elixir field* is in the area of the lower organs,
from the diaphragm down to the pelvic floor. This elixir

field strengthens the lower visceral organs. The *second elixir field* is in the area of the upper organs of the torso, from the diaphragm up to the top of the lungs. This elixir field strengthens the lungs and heart as well as the thymus gland, one of the major sites of the immune system. The *third elixir field* is in the head and strengthens neurological function.

Certain forms of Taoist alchemy draw chi into these areas (collecting) and then circulate the chi through the corresponding organs and up towards the head (cultivation). As the chi is refined and drawn to the next elixir field, the organs within that field are strengthened and the circulating chi is refined.

The ancient Taoists also explored the subtle energy pathways of the body and mapped them out with considerable detail. The *meridians* used in acupuncture were discovered and described by the Taoists. They are similar to the nadis of Yoga, and scientific research on the meridians, most notably in Japan, has demonstrated that they are an energetic phenomenon.

In addition to the meridians, the Taoists described a pathway that became crucial to certain types of alchemy; they called it the *microcosmic orbit.* This pathway circulates chi from the perineum up the spine into the head and then down the front of the body back down to the perineum. As the microcosmic orbit makes its way through the chi body, it passes through the three elixir fields. By moving *chi* through the microcosmic orbit the practitioner stimulates the higher brain centers, and greatly refines the quality of the circulating chi. The refinement of chi is crucial in Taoist Alchemy since it is only through refined chi that one can enter shen, or the spirit world. It is also said in the more esoteric schools of Taoism that practicing the microcosmic orbit dissolves negative karmas (negative effects arising from past actions).

Sexual Essence into Spirit: Jing and Shen

If we look at the transformation of consciousness
through Taoist metaphor, we could say the task is that
of changing water into mist. The energy of embodied life is refined through alchemical processes to the
point that it becomes like mist. When one has attained
this highly refined state, one's essence is now more
spirit than that of man or woman. And the key to this
remarkable transformation from a biological into a spiritual being begins with sex.

The transformation of sexual essence into spirit is a
key component of many types of Taoism. In Taoism,
the male's sexual essence is called *jing*. One's spiritual
nature is called *shen*. By drawing the sexual energy of
jing up the spine through the microcosmic orbit, it is
refined and eventually becomes shen. This movement
of chi up the spine is, of course, reminiscent of the raising of the djed in Egyptian alchemy as well as the concept of the sushumna or central pathway of the chakras
in Yoga. I have not read any existing traditional Taoist
writings for women in regards to the transformation of
their sexual essence into shen (spirit). This does not
mean, of course, that such writings don't exist, just that
I haven't seen them. Nevertheless, I believe the process
is similar to that of the male in many ways.

As in nature, there is always more than one way to
accomplish a task. And the transformation of one's
sexual essence into spiritual illumination (shen) is no
exception. In some forms of Taoist alchemy, the practitioner focuses on the collection of chi into the first elixir
field. When there is an excess of chi in this area, meaning not needed by the visceral organs, the alchemist
will activate the *first alchemical furnace* in which the
dross or impurities of the chi are removed. This refined
chi is then progressively circulated into the second and
third elixir fields. This movement also refines the chi,
making it more subtle. By the time it reaches the head

(third elixir field) it is transformed into shen, giving the Taoist access to the spirit worlds.

When a Taoist alchemist has successfully transformed his or her sexual essence into shen, he or she has attained a very exalted state of being. Myths and legends abound from ancient China in regards to these high Taoist sages. Legend has it that these beings lived in the high places of mountains (Dragon Points) sustaining themselves off of dew and herbs.

From an alchemical standpoint, morning dew collected on the leaves of plants is highly concentrated chi. A being who has transformed his or her sexual essence into shen would have no trouble sustaining himself or herself on such a refined food. For such a person, the digestive system would be highly refined and could easily metabolize the chi of dew into usable energy.

Here on an island in the Cyclades, there is a wonderful melon, a cousin to the honeydew. But unlike other melons that need watering, this melon grows on the barren, dry, and windswept soil of the island without any water whatsoever. Amazingly, it draws its water from the air. And it is one of the most extraordinary melons I have ever tasted. One can sense the intensely concentrated chi, and the taste is sweet.

There is another botanical wonder on the island that does something similar. It looks like our cedar trees in the Northwest, but like the melons it does not need any water. This is good because there is precious little on the island. These trees grow near the ocean and draw the salt-laden air to their leaves, extracting the moisture and leaving the dried salt behind. I had never thought about plants being alchemists (other than the obvious process of photosynthesis), but these two plants have obviously attained a high degree of alchemical mastery.

But let's return to our human alchemists. When a Taoist has refined his or her sexual nature into the state of shen (spirit), he or she becomes a very different order of being. And how this miraculous transformation takes place is through balancing two opposing cosmological forces: *yin* and *yang.*

Yin and Yang

The deeply intuitive sages of ancient China explored the patterns of creation within nature, and one of their discoveries was the existence of two subtle, complementary and at times opposing forces called yin and yang. In Taoist symbolism, the sun and moon are sometimes used to denote these two elements of creation.

Yang (the sun) is associated with light and heat. It is kinetic, meaning energy in motion, and it moves decisively. Lightning is yang. It lights up the sky, has tremendous force, and when it strikes, there is no hesitation.

Yin (the moon) is moist, cool, and dark. It is potential energy, not kinetic. A seed sitting under ground is under the influence of yin. It is surrounded by moisture. It is dark and it is cool. But when the sun (yang) comes out, its heat warms the soil and the seed begins to grow. It is the balance of yin and yang that produces life. Too much moisture (yin) and the seed will rot. Too much heat (yang) and it will shrivel up and die.

Yin and yang are not static forces. They are continually transforming into each other. Yin becomes yang and yang becomes yin. Although we can never see yin or yang directly, we can experience their effects.

For some reason, I am reminded of an experience I had during my freshman year at Belmont Abbey. Although I did not know it at the time, it is an example of the ever-constant transformations of yin and yang.

It was October and the trees on campus were brilliant with the mottled reds and yellows of fall. Everywhere one stepped, the grass crackled with the sound of dead leaves under foot. A stiff breeze was blowing across the quadrangle, an omen of winter just ahead.

I had stepped out into the brisk air from my dormitory, en route to an afternoon soccer game. I don't remember who we were playing, but it was homecoming and the campus was humming with activity, a state rarely experienced in this Benedictine run college.

The lanes were full of parked cars with alumni returning to their alma mater. The trunks and backs of station wagons were brimming like some kind of modern cornucopias laden with fried chicken, potato salad, and iced tea. This was, after all, the South. Here and there a make shift barbecue was obscured by smoke. And the smell of hot dogs and hamburgers wafted through the air.

Students walked with their parents in a kind of spontaneous parade. Some seemed proud of being seen with their families. Some slinked back, pretending not to belong to the parents who had borne them.

This menagerie of humanity flowed into the soccer stadium like a river and I joined it on the last rung of the bleachers. As the game ensued, I remember being oddly detached, as if watching a ballet. The sky was a bright Carolina blue and the sun was hanging midway in the sky. Its warmth was just enough to be pleasant against the cold air, and I suppose it was this balanced force of the elements that created the odd effect in me.

The soccer team came onto the field and we released a hullabaloo like only a group of suppressed Catholic boys can muster. We had become yang. We were full of energy, yelling and whooping, the sound of our catcalls no doubt heard in the small town miles away.

And then the team took their positions, waiting for the ball to be tossed in the air by the referee. We stood breathlessly still. We watched with rapt attention. We had become yin.

Then our team miraculously got the ball. I say miraculously because almost every game we played that year, we lost. Not only that, but we had lost the homecoming game to this same team every year for the last five years. You can imagine the tension.

Suddenly we sprang to our feet. The aluminum bleachers groaned from the weight. We had transformed, in the twinkling of an eye, from yin into yang. We were screaming with delight as our team got closer to the goal, and then, in a moment, our glory was taken away by some blonde punk who stole the ball and the game headed off in the opposite direction. After some catcalls from a few of the alumni, we settled en masse back into our seats. Yang had become yin.

I watched this constant ballet of yang into yin and back into yang the whole afternoon. When the game was over, I watched the last glimmer of the sun as it sat behind the large oaks on campus. The air was still. The alumni had gone home and most of the students were in the pub or in their dorms. I walked the strangely silent grounds. The sliver of a new moon was rising through the last remnants of sunset. Yang had turned into yin. Oh, and the ballgame? We lost.

Cultural Attitudes and the Cultivation of Chi

We live in an ocean of chi. Some of it is yang, full of power and direction. Some of it is yin, receptive and resting. For the most part we are unaware of it, though it affects us on many levels.

A Taoist alchemist is one who has become aware of this all-pervading sea of chi. And through the practices of alchemy, he or she learns to draw this energy into his or her body to transform consciousness and to enhance health and well-being.

Our modern lifestyle in the industrialized West is destructive of well-being. We are overly fixated on yang. We honor productivity and action. We do not, as a culture, understand or appreciate inaction. It is considered weak.

We jazz ourselves up with caffeine and other drugs. We are obsessed with speed. We are yang and proud of it.

But there are problems with this.

For one, it is out of balance, and two, it is ultimately destructive. We don't generally understand this, but yang comes out of yin.

In the state of Washington there is a powerful hydro-electric dam. There is nothing more yang, perhaps, than electricity. But the source of this yang power is watery yin. The lake that was dammed to make the hydroelec-tric plant is now a vast body of water. It sits absolutely still most of the time, except for little wavelets created by the wind. It is yin. It is potential power, but it is unmov-ing. It is *all* potential. But when the sluice gates open at the plant, this watery yin is transformed into yang and the rushing water turns the immense turbines of the power plant. This, in turn, produces another form of yang, the electricity that runs our lights and TVs and our other "time-saving" appliances. Of course, we don't have enough time to enjoy those time-saving devices, but that is another issue.

We are caught up in a cultural whirlwind of yang-mad-ness. Fast food restaurants abound and are painted with yang colors like red and yellow to encourage customers to eat faster, making room for more customers. Mindless repetitive techno pop blares in the background and fast paced ambient music encourages us to do everything a little faster. I use the term *music* rather loosely, since this post modern crap bares little resemblance to the loftier attributes of music like healing and inspiration. But you see, music or the bastardization of it, is one of my pet peeves. So please do forgive me and let's get back to yin and yang.

To summarize my main point here, I would say that many Westerners, especially those in the United States, seem to be uncomfortable with leaving any space or moment in time unfilled.

The net affect of all this is that we are seeing an immense increase in stress-related illnesses. The body is simply not equipped to remain in yang states for long periods of time. It needs yin. It needs time to do nothing, to rest, perchance to dream.

But in our Western culture, doing nothing is seen as being lazy. Yet this is sometimes the wisest thing we can do. If you want to be yang, then you had best spend some time being yin.

A Taoist would never be caught dead having expended too much yang, if he or she can avoid it. The reason is that Taoist alchemy requires an exquisite balance of these two forces.

The ancient Taoists understood this phenomenon to a great extent, and if anything characterizes Taoism, it is the concept of poised balance. This concept becomes second nature to a practicing alchemist, since the success of Taoist alchemy requires that the forces of yin or yang be used correctly.

Dual Cultivation

Dual Cultivation has some striking parallels to methods discussed in the *Manuscript*. There are also some very significant differences.

In order to understand this type of alchemy, we must return to yin and yang. According to Taoist theory, a healthy female possesses a virtually unlimited amount of yin-chi (chi that is yin). This is part of her nature.

A healthy male, on the other hand, has a limited amount of yang. Unlike the female, his nature does not grant him an unlimited reservoir of yang-chi.

In the advanced forms of *chi cultivation*, the female alchemist must collect yang energy in order to balance her excess yin. And the male must collect yin energy in order to balance his excess yang. In actuality, it is much more complex.

The ultimate balancing of yin and yang within a practitioner is paramount, since it is only when yin and yang have been balanced that certain alchemical practices can be engaged. Thus, all Taoists seek to balance the forces of yin and yang within themselves.

Those alchemists practicing alone must accomplish this task through elaborate alchemical meditations and energy work. Those who do this with a partner of the opposite sex can simply collect the desired chi during the act of sex.

During sexual contact there is an abundance of excess chi. The acts of stroking and fondling set off flows of chi both inside and around the body. An alchemist trained in the methods of Dual Cultivation can draw the excess chi into his or her chi body, thereby greatly enhancing his or her alchemical work.

During Dual Cultivation, the male avoids ejaculation as this would deplete his yang energy and bring the act of intercourse to an end. In this type of alchemy, long periods of intercourse are desired. The reason is quite simple and pragmatic: prolonging sex generates massive amounts of chi, and since the goal of Dual Cultivation is to collect excess chi, the more the better.

To assist in this process, the ancient Taoists developed something called the *valley orgasm*. When the male starts to feel that ejaculation is close at hand, he backs off from genital stimulation. He rests for a moment until the desire passes. Then he returns to intercourse. This continues in cycles of stimulation and rest for as long as the partners desire. The result is that both partners enter highly altered and deeply sensual states by which their sensitivity to chi is greatly increased. In addition, the amount of excess yin and yang generated from such continual sexual contact is considerable.

The Final Attainment: Land of the Immortals

The ultimate goal of Taoist alchemy is immortality. Having attained quiescence of mind through the stillness practices, the Taoist alchemist has trained him or herself to be aware of the many types of chi. And with this knowledge he or she has been able to *collect* and *cultivate* beneficial chi through the subtle pathways of the body. He or she has learned how to distill the essence of this excess chi into energy for the purpose of increasing health and generating enhanced consciousness.

Along the way, the alchemist gets healthier and more vital, a result of collecting chi and circulating it into the major organs of the body. This is, gratifyingly, one of the key benchmarks to progress in this way of alchemy. And even if he or she does not attain the Immortal Body, the work of alchemy has been well worth the effort.

Eventually, through persistent practice, the subtle chi body is charged with vital force as well. It becomes as real to the Taoist alchemist as his or her physical body, and through it he or she can, in meditation, enter the Heavenly Abodes where master alchemists abound and one can greatly accelerate one's progress through the grace of instruction.

Finally, the great alchemical task of transforming sexual essence into spirit (shen) is coming to fruition. Long years of practice are bearing fruit and the alchemist is, in some ways, more spirit than flesh, though he or she still has a body.

The moment comes when the Taoist, now a sage, senses a moment in time. All the forces have come together in perfect timing. Yin and yang are perfectly balanced. Death might be near, or the alchemist might simply choose to leave the earth plane at will. Entering into deep meditation, the sage passes beyond the grips of time and space. The breath stops. Attention is shifted into the chi body, as it has been done so many times before. The Taoist has mounted *the Dragon*, his or her own transformed nature, and flies off into the Heavenly Abode.

The alchemist is now an *energy-being*. He or she might remain like this for a very, very long time. The moment may come, however, when no longer desiring even the subtlest of forms, the sage leaves the Heavenly Abode behind. The master alchemist refines his or her (already subtle) chi even more. Attaining the subtlest form, he or she returns to the *Formless Heaven* from which he or she originated. And as the sage slips into this primal space, all traces of the self disappear. The drop has slipped into the shining sea. There is no form; there is no sage; there is only the Tao.

Tibetan Buddhist Alchemy

Of all the forms of Buddhism, and there are many, I personally find the Tibetan forms to be the most vibrant. Part of this is due, no doubt, to the fact that Tibetan Buddhism is actually a synthesis of both Buddhism and the *Bon* religion. When Siddhartha became the Buddha, the Bon had already existed for many centuries.

The Bon were known as master magicians and sorcerers, and today there are still persons practicing this ancient religion. Much of the Bon deals with the residing spirits of the primal elements (earth, air, sky, water) as well as spirits and beings that reside in places of power such as mountains and openings into the earth.

When Padmasambhava brought Buddhism into Tibet, he encountered many of these spirits. Some of the beings were quite negative, and Peme (as the Tibetans call him) transformed these demons into Protectors of the *Dharma* (the way of Buddhism), which is why some of the Protector Deities look so fierce.

I imagine that it is due to the Bon that the Tibetan forms of Buddhism have so many more deities (energy-beings) than do other forms of Buddhism. And the various forms of Tibetan Buddhist alchemy reflect this abundance. The idea of energy-beings may seem foreign to Westerners, since these beings are non-corporeal (meaning without physical form). However, they do have bodies of a kind. They are more energy than mass, and for the most part we are unaware of them. However, if a person's awareness is refined enough, as through meditation practice, one can, not only sense these beings but one can interact with them as well. The attributes of such beings were catalogued by lamas centuries ago in highly secret texts which, for the most part, have not found their way into the West. In certain types of advanced alchemy practiced by Tibetan hermits in their remote, high mountain retreats, some of these beings were utilized in secret Tantric rituals. I will speak more on this later, but first I think it would be good to discuss the fundamental insight of Buddhism in general, since this forms the foundation upon which the alchemical practices of Tibetan Buddhism are engaged. Indeed, without this foundation of Buddhist philosophy, the practices of Tibetan alchemy can lead to misunderstanding and abuse.

Emptiness

From the many insights offered by the Buddha regarding samsara (this world of illusion), perhaps the most penetrating is the concept of emptiness. For many Westerners, hell-bent to fill every quiet moment, this concept is strange indeed.

But a cursory glance at quantum physics shows that this modern science is utterly and completely in agreement with the Buddha's assessment. According to the quantum view, there is very little solidity to matter. Take your body, for instance. It has been estimated that we are comprised of +/-99.9% space. If all the actual physical matter of your body was put in a pile, it would fit on the tip of a pin! To our physical eyes and to our physical touch, we seem solid. But this is illusory, a smoke-and-mirror show created by our physical senses. In point of fact, we are mostly emptiness.

According to Buddhism, if you go deep enough into the heart of all things, there is only emptiness. And therefore no thing is ultimately real since it is, at its heart, empty and devoid of form or identity.

Take your body again. It has senses through which you make contact with the world around you. Out of these five senses you create your experience of yourself and the world around you. That wasn't a typo, by the way. You *are* the creator of your experience. You tend to identify with what you like and distance yourself mentally from those things you don't like. Perhaps you like the color of your eyes, but dislike the texture of your hair. When you see your eyes reflected back to you in a mirror, you might pause for a moment to enjoy looking at them. But when you catch a glimpse of your hair, you may find yourself feeling uncomfortable or self-critical. These emotional responses to ourselves and the world are experienced as quite real. They have a punch and a power that is sometimes difficult to avoid.

However, all of this is based on nothing. For if you go deep enough into the brain, for instance, into the neurons responsible for holding the thought and emotions of self-criticism or self-glorification, you will find that eventually there is nothing. In other words, at the deepest levels of the cells, i.e., the atomic and subatomic levels, there is no mass, no solidity, only space and emptiness.

Relative and Absolute Existence

To summarize an essential concept in Tibetan Buddhism: "Form is emptiness, and emptiness is form. Neither is real nor unreal. They are both existing and non-existing."

To the Western mind this may very well seem like nonsense. How can something exist and non-exist at the same time? Well, what this statement refers to is both

absolute and relative existence. You and I exist at the relative level of creation. We have a common illusion of solidity, but at the deepest levels of our very physicality there
is nothing, only emptiness. Therefore, at the absolute level
of creation, you and I do not exist. We are like mirages,
like clouds; we come and go. For a moment we seem
quite real, and then we pass away. Thus not only are we
essentially empty, we are impermanent as well.

The Cultivation of Bliss

This could very well lead to depression, except that
through the practice of Buddhist alchemy we also make
contact with another aspect of our intrinsic nature: bliss.
This is one of the hallmarks of Tibetan Buddhist High
Tantra (or alchemy). Through meditative practices, the
yogi or yogini self-generates bliss. While resting within
this field of self-generated bliss, the yogi or yogini contemplates the nature of emptiness. In other words, raised
up on feelings of bliss and ecstasy, the yogi or yogini
thinks about the essential emptiness of all things, including his or her own body. This union of bliss and emptiness generates enlightenment.

The goal of Buddhist practice is to penetrate the
depths of consciousness (called *the Mind* in Buddhism).
For when this occurs, one is no longer deluded by the
play of the senses or the illusory nature of samsara. One
is then free and aware. In fact, when someone asked the
Buddha if he was a god, he said, "No. I am awake."

The metaphor runs very deep here. From the vantage point of illuminated consciousness, we are all in
various degrees of sleep. We think we are awake, but
we are actually dreaming. Through the power of *bodhicitta* (literally Buddha mind), we awaken from the
dream and see that we are creating our reactions to all
that we survey.

This power to recognize life as a dream, and to awaken from it, is an inherent power of bodhicitta. Now, it is important to understand that we all possess bodhicitta (or Buddha-mind). We are all Buddhas (awakened beings) in latent form. But some of us, due to mental and emotional obscurations (blocks), are more removed from our blissful and compassionate natures than others. And this is precisely the reason for practicing Buddhist meditations—i.e., to remove the obstacles to our essential natures.

There are many schools or lineages within Buddhism. Each lineage has its own ways of imparting the essential insights of the Buddha, and each tradition has its own ways of imparting the dharma (literally, the Way of Buddhism).

Our concern here is with a particular type of Tibetan Buddhist practice that is alchemical in nature. It is called *Highest Yoga Tantra* and is considered by some to be the rapid path to enlightenment. In this regard, it shares its reputation for swiftness with *Dzogchen,* another form of Tibetan Buddhism.

The focus of Highest Tantra is fourfold: 1) Secret Mantra, 2) alchemical meditation, 3) bliss generated from distilled sexual essence, and 4) embodiment as a Buddha.

Secret Mantra

First, let us take a look at *Secret Mantra*. The Sanskrit word, mantra, literally means protection of the Mind (*man* meaning mind, and *tra*, meaning protection). Within this practice, the term mantra does not mean words of power as is normally associated with this word. For instance, the *bija* (or seed sound) Om is a mantra, a mantric word of power. By chanting this mantra silently or out loud, one alters awareness and protects one's Mind from the delusions of samsara (the world of sensory illusion). However, the practices of Highest Yoga Tantra also protect the Mind. How do they do this? This dazzling feat of protection is accomplished by keeping the Mind free from identification with the illusion of the mundane. According to Highest Tantra, we are (in our natures) luminous, blissful beings (utterly and perfectly divine). However, one of the effects of samsara (the illusion of this world) is to defile our Minds with the impression that we are ordinary. We believe ourselves to be mortal rather than divine beings. Thus, Secret Mantra is a means to remember that we are divine Buddhas currently residing in the ocean of samsara. This is a very different strategy from that of striving to become Buddhas, and it has vast implications—one being the rapidity with which enlightenment can take place.

The Secret Channel

Next, let us consider the alchemical meditations of Highest Tantra. The goal of this alchemical method is nothing short of enlightenment, which requires that the Mind withdraw or be freed from the sensory illusions of this world. In other words, as long as we are bedazzled by the sensory displays of our embodiment, we will not be able to make contact with our essential bodhicitta (Buddha mind). To do this, our Minds must be still, quiescent.

The yogi or yogini within Highest Tantra accomplishes this formidable task by driving the *winds* of their senses inward, away from the objects of their desires and into the inner sanctum of their energy bodies, into what is called the *Secret Channel*. The net result of this action is that the Mind is brought to a deep state of quietude. It is only within this profound stillness that bodhicitta can be directly experienced.

The winds are subtle energies that move through the energy pathways of the body (called meridians by Taoists and nadis by Yogis). My experience is that if I listen (clairaudiently, i.e. inner hearing) to the movement of life-energy through these subtle pathways, the sound is very akin to the sound of the wind.

According to Tibetan anatomy, the winds (lhung) are responsible for the five senses. Each sense has its own peculiar type of wind, and when the winds stop, the corresponding sense ceases. Death, from this perspective, is a dissipation of the winds. As a result, the death process is one of successive disconnection from the five senses. Ultimately, with no input from the senses, there is only consciousness. And with no sensory object to focus upon, consciousness focuses upon itself. For a moment, depending upon the clarity of the individual, there is a spontaneous arising of bliss and clear light (light without attributes). If one has been trained in the yoga of the *bardos* (states of being, especially those in the death realms), it is possible to remain in this clear light without the need for re-embodiment within samsara.

Tibetan alchemical yogas, such as Highest Tantra, are an attempt to accomplish this feat of self-realization while alive by driving the winds inward, into the Secret Channel. This subtle energy channel runs through the center of the body from the perineum up into the head. By sending the winds into this channel through the power of meditation, the senses cease to generate sensory experience and the yogi or yogini experiences *pure Mind* without dying. Repetition of this radical shift in perception eventually results in high degrees of spiritual illumination, and an ability to remain aware during death and the after-death experiences of the Bardos.

Sexual Essence: The Red and White Drops

Another stage in Highest Yoga Tantra involves the distillation of sexual essence into bliss. One way this is accomplished is through a specific form of *tuomo,* or *psychic fire.*

In this form, one focuses on the sound *Ah* while concentrating on the navel wheel (chakra). This action causes a psychic fire to rise up the Secret Channel into the head. Here, the "heat" of the psychic fire causes the *Red and White Drops* to fall down from the crown wheel (chakra). The Red Drops are related to the sexual and spiritual essence of one's biological mother, and the White Drops to one's biological father. As the two drops join, bliss is generated. The longer the practice is engaged, the more powerful the bliss. As the bliss arises within one's mind, one contemplates the essential emptiness of all things. This union of bliss and emptiness produces a type of enlightenment.

There are dangers with this practice. According to Tibetan Medicine, *Nectar Gathering Practices*, like this, can create imbalances in the subtle bodies due to an overabundance of the fire element. For this reason, it is traditionally stated that this form of alchemy should only be undertaken under the guidance of one's tantric guru or teacher. I don't say this to discourage anyone from experimentation, but to be responsible in how it is shared. If you wish to try this practice and you do not have access to a qualified tantric master, I strongly suggest you at least read some of the available texts on Tibetan Tantra.

In the *Manuscript*, Magdalen shares a meditation that has striking similarities to the Nectar Gathering practice just described. In this case, however, the blissful states are used to strengthen the Ka body rather than to contemplate emptiness. The goals are somewhat different, but the methodologies are uncannily similar.

Sexual Essence Initiations and Practices

The concept of sexual energy as being tied to the attainment of enlightenment shows up in Highest Tantra in other forms. For instance, one of the first Initiations is called the *Vase Initiation*, in which the sexual fluids of a deity and his

or her consort are imagined. This is then poured over the
head of the Initiate for the purpose of generating bliss.

In another type of Initiation, a particular mandala (a
specific geometric pattern) is used: called the *Vagina
Mandala*. This association of the feminine with enlightenment shows up in many forms of Tantra. The implication
is clear. Without the aid of the feminine principle of consciousness, liberation cannot take place.

One of the tools of Tantric Tibetan Buddhism is the
bell and *dorje*. The dorje is a stylized thunderbolt or dia-
mond. It is held in the hand and used as a device for
accumulating energy. Metaphorically, the bell is associated with the feminine and the concept of emptiness. The
dorje is associated with the male and the concept of right
method. When emptiness and right method are joined
together, you create illumination.

But back to bliss. It is, quite frankly, one of the fundamental experiences sought after by Tibetan Buddhist
Tantric yogis. The reason for this pursuit of bliss is that
it is a part of our bodhicitta (or Buddha mind). When
joined with awareness of emptiness, enlightenment
begins to dawn. Thus, bliss is sought after not for its own
sake, but as part of a larger alchemical pursuit.

In an exotic form of bliss generation (an aspect of
Deity Yoga), some yogis or yoginis call their chosen
deity into vivid manifestation within their minds. They
then imagine having sexual intercourse with these highly
refined beings. One result of such merging is that they
take on some of the qualities of that being.

Up in the high mountainous and remote areas of Tibet,
there were reputed hermits who cultivated bliss through
a type of sexual interaction with energy-beings known
as *dakinis*. The dakinis are feminine beings who exist in
the subtle realms of existence but who have the ability
to manifest quasi-physically, especially at high altitudes.
The dakinis are acknowledged by Tibetan Buddhism as
a reality, but some of the stories and legends about them
stretch the imagination. Sexual intercourse with a dakini

reportedly imparts special powers and unusual abilities to the practitioner, but it is a practice fraught with danger. The practice of Deity Yoga as described above is much safer in this regard.

In some forms of Tibetan Buddhist Tantra, a yogi or yogini would engage in these practices with an actual physical consort. But such practices were forbidden to renunciants such as monks and nuns.

As intriguing and outlandish as some of these esoteric sexual practices are, they need to be placed within the greater context of the Dharma, the Way of Buddhism. Without the tempering of these practices by the sobering task of attaining enlightenment, they can become seductive traps rather than portals to liberation. Thus, those undertaking these esoteric practices are first trained in *sutra practice* (the teachings of the Buddha) as well as moral codes of conduct. Without this understanding and personal ethical constraint, the more esoteric sexual practices can be quite dangerous.

Signs of Progress

There is one final element that needs to be added here. It arises spontaneously when bliss is joined with emptiness. Somehow, as the two are drawn together within the alchemical container of the Mind, there is a reaction. Something new emerges. Although one is still embodied, one is increasingly free. One begins to see through the smoke-and-mirror show of the senses. One becomes less attached to things, for one sees clearly that all is emptiness. And nothing is worth losing oneself over.

But there is also a strange paradox. Although one begins to see more clearly and awakens somewhat from the dream, one still loses sight of it and falls back to sleep again and again. From this struggle with one's own obscurations, one develops compassion for others.

We are all in the same boat. We are all lost on the ocean of samsara. Believing ourselves to be real and fighting each other over illusions, we are like floating clouds, for a moment so vividly real and then passing away into nothing.

For those lost in the samsaric sea of illusion, this passing away of all things into nothing can be quite painful and terrifying. But for the yogi or yogini who has awakened from the dream, there is an arising of unfettered bliss and unbounded compassion.

And...there is laughter.

A friend of mine once had the honor of preparing tea for two lamas who had not seen each other in a very long time. They had been at the same monastery in their youth, and now their work took them all over the world. They had been friends all those years, and they were happy to be reunited.

She said that they sat for the longest time in silence, then chuckled, seemingly at nothing. This went on for some time. Then one of them pointed to a blossoming redbud tree, not far from where they were sitting. "And they call that a tree!" one of them said.

At which point they both started howling and slapped their thighs.

As consciousness reveals its natural bliss and compassion, life becomes inherently amusing. The horrors of samsara still exist, but they are counterbalanced by the unimaginable and unfathomable bliss of bodhicitta (Buddha-mind). Perhaps by the time one reaches this level of alchemical attainment, life must seem very odd indeed. Can we even imagine the inner life of such a person? What must it be like to know oneself as unbounded consciousness while still living in a body that is tethered to time and space? If you look at Buddhist practitioners who have attained Highest Yoga Tantra, a clue can sometimes be found. They often have smiles on their faces.

The Alchemy
of Relationship

Many of us do relationships the way we play poker. We do everything possible to get the upper hand. And if that fails, we bluff. We pretend to hold cards we don't have. We cheat. We lie.

And while this is the model for many a relationship in our post-modern era, it is not the model for Sacred Relationship as described in the *Manuscript*.

Let me be very upfront here. Sacred Relationship is not for everyone. In fact, I suspect that there are far fewer persons capable or even willing to undertake it than there are those who prefer to play emotional card games.

This type of relationship demands utmost honesty, both with oneself and with one's partner. Instead of hiding our cards, we lay them all out on the table. All our hopes, all our fears, all our petty and jealous thoughts, all our connivings—all of it gets laid out in the clear light of awareness for our partner to see. And he or she must do the same. It will not work if there are *back doors* unlocked with mental escape in mind. It will not work if both partners are not absolutely impeccably honest with each other.

And the reason for this radical type of honesty is that without it, the Alchemy of Relationship cannot take place. Now this may be a new term to many, even students of internal alchemy, since the dynamics of intimate relationship are rarely discussed in the four major alchemical streams (Egyptian, Taoist, Yoga Tantra and Buddhist Tantra).

So I think it might be good to define what I mean here, and to lay some type of foundation. Like all types

of alchemy, this type of work is about changing one form
into another. The form, in this case, is the inter-dynam-
ics that have become habituated between two people.
After a while, people tend to get into ruts. The liveliness
that existed at the beginning of the relationship begins
to fade. Both people become more or less unconscious.
The harsh reality is that it takes continual vigilance and
effort to keep a relationship conscious and alive.

Many relationships drop by the wayside because
the partners are either unwilling or unable to make the
efforts required to sustain them. Instead of experiencing the newness of each moment within the relationship,
a kind of dullness seeps in over time; what used to be
exciting is now boring. And worse, a kind of psychological and emotional lethargy sets in, and both partners
succumb to the dulling effects of unconsciousness.

This type of unconsciousness is a death knell to
psychological awareness and insight; and although it is
rarely mentioned, this type of unconsciousness has a
negative effect on one's spiritual life as well.

So the form that needs to be changed within a relationship is literally the form of interactions that habitually
take place between the two partners.

Like all types of alchemy, there must be a container
for the reactions to occur. And in this case, it is the container of safety and appreciation that provides the reservoir for transformation.

If there is a lack of safety or appreciation, this type of
alchemy cannot be undertaken. And if you have decided
you wish to try this type of alchemy in your relationship,
I suggest you do an analysis first. Honestly assess if you
feel safety and appreciation in your relationship. If you
don't, you will be wasting your time trying to undertake
this type of alchemy with your current partner. I suggest
you focus your efforts, instead, on the solitary practices
mentioned in the *Manuscript*. If you still want to give it a
try, get your partner to talk about these feelings of danger and lack of appreciation that you are feeling. Only if

and when they get resolved, should you consider taking on this type of alchemy.

So now we have two of the three elements needed for alchemy: something to be transformed (the habitual patterns of interaction) and the container (the safety net, if you will, of the relationship itself). A third element is needed; and that is, of course, energy to drive the reaction. There is usually plenty of energy in relationships in the form of neurotic patterns, hopes, fears, and desires. We'll get to those in a moment, but for now I want to talk about steel.

Our psychological selves are much like swords made from steel alloys. They have been forged in the hot searing foundry of our childhood, in the formative pressures of our early experiences. It is this early period of life that bonds the elements of our psyches together. And like steel, this was done under immense heat and pressure. Some of us were abused by overbearing or downright hostile or even destructive parents. Some of us were left to our own devices without any kind of support or guidance. And every kind of parental/child relationship falls in between these two polarities. The possibilities of childhood pressures are virtually endless, and so too are the psychological alloys that result from these types of experiences.

There is a lot of talk about *the child within* in many personal growth groups, and while there is certainly value in making contact with this *younger self,* it is not always pretty. Our cultural myth is that childhood is a time of innocence, a time in which everything is *right with the world.* For some children this is true; for many it is definitely not.

I remember being at a fellow therapist's house for a party quite a few years ago. Most of the adults were practicing therapists, psychologists, psychiatrists, and several clinical social workers. I had just plopped myself in a big oversized sofa; and sipping my iced tea, I noticed a remarkable event. One of the therapists had brought his son and his son's best friend to the party. It was clear that the two boys were buds. They were playing some kind of card game and respectfully giving each other a turn. There were no attempts at cheating, and they seemed to be in a bubble of camaraderie.

Then the boy's father came into the room and asked both kids if they needed anything. They both looked up with cherub faces and smiled. No they said, in the cutest little boy voices. The father patted his son on the back and as he walked off, he nonchalantly patted his son's friend on the back as well. For a moment, his son looked at the incident in abject horror. You could see that he could not believe his eyes. And then as his father turned the corner into the other room, his son pulled back and hit his best friend in the face!

This was not childhood innocence. This was childhood rage. He was not willing to share affections from his father, not even with his best friend. This type of jealousy is typical of higher mammals, and we are, for all our self-righteous self-congratulatory delusions, still mammals. No matter how high we get spiritually, we will, for as long as we live, share traits with our mammalian brothers and sisters.

The inner life of a child is often far different than those around him or her imagine it to be. Surrounded by both dangers and opportunities, the psychological life of a child is directly shaped by how he or she chooses to deal with them. Whether it is something as life threatening as a deranged parent or a child molester, or seemingly innocuous as whom to go to the prom with, does not in some ways matter. While the impact of fighting for one's life may very well imprint a child's behavior well into adulthood, the little decisions of life, like who to socialize with or not, also have impact. All these major and minor decisions create internal psychological heat and pressure. The alloys of one's personality get bonded together or burned away. The sword has been tempered by the time we reach adulthood, and the alloy of our personalities has been set.

Some of us emerge from this childhood foundry with sharp edges, others of us are blunt. Some of us hold our edges and some of us can never seem to hold anything.

The thing about steel is that it tends to remain in its original form once it leaves the foundry. And one of the few things that can ever re-configure the alloy is if the steel gets as hot as it did when it was first formed.

In the alchemical work of Sacred Relationship, we voluntarily put ourselves back in the foundry. The heat that arises between two people when their neuroses rub against each other can get quite intense. If both people can find the courage to be *radically honest* with themselves and with each other in these searing moments, the psychological alloys can be altered. A new type of aliveness then enters the relationship fueled by the energy of psychological truth.

The thing is—most of us will do almost anything to avoid psychological heat. When we get uncomfortable, many of us get the *hell out of Dodge.* Now for some of us this means literally packing up and getting out of town or at least out of sight. For some of us it means that we are physically present, but no longer emotionally present. We numb up. We become automatons. We move and talk, almost like normal, but we have retreated far, far inside. Others of us numb ourselves with alcohol or drugs. And some of us do it with television. We humans are, after all, quite clever and creative. We can find all sorts of ways to avoid facing ourselves. In fact they are far too numerous for me to list here. But I suspect you get the idea. I guess the real question here is this—what do *you* do when things get psychologically too hot for your taste? What do *you* do when you are on the verge of feeling something that you don't want to feel?

For those in Sacred Relationship such feelings are *a call to presence.* It is a time to be *radically honest,* and for both partners to express their true feelings no matter how embarrassing or scary they might be. By speaking their truths to each other, an enlivening element enters the dynamic. Psychological honesty results in psychological insight. And with insight there is hope for awareness, and with awareness there can be change.

This chapter is hardly a manual for the Alchemy of Relationship. It's mainly, I think, a warning. Magdalen alluded to this in the *Manuscript*. She called it *obscurations to flight*. That sounds wonderfully exotic doesn't it? Well it isn't very exotic when the obscuration is clearly in your face. And it isn't very exotic feeling when the foundry of the relationship gets so hot that you feel you are dissolving (psychologically that is). It takes courage and fortitude to stay in the foundry when the heat begins to weaken the stability of one's self-perceived image. Few of us care to look foolish, scared, petty, or jealous. And we will often go through elaborate means to hide these feelings from ourselves or others.

But in Sacred Relationship these things invariably float to the surface like mud that has been stirred up from the bottom of a barrel. The thing is to realize that this does not mean you are doing it (Sacred Relationship) wrong; it means that you are probably doing it right. As Magdalen said in the *Manuscript*, the power of the alchemy extrudes or pushes out the dross. This can be fascinating when the dross is being pushed out of your partner, but it is truly horrific when it extrudes out of you.

What makes Sacred Relationship *sacred* is that it is truly a holy way of being. The root of the word *holy* actually means *to make whole*. So...when we do something that creates wholeness (in this case psychological wholeness), we are engaged in a sacred or holy act.

In the crucible of mutual safety, honesty and appreciation, it is possible to forge a new kind of self. This new self is psychologically more honest, more aware, and freer than its counterpart before entering *the foundry of relationship*. And like the phoenix that arises from its own ashes, this self has wings. It can fly places that it could only imagine before.

There are mysteries here, and treasures that await those who have the courage to enter the depths of themselves and their partners. It is not, as I said, for everyone.

You will probably know if you are a likely candidate because you will feel it in your soul, your heart.

If you enter this path, know that there are no manuals. There is precious little guidance out there. The path to spirituality has traditionally been one of solitude. And while times of solitude may be necessary for those in Sacred Relationship, something has turned. They agree to walk the path to godhood together, side by side, through both heaven and hell, through the brilliant summits where all things are suddenly crystal clear, and through the dark valley of psychological death where it is hard to even see one's foot in front of the other. And yet through the darkness of not knowing, a deep primordial force begins to rise up. It requires an unusual type of *holy trinity*—three things for it to do its most holy task—*mutual safety, psychological honesty,* and *appreciation of the Beloved.*

Have a good journey!

A Note to the Reader:

There is an implicit danger in writing about such things as sacred relationship. For one, some people might assume that the writer (moi) is an expert on such matters. I assure you that I am not, and I wish to place into written record this fact.

I have found myself, several times, running from the heat of the foundry of relationship. For as I mentioned earlier, when the emotional and psychic heat of sacred relationship gets really hot there is a tendency to feel that oneself is being obliterated. Of course what is being obliterated, or at the very least challenged, is our own neurosis, not our existence (which is what it feels like). Our neurotic habits are tenacious and they don't give up easily. My experience is that they often fight to the death, so to speak, rather than fade gracefully into the past. But that is just my personal experience, and I don't wish to imply that this might be your experience as well.

The art of sacred relationship, I believe, is learning how to be in the "heat" of transformation and not automatically run from it. I also think that this way of being in relationship with another is one of the most challenging and rewarding things I have ever asked of myself. Because this way of relationship is so dynamic and life-changing, I think the entrance into this path should have a warning sign, so here it is.

WARNING...ENTER THIS PATH WITH SOBRIETY AND ABANDON. KNOW THAT THOSE WHO ENTER THIS PATH WILL NEVER BE THE SAME...NOR WILL YOU. (I was redundant here for those of you who think you are an exception to everyone else.)

One Woman's
Story

Judi Sion

In this story of one woman is the story
of every woman. May you find the pathway
into the spirit by which it was written.

—Mary Magdalen

Tom's Introduction to One Woman's Story

Some might wonder why we included something so personal in the last section of this book. After all, we all have our stories, and none of us is any more important than anyone else. Indeed, this is what we posed to Magdalen over and over again after she asked Judi to write "her story." And even after the book had been completed and was ready for press, we asked the Magdalen one last time, thinking that perhaps she had changed her mind. She had not. She was, in fact, quite emphatic that elements in Judi's personal story would *speak* to many women, that many of her experiences were shared by women universally. And this was, Magdalen reminded us, about the return of the feminine to a place of honor and power.

But first the patterns of abuse, betrayal, lack of honor, and disempowerment need to be owned and accepted.

Now, after sitting with the material for these many months, I think I understand what the Magdalen is talking about. It has to do with the principles of *Sophia* and the *Logos*. For those familiar with these terms, please forgive my taking the space here to discuss them, but I find many people do not understand them. This lack of general understanding about the Logos and Sophia is, I think, a result of the Church Fathers' attempt to erase the feminine from the theology of Christendom, an act that stretches back in time to the first century A.D.

Many are probably familiar with the term "Logos" as it sits at the core of the Church's two thousand-year-old theology. The Logos is the intelligence (the logic) of the cosmos itself. It is the fundamental creative force (or God). Traditionally, theologians and philosophers have considered the Logos to be a masculine principle. This concept actually goes back thousands of years before Christ into the ancient pagan world. At a mythological level, gods were viewed as solar, while goddesses were seen as being more related to the moon (lunar). In this context, *spirit* was conceived as being in the solar realms of consciousness (male), and the *earth* (matter) resided within the lunar realms of consciousness (female). Thus the sky (heaven) became associated with the masculine while earth became associated with the feminine.

The pagan consciousness understood that all creation was the result of an interplay between the cosmological forces of the masculine and feminine (spirit and matter; sky and earth). Neither force was more important than the other. Without both of them, creation was not possible. The key to a fruitful creation, whether it be cosmic or individual, was seen as a balance between these forces.

In the earliest period of Christianity, before the political aspirations of the Church, this was commonly understood and accepted. This understanding of the place of the feminine shows up nowhere more clearly than in the concept of Sophia.

Sophia was viewed as the feminine aspect of the godhead. She was the holy bride to the Logos, and they were viewed as inseparable. When the Logos generated an impulse (the thought) to create, it was Sophia that implemented it. Without her, creation would have been impossible. They were two sides of the same coin. One remained aloof in the realms of spirit, forming the ideas of creation. But it was Sophia who received the seed (the thought of creation) from the Logos. And it was she who gave it birth into actuality in the realms of matter.

Sophia was known as the *Cosmic Mother*, and as such, she shared the same place of honor as *Isis* in Egypt and other Goddesses in other ancient cultures. According to the *Sophionic* understandings, she incarnated as Mary, the mother of *Yeshua*. And through this embodiment the word (Logos) became flesh (Yeshua). God/man had been actualized. But it could not have happened without the sacred act of Sophia incarnating as a woman. Only then could God (Logos) incarnate as a man (in the womb of Sophia/Mary).

This understanding was common among some of the early Christian theologians. And although many of their writings were destroyed during the Dark Ages, a few of them have survived.

But something ominous occurred over the first few centuries A.D. in regards to the feminine teachings regarding Sophia. We see a concerted effort to remove all traces of her from Christian religious writings and thought.

Metaphorically, we could say that the Church subdued the moon with all of her dark mysteries. The Goddess became veiled and hidden. Not only this, but it became a heresy to even talk about her. One could lose one's life simply by uttering her names.

The sun was at its zenith. God (the Logos) was all there was. Then came the mysterious Holy Trinity—the Father, the Son, and the Holy Ghost. There was no mention of Sophia, or Mary. There was nothing feminine in the Trinity. And the feminine was relegated to a place of unimportance.

But worse, she was scorned. In the official version of Genesis adopted by the increasingly patriarchal Church, the source of mankind's downfall was laid squarely on the shoulders of Eve. She had, after all, taken the apple from the serpent of Satan. And with this one fateful act, she (a woman) cursed all succeeding generations.

But wait a moment. There are other versions of the creation myth. The censored version we have inherited is only one of them. According to one Gnostic account, the serpent was a good guy. He was actually trying to help Adam and Eve get out from under the tyrannical rule of a jealous God (Jehovah). And in this version, the snake simply opened the path to the godlike powers of consciousness that were part of Adam and Eve's rightful inheritance.

The Gnostics, for those unfamiliar with them, were a long line of luminaries whose traditions, in various forms, stretched back into ancient Egypt, if not before. They believed in the power of direct revelation without the need for an intermediary (a priest). Of course, this did not fit in with the political and monetary desires of the Church, and so the Gnostics were branded as heretics and summarily imprisoned or killed on a regular basis.

In the view of the Gnostics, Eve was a heroine who, through her act of accepting the apple, raised humanity closer to ownership of its godlike powers. In the myth propagated by the Church, however, she was weak and cursed for having tricked her mate into accepting something from Satan.

Myth has power. It gets laid into the fabric of a culture and colors its attitudes and beliefs. And as a result of the officially sanctioned creation story, women have suffered considerably as the dark dangerous creatures of the moon, who by their natures consort with evil. Just read the medieval hogwash of scholars and theologians justifying their witch hunts and other admonitions against women. This incendiary madness even extended into the fledgling colonies of the United States during the Salem witch trials of the 1600s.

But I think the damage of the overly solarized mythos of Christianity extends far beyond the labeling of women as evil. All of our society suffers, men as well, and here's why.

By cutting ourselves off from the feminine aspect of creation (matter itself), there is a deep spiritual dis-ease (discomfort) that has been infecting Western culture for two millennia.

We long for the realms of spirit (heaven), but reject our experiences in the world. We have set heaven and earth at odds. Earth is, after all, tainted. We are only here because we have fallen from grace. If we are truly born in sin, just through the act of being born, then all that follows our birth is a lie. The truth lies above us, not here among us.

The expression of spirit in the form of earth experience is denied by our current cultural mythos. Thus,
we can rape and pillage the earth with seemingly little
regard. At a mythological level the earth is feminine. And
women are, after all, just to be used.

But the danger in this fallacy is that by pillaging our
earthly mother (Gaia), we are destroying the very ecological
roots that support us. And the biological sciences are full of
dire warnings concerning the exhaustion of our ecosystem.

Does it dawn on us that the disappearance of animal
and plant species at its current alarming rate is a threat
to our very survival? No! We are above it all. We consider
ourselves to be at the apex of nature, with an inherent God-
given right to dominate and subdue it according to our will.

The idea that other forms of life might have wills of
their own just as significant as ours does not occur to us.
And the concept of equal coexistence between us and
other life forms is barely a part of mass consciousness.
This is essentially because we do not see life forms as
expressions of spirit. At an unconscious level, we separate them. There is life and there is spirit. Heaven and
earth do not meet. At the mythological level, many view
the earth as a kind of in-between place, a test to see if
they deserve an eternal hereafter in heaven or a hellish
eternity in the bowels of—where else—the earth!

This *koyaaniqatsi* (a Hopi term for being out of balance
with the world) may very well destroy our civilization. We
must come back to a place of balance if we are to survive.
Mythologically, the moon must be unveiled within our own
psyches. The feminine principle must be put back in her
rightful place as a co-creator, not as a dominating force
nor as a subjugated force, but as an equal force.

All of this brings me back to the personal story of
one woman you are about to read. Why would this be
so pertinent?

Well, I believe, for one thing, that it goes back to the
distortion of spiritual values we have inherited. If our
life, as an embodied soul, is tainted (by the mere act of

being in a body), then there is psychological discomfort with our experiences. They are, after all, of the earth, not of the spirit.

And yet, in the balance of spirit and earth, both are valued. The shimmering visions of the spirit world and the earth-caked experiences of life in a body are both seen as inherently sacred. Hanging the laundry can be just as enlightening as reading scripture.

It's all in the attitude.

Someone once asked me what "the return of the Cosmic Mother" meant. I suspect it means many things, some of which we won't recognize until we are well into it. But I imagine it will bring at least one cultural shift. We will come to recognize our earthly life and all its experiences as an expression of spirit in matter, not as a battle between the two, but as a sacred marriage.

This sacred marriage between spirit and matter is sometimes called the *Opus Magnum*, or the Great Work. It is the alpha and omega in which spirit (Logos) descends into matter (through the grace of Sophia) and returns back to itself transformed.

Our lives are forged in the alchemical furnace of experience. For those of us who willingly choose to enter the Great Work of self-illumination, our life experiences can become great teachers unto ourselves.

You are about to read the story of one woman. She shares something in common with all women undertaking the Great Work of self-illumination in this, our time. Re-storing the feminine to a place of honor in our culture begins with women honoring both themselves and their stories.

The pain and lies of the last two thousand years are brought closer to their end each time a woman takes her own power. The return of Sophia draws closer each time a man honors the women in his life as well as the feminine within himself.

Those of us striving to live this realization *are* a part of the Cosmic Mother's return. We are the moon becoming unveiled in balance to the sun, and we are the restoration of the feminine in balance to the male.

May heaven and earth be joined in this, our time.

Judi's Preface to One Woman's Story

T he first night that Mary Magdalen came through, her power and strength were as palpable as her words were audible, and it continued that way throughout the whole process. There was never a stumble over a word. Her words carefully chosen before she spoke, she spoke with authority and with definition. She was here to do a job—to set the story straight, and to go back home, which she said was a place we call heaven, but she called a "place in the soul," where she rests forever with her Beloved, Yeshua.

Hers was the most powerful presence I have ever experienced, and from her first words I was deeply moved and my consciousness profoundly altered. I typed what she brought through sitting in bed with a computer propped on a pillow, my hands trembling both with excitement and with fear that I might not get it all correctly.

When she was leaving that first night, after she had completed the information, she "turned" to me, so to speak.

I felt the definite shift to the personal, almost intimately to me, and she said, "I agree to give my story because of *you*—because you sense the importance of the relationship, the Sacred Marriage. And Metatron requested also that I give you my story." In a subsequent transmission, within the *Manuscript* itself, she stated that Isis had specifically asked that she tell her story, in this, "the beginning of the end of time."

Later we asked Magdalen for the best way to bring this information forward, considering the format of the book.

Her *Manuscript* is compact. There are no extra words. She doesn't go on and on. She clearly wants to give only the necessary coded information to awaken the memory, and those few who are ready will hear it all.

But everything you *need* to know, *all the secrets*, are here in *her* few pages.

Tom felt it was important to add an overview and to fill in some blanks, which he is well qualified to do. He is one of the most astute and erudite beings on the face of the Earth at this time regarding the entire subject of internal alchemy, as streamed from many different sources, as this has been his lifetime's work.

And me? Why am I here? Why am I privileged to be taking space to write words to you? Of what am I a lifetime student?

Relationship. And Sacred Relationship and the inherent power and mystery of the feminine are what this book is about.

And so when we asked about the format, over and over, we were told that I must write my story. I argued the point and avoided the opportunity until the book was ready to go to press and only my story was holding up publication of the *Manuscript.* The pressure mounted. I started it over and over. I wrote and rewrote. I added sections and fleshed out parts, and I still felt inadequate to the task of adding anything of value to this magnificent document, this truth that Magdalen gave.

I recapitulated my life through desert and mountains, through blizzards and sunsets that would set your heart on fire. I initially began the process under her instructions back on little Oudish, in Malta. I struggled with it in southern France and in the Cyclades, on Paros Island in Greece. I deleted and added to it like you add ingredients in soup. Too much salt. Add a little sugar. Too much drama and violence. Add the humor life always provides.

Yet, I wasn't going to include it. I still struggle over its relevance and your criticism. One day Tom said to me, "Shouldn't you be working on the *Magdalen Manuscript*?"

I said, "Oh, I just don't get it. I'm not about to include my life story. What will people think I'm trying to do?"

He handed me a card that had just arrived. It said, "Please write your story and include it in the *Manuscript*. When you write your story, you will be writing my story. You aren't writing it for yourself. You're writing it for all of us."

And so with all my flaws and fears on my shoulder, I honor what the Goddess requested.

The first section contains my story. The diary entries at the end share some of what I went through experiencing the "process" of receiving her information and the "obstacles to flight" we experienced living with this material, for it brought up, as it well should have, all my unfinished relationship issues.

In my case, these were essentially jealously, fear of abandonment, fear of betrayal, and general and pervasive unworthiness. And—to place that information in true context demands that I also tell you my story, as Metatron, my beloved advisor, has told me to do now for years.

And so I write this for Magdalen, for the Hathors, for Isis, for Metatron, for all my daughters—and for Tom who plays guitar and writes songs—because he dared to cross the dark, moist, and dangerous abyss to the portal of the feminine to risk asking me to dance in Sacred Relationship, in the chalice of the Holy Grail.

One Woman's Story

Life spit me out of my mother's womb in Appalachia, not to find waiting hands but a cold floor, as she was unattended at my birth. My mother and I shared this experience in a little clapboard house by the side of railroad tracks in Pennington Gap, Virginia. My birth name was Phyllis Elizabeth Zion, originally Sion.

Within months I was thrust into another environment, as my birth mother left home with me and my older brothers and sister to escape an abusive marriage and in search of her dream.

She wanted to be a country singer. And so when I was a month or so old, and my father was at work, she put us all on a bus, and we traveled across the state to south central Virginia where she left us with her parents while she went to find a singing job.

But as life would twist, very shortly after our arrival, grandfather's tractor pinned him underneath when he took a hill the wrong way. My older brother told me the story only a few years ago, when we found each other finally. He was running alongside the tractor so he ran to the house for help. He remembers grandmother running with her big, black nurse's bag. She took out a huge, hypodermic needle, which she filled with morphine for the pain. He watched her first squirt the liquid into the air and then inject it into grandfather. Then she tried to lift the tractor off him, breaking her back instead.

My grandfather died underneath the tractor, and grandmother never walked again.

I never knew these people. I was an infant as this drama played out, left inside the house while life and death called to its side who it wanted in the moment. We were handed out in the four directions, like leaves caught in a swirling wind.

I wound up at a motel/restaurant owned by a distant cousin while family frantically searched for someone to take an infant. There weren't many adoption agencies in the tobacco plains of Virginia in those years, and I suspect families preferred to take care of their own, as best they could.

And so it was that I was ultimately farmed out, like the tobacco I grew up around, and raised by Queen Victoria reincarnated—a staunch and severe woman, a schoolteacher, who couldn't have children of her own. At this apocalyptic juncture of fates I was still quite shy of one year, and I had already earned another equally portentous name, Judi Lee Pope.

Ruby Carter Pope loved me dearly; there is no doubt of that. Her life, and therefore the life of her husband, who became my father, centered around her Church, her family, her schoolchildren—and the constriction of me.

But her God was a fearsome and jealous thing I couldn't tolerate. And as soon as I got old enough to question, which in my instance was quite young, we came to loggerheads.

I grew up almost totally without playmates, wandering the tobacco fields of the Piedmont Region of Virginia with a St. Bernard dog and a borrowed horse. She sewed many of my clothes from flour sacks and never did anything herself but work and sacrifice. These were my models.

Oh, and judgment. They do a lot of judging in the country of Virginia.

We were very poor, though measured against the poverty of Brunswick County, Virginia; we were middle class, I suspect.

My father ran a country store that essentially served the abysmally poor black families that lived around us. I remember one barefoot woman who came in daily. She wore one single stocking over her head and ate one can of sardines and an "urnge" soda every day. It never occurred to me then that this was probably all she had to eat. And it never occurred to me then either that she never paid. Dad wrote up little pieces of paper that represented bills.

He died when I was eighteen and I found boxes of
these unpaid bills, totaling well over $20,000, which was
a staggering amount of money to be owed in those days.
He must have fed half of Rawlings, Virginia and simply
never told anyone.

I grew up being schooled in the fork of a pear tree.
My teachers were a voice in the wind and whispers in the
forest. I fashioned a bow and arrows myself and when
the horse across the road was offered to ride, I left home
for hours every day to find something. I don't know what.

I never had riding lessons. The horse taught me.
The saddle and bridle anyone could figure out. And
when the saddle slid underneath him, with me in it,
on my first attempt, I had a little talk with him about
letting the air out of his stomach before I cinched the
saddle. I had to have this little talk with him often, but
it worked.

And when his ears pricked up one day when he saw a
fallen tree in the field, I knew what he wanted.

He wanted to fly.

And so we flew over it. I leaned into him; it was the
logical thing to do. He jumped the tree; I just got to
fly along with him. After that, there was nothing that
stopped us. We forded rivers and trotted right down the
middle of creeks. We wandered for miles through dense
forests and galloped over fields and meadows, and if
anything got in our way, we jumped it.

No one ever knew where I went on this horse. You
could travel for days and not see another human being
if you knew where to go through the forests and back
roads of Brunswick County then.

I lied to my mother, of course; she wouldn't have
allowed me to leave the yard but for well-crafted lies that
became a necessity of life very early. She objected to
everything and anything. To her, almost everything in life
was either sinful or dangerous.

I never went to a birthday party or slept over at a
girl friend's house. No one ever slept over at my house.

These were fantasies other people lived on the television. I had no idea people really lived like that.

My adopted mother chose my clothes and told me what to wear every day to school, even when I was much older. If I put on a sleeveless dress in June, she said I would get cold, and she added layers. If I put on a sweater in January, she told me I'd be too hot and dressed me down. The ultimate effect of this control was that I didn't have any idea what I felt or what I wanted. I wasn't allowed to date until I was 17, and she sat, stony-faced at the window, watching for me to come home even then, so she could approve my appearance when I returned, to make sure I hadn't discovered anything sinful, I'm sure.

Once, my date walked me to the door with his shirt not properly tucked in. I was never allowed to date him again. I think I was still in love with him a decade later, when we met and released each other from the fantasy we had each held, in our own way, for all those years, simply because we had never been allowed our time.

My father and mother slept in separate double beds in one bedroom. I slept with my mother until I left for college. My grandmother had the other bedroom. Ruby refused, heralding a variety of excuses, to ever finish the room upstairs. Thusly, she even managed to control how I slept at night. And she managed to never have to sleep with my father.

"Quit fidgeting," she used to say to me when I turned too often. "Lie still." Summers were endless, drenched in suspensions of tepid, stagnant pools of humidity. I lay for hours on end, too hot to sleep, not allowed to move, only my mind free to move about. Winters, I lay weighted under piles of ancient quilts, unmoving then due to the oppressions of stiff blankets from the Civil War holding me in their spell, haunting me with their visions, yet still cold in the depths of a Virginia winter.

But I had my music and dance, and I had the forest, which instructed me to dance on her naked skin bare-foot, until I could waltz across the forest floor without making a sound. I had a borrowed horse, a beloved St. Bernard, named Micky, a teacher in a pear tree, a little friend in the Jack-in-the-Pulpit plant and another in the Pink Lady Slipper.

These were my childhood advisors.

There is one lesson I will never forget and now I watch it come to pass as a prophecy in my own life. From my memory, it was my first lesson delivered in the fork of that pear tree, where I wedged myself daily for years, dialoging with what I called, "words without a voice."

I was told that about every possible life experience would come to me, so that I would ultimately understand and have compassion for the human experience. And I was told that someday, when I was full of these life experiences, my voice would travel around the world, sharing what I had learned and that what I had to say would have a tremendous impact, but only when I really didn't care about such influence.

I was also told that there was another part of me out there somewhere and that someday I would meet the "mate to my being," and that our work would be together, that I wouldn't "get up in the morning and go to a job" like other people. I was told that he was part of my soul and that our work together would have a vast and beneficial influence on the world. This is, essentially, what I care to share of what I remember.

And there is one other early awareness that I distinctly remember.

I *knew* that the secrets of the universe lay in the physical experiences possible between a man and a woman—when they truly loved each other. I knew that *love* was the greatest gift you could be given. I knew there was a place you could go, a road only opened through that gateway of physicality, that few have ever walked. And I knew that was why the Church shamed sexuality and why governments had such rules and regulations to govern what they called "marriage," and why the whole subject has been both "tabooed" and regulated throughout this age of civilization.

I suspected the serpent wasn't evil, and I knew that Eve must have been brilliant to want more knowledge, and I knew it was illogical for the loving God who had created us to not want us to know everything. I suspected if there were such a beast as the devil, the smartest place for him to hide would be in the Church!

I *knew* the deepest secrets had to do with love, with what I now call Sacred Relationship. I knew that my purpose was somehow tied to reintegration of these secrets.

And I also *knew* there was another part of me out there somewhere. And I began a lifetime search for him.

I thought I saw him once, his face pressed against the window of a bus that slowly passed us on Route 1 on the way to Petersburg. For a minute, the bus and our car traveled at the same speed and our eyes met. We linked in that brief moment at some place that was holy, though we were only maybe—I don't know—eight, nine or ten years old. It would be another forty years before I touched such a holy place with a man again.

I knew *he* played guitar and wrote songs and had the voice of an angel. I always thought I'd know his voice if I ever heard it.

I n terms of what shaped me, I can look back and remember the incidents that made me question the veracity of what was presented as authority. In the church I was forced to attend, I heard preaching on Sunday about love and non-judgment. I heard preaching about how God didn't care what you wore, but only saw what was in your heart. But I frequently overheard parishioners and the preacher criticizing and demeaning each other before they even got out the door!

"Can you believe she wears *that* to church," my young ears heard when my logic knew *that* was all the poor woman in question had to wear. I could *see* hearts then, and I saw purity in that old woman, but they only saw clothing.

"Well, you know where she comes from, don't you? I wouldn't expect much out of her! Her family is trash." I couldn't understand blaming someone for the actions of their parents or their distant cousins. And I remember hearing, "Always be good to your family. They're all you've ever got. And always remember that blood is thicker than water." Hmmm. That's a funny thing to say to an adopted child who had no blood around.

I simply never believed what I was told by the humans around me. And there were extraordinary events that made me look elsewhere for answers. I don't remember how old I was, maybe eight or nine. I had just gotten into bed one summer night. My mother was grading papers and my father was reading. I distinctly remember pulling a single sheet up to my chin when a glow appeared in the room. It transcended the darkness, creating an unmistakable luminescence, a pregnant "wetness" that made the very air seem visible, like floating molecules of moist light. A fear rose in me that was incalculable, beyond my wildest imagination. I had no backdrop for a mystical experience, though I am sure now that is what this was. Three lights appeared in the room, one on either side of the bed and one in the very center at the foot of the bed. A form appeared below the center light and it seemed to rock, though now I understand that was probably a pulsation.

I was frozen, completely unable to move, which exacerbated my fear. I told myself that if I could only move one digit of a finger, I could break this terrible spell and so I focused all my energy on moving one finger. It was impossible. So then I tried to focus all my will on my throat, to scream for help. I could make no sound. I thought I would surely die there, frozen to the spot. My father came down the hallway toward the bedroom, and I knew that if he came into the room he would break the spell, and I sent him every thought I could muster to please enter the room. But he stopped at the door, as if he'd forgotten something, and he turned around and never entered. I knew the "lights," whatever they were, had planted a thought to change his mind, and I knew I was dead.

I don't know how long this otherworldly spell lasted, but slowly the lights on the side dimmed. The pulsing of the center "figure" slowed in direct relation to the dimming lights. The lights on either side disappeared at the same time, blip! I was now transfixed by only the central light above the rocking figure. Imperceptibly slowly the rocking slowed, in direct proportion to the light slowly extinguishing. Finally I was held only by the unmoving apparition, a formless form, underneath a single dim light. As immediately as it had begun, simultaneously the figure disappeared, the light left, and I was free to bolt out of the bedroom and tear down the hall. I threw myself into a chair, hanging on for dear life and told my mother what had happened. I refused to go back to bed, though eventually exhaustion won out.

In the morning we received a phone call from an aunt, to say that her aged mother-in-law had died at precisely the same time as my incident occurred, and so it was that it became legend in my family that Great Aunt Somebody or Other had visited me when she passed. My only memory of her was of her sitting in a rocking chair, slowly rocking back-and-forth. And perhaps it was she, though I prefer Metatron's explanation. He says it was an Initiation from three Masters from other dimensions, and that it could only be given after I had finally decided to stay in a body; though that decision, if Metatron is right, has been questioned many times since.

I suppose that because Ruby had not allowed ordinary life to touch me for so many years, I rushed headlong into it when my father died, and I left for college at 18. I clearly began to have those "life experiences" the voice spoke to me about. I fell in and out of love like children learning to walk fall down. I was desperate for love,

desperate to be touched, desperate for passion. The love
"toddler" landed safely on her bottom until one night
when a date refused to take me home.

I remember the feeling of fright when he drove past
my street and turned instead down a dark road toward his
own apartment building. His intentions were made clear
when he used a martial arts grip on my arm, forcing me
inside his apartment. When he turned his back inside, I
bolted, running for my life. He took chase. As I ran, I had
to make a choice between staying in the shadows or trying to make a phone call. The phone booth lay in light,
clearly visible to anyone chasing a frightened young girl.

I chose the lighted phone booth, hoping that I could
make an emergency call before he spotted me. But
when I got to it, the phone was broken, and he had spotted me. I then ran toward the beach, sinking deeply into
sand with each stride and exhausting myself trying to run
through marsh grass and sand dunes.

But I got away.

After walking several miles along the beach, I saw
figures approaching in the dim moonlight, and I pan-
icked and took back to the roadside to cover the last
five or so miles home. It was now the middle of the
night, closer to dawn than night. It had been a long
night of escape and terror.

A car pulled alongside me, and a voice said, "You
must be crazy walking out here in the middle of the
night. What's wrong? Let me give you a lift home. You're
not safe out here walking like this." I peered in to see a
safe-enough looking face; one I had never seen before.

I must have been crazy. Because I got into the car.

He immediately sped up to a pace that left no possibility of jumping and pulled out a blade that gleamed
in the moonlight, leveling it sideways at my throat. He
drove somewhere deep into the Dismal Swamp, as far
as the road went then. The rest of that night and into the
dawn are a blur of blood and contusions and struggling,
with moonlight sharding off a knife blade.

After the battle was over he drove me back to the very street I had tried so hard to get to that night, and dropped me on the corner.

I wore a fencing mask for weeks, ashamed somehow of my cuts and bruises. As if a girl trying so hard to get home had done something to deserve the terror of that night. I ultimately went to the police, but at the time Virginia Beach had a policy of printing all rape victims' names in the local paper, and I knew Queen Victoria would hear what had happened, and I just wasn't ready for what that would create in my life. The thought of her accusations, of her screams of sin and guilt were more oppressive, more terrifying than anything that had happened to me that night.

I closed that door and went on with my life with a passion. I went to work at a radio station and moved into a phase of success in media and communication that was to continue through all the emotional turmoil of the next thirty years.

I met a handsome young man, and we began to date, getting more and more serious. He asked me to marry him. I was thinking about it, though there were signs I was ignoring, things about him and other issues with me. I had been having problems with my period, but nothing else seemed wrong. So I ignored these sporadic appearances and continued my life. Finally I sought help. Initially I was told I had a tumor. Then I was told I was seven months pregnant.

This was not in my life plan. I suppose because I had not enjoyed my own childhood, I had no intention of ever having children of my own.

Children, from what I had seen around me growing up, are what kept women from having a life. I viewed women as trapped in an endless cycle of sacrifice, not to mention that I was scared to death of the shame and the pain.

I married the handsome young man and spent a terrifying night giving birth to a girl, I was told. Perhaps it seemed the only solution at the time. My doctor had

arranged a private adoption, and I never saw her. It was
the best choice I felt I could make, under the circumstances. I had no money at all, and I felt she would be
much better off with a family that could afford to raise
her. I suppose my own childhood of flour sack clothes
and few opportunities was still too fresh in my mind. And
it was the only way to keep Queen Victoria from knowing and avoid sinking the illustrious and noble, but poor,
southern family into shame!

I hid the last two months of the pregnancy, never leaving the apartment. I had learned at a very young age to
draw the shades on things that are not supposed to be
seen, and I had become that.

My handsome young husband turned out to be gay,
and though he loved me as much as a gay man can love
a woman, I was, after all, still a woman.

Through all of this I had managed to work my way
through college in music, drama, and philosophy. I
had stumbled into radio as a DJ when women were
first "allowed" that joy and from there I discovered the
"power" of advertising. I moved into one of the most creative ad agencies in North America and worked my way
into a position of authority and respect at a very young
age, in what was still a man's world there as well. I won
awards and honors and was highly paid. I had a magic
touch that translated into high profits for my clients, and
I loved what I did.

I lived what was, I suppose, a dual life. My days were
filled with producing television commercials, planning
campaigns, writing radio jingles, buying media, negotiating with clients and reps. My terrain ranged from the
Board Room to the studio. I was a rare duck, equally
adept at the creative end and the "business" end. I
almost seemed to possess a psychic ability in advertising. Once I knew the soul of a client, I could "see" how
the business or product or image flowed out of who
he/she was and could just as easily see what ingredients
were needed to position that image or message. Then I

could "write" and design the "piece," whether it was print or audio or video. And much to my surprise, I could just as easily sense the budget and skew it where it belonged, holding huge traffic patterns of media in my mind. I thrilled at filling in the mental crossword puzzles, where the demographics of listeners/viewers/readers cross-matched certain words in a spot or a visual designed to reach a certain segment of a market, thus assuring sales.

But my nights were not as successful. We looked good together, and we had bought a home that was way over our heads, as all young yuppies are expected to do. It was a "Spanish Mansion" with a hand-painted tile fireplace and picture-frame molding. There was a fountain in the back courtyard, a marble foyer that ran about forty-feet-long to the foot of a staircase that could easily have been the scene for *Gone With the Wind*. It even boasted a servant staircase. Of course we had no servants, and our nights were spent trying to clean the alternating black and white marble tiles in the front foyer. The roof leaked and sadly needed replacing, and the kitchen had never been brought into the 19th Century, much less the 20th. The illusion was great but you couldn't cook there. And so after working all day, I worked alongside my husband to renovate this ancient mansion at night. We had lots of parties. He loved parties. But I always worried about who he'd fall in love with before the night was over. His depression seemed to get worse when he was drinking, and I knew our marriage was as much of an illusion as the Spanish Mansion.

But you never know what will break the camel's back. One morning on the way to work, I skipped along the sidewalk toward my car, trying to admire my dark green Buick Electra. It looked good in the sunlight and clients liked it, though my heart ached for my old MG.

A construction worker sat forlornly on the curb by the fender of my car. I ignored him as I stepped to the other side of the car and jumped back in shock. The driver's side had been sliced open, as if a giant had mistaken it for a can of green peas. I stood there gawking, my jaw hanging against my chest. The construction worker stood up, hardhat in hand over his chest, as if in respect for my now deceased vehicle.

"My demolition crane was on the way to a job, and when we took the corner, it just jumped off the truck and did that to your car. We had the knife on it instead of the ball. They left me behind to wait for the owner to show up."

I don't know why I cracked at that moment. But it was at that precise moment that I decided I needed to make a change. I managed to get to work only to be called into the President's office. He announced that he was leaving advertising and closing the business that month. I had been there five years, and I loved my job. I was a writer and creator. I produced radio and television commercials and planned campaigns and managed huge budgets for clients. These people were more "family" than I'd ever known.

I had just been given up for adoption again.

When I got home that night and my husband was "no-emotional-where" to be found, preferring liquor and a few ice cubes. I snapped.

Women keep score retroactively. Men erase their bad marks at the end of each day. So I was at five years and not much rope left; this was the three millionth time he hadn't been there for me. He figured he hadn't done anything wrong yet that day. Besides, he'd always gotten away with it before.

When he drank, he always threatened suicide, and I always hid the keys to his car and pleaded earnestly for him to come to his senses, which usually meant staying up all night negotiating deep passages of his inner turmoil, after which he usually celebrated by cleaning the marble tiles or stripping furniture. But it had been a bad day and that night, I was a new woman. This time I threw the keys at him, suggested he take a long drive, preferably off a short pier, packed my suitcase and walked out the door. I left him the Spanish mansion on the lake, the antique furniture, the statue of David, and a slightly damaged Buick Electra.

Luckily I had built a good reputation in advertising and was quickly offered a job in television. The day I signed my contract at the TV station, management walked out, leaving me the only person on staff at a management level. And so it was that I ran a television station for a year. I had "stumbled" into radio on bluff and bravado and gained a tremendous education, spent five years in an award-winning ad agency, and now fate had rounded out my resume quite nicely.

Fate had a few other surprises in store for me in my personal life as well. I went to a Unitarian cocktail party and saw the most handsome man I'd ever seen across the room. Judging him to probably be equally egotistical and no longer trusting very handsome young men, I spent the night crossing the room in the opposite direction he went, determined not to run into him. I survived the party without encounter and joined a group for dinner, only to find myself seated right across from him.

In the end, I took him home and ultimately we married. We were deeply comfortable together, he and I. He was an intellectual, with a great sense of honor, deeply wounded from his childhood—but who isn't.

I didn't understand the "drivers" implanted from my childhood, and I had already fully embarked on my "you need to be more giving, smarter, prettier, sexier, nicer, funnier, and more talented than anyone around you to be equal and deserve life" phase. That translates to a woman headed for being Super Woman and to a potential victim.

I subbed for a late-night radio talk show host on occasion as well during those days, and I remember an incident that foretold a lot but which took another twenty years to finally make sense. The regular talk show host was a conservative and needless to say, I considered myself a liberal. I received great joy in what I considered opening the minds of his listeners when I did his show.

On one particular night I chose to talk about a very controversial legal situation. It was a court case in a nearby state in which a black woman had been jailed as an accomplice to a burglary. Her boyfriend had stolen something while she was riding in the car. During the night her white jailer entered her cell and raped her. During the rape, she managed to grab a knife from his belt, stabbed him and ran. He died, his semen splayed on the walls and his pants around his knees. She fled to another state, fearing southern justice and an extradition process was begun to bring her back to face murder charges.

Feminists were appalled. Rednecks wanted blood. I merely brought the circumstances to the attention of my listeners that evening, representing both sides of the argument, though I admit my obvious bias toward what I considered to be an enlightened and compassionate point of view.

I interviewed a local judge regarding the legal issues and also interviewed area feminists, to get the argument on the woman's behalf. When the show was over, I switched the FM to automatic, as I did every night, checked the logs, and closed down the station. I exited the side door, shutting the lights off behind me. I was alone in the station, as always at that hour. I walked out into the huge parking lot to find a row of cars down one side of the parking lot, another row of cars down the other side of the lot and a row of police cars down the middle, holding them apart from one another. The cars on the right were there to hurt me. The cars on the left were there to defend me. And the police were there to keep order. I slunk to my car and drove home and sobbed all night. How could anyone have been angry at the truth? And how could they hate me so? I was only shedding light on the dark truth. Why didn't people want to know the whole story? It was a crisis point in my southern life, a life where a woman is not supposed to offend or question.

By dawn I had come to the realization that essentially I had a power which I hadn't wanted and didn't know what to do with. People, I sadly realized, either really, really liked me, or really, really disliked me. There was, for whatever reason, no middle ground. This incident pointed this out regarding my speaking voice. I was later to realize I had the same effect on people with my writing and even my sheer presence.

That night and for many years to come, it brought me great pain to imagine having such a presence. I was frightened of power and wanted nothing to do with it. I much preferred to be loved by all, seeking only approval. It was years later and many more tearful nights before I came to respect and accept this particular power as something to *own*, something to use to make a difference. It would be decades before I realized that people who make a difference usually offend someone. "People Pleasers" seldom trigger change.

My husband's government career moved us to Washington, D.C. and I began a consulting business, incorporating everything I had learned in my years in advertising.

Perhaps it was the sands in the biological hourglass and their ever-present descent from future into past, but my husband and I began to speak of children and ultimately had two exquisite daughters. But our life began to unravel with the intrusions into our private time. First Jennifer developed allergic reactions to milk, soy, all protein, and all sugar. As I struggled with that diagnosis and some system of nutrition for her, Adrianne began a series of ear infections that continued until she was about 12 years old. Nights became a blur of shuffling from one room to another, from rocking one while she screamed in pain to cross the hallway to lift another crying infant into my arms.

These were my Superwoman days as I lived on about four hours of sleep, broken by feedings and disruption, and then served my clients during the day. My office was in my home, and I had full time help, which meant I could be with one daughter while the help was with the other. That way I could be with the girls when I wasn't on a deadline

and make sure no one hurt them. The oldest, Jennifer, literally cried most of the time, due to the stomach discomfort
she was in; and from ten days of age, she never napped.
She finally fell asleep, crying at midnight. She woke crying
at 2 AM and again at 4 AM and was up for good at 6 AM
every day. The youngest simply cried all the time when she
had an ear infection. She had twelve in her second year.

When I visited my clients, I frequently took the girls
and the sitter along, stopping along the way at a play-
ground or a Children's Museum or a mall. That way they
could play while I handled business meetings.

We were living near Washington, D. C. at this point,
and so it was only logical, as I was prone to stumbling
through life now, that I fall into political consulting. I had
a gift there too, it seems. I treated the politicians the
same way I treated a shoe company. It was really quite
simple. It's all just understanding what the client "stands"
on and what his "soul" is made of, and how to out-pic-
ture that in the marketplace.

It was during the management of a particular campaign that I became painfully aware of the encroaching
power of the right wing evangelical agenda. The ominous
and obvious portends terrified me. My crystal ball foretold a future ahead with chiseled Constitutional Rights. I
foresaw a horrible future world dominated by the kind of
consciousness I grew up around, narrow and bigoted and
ignorant. I saw censorship ahead and loss of freedoms,
all in the name of God and righteousness, mind you. I felt
totally helpless in the face of this rider, as I felt in my life
in general. I was astride the back of a horse nothing like
the horse of my childhood. Where this one was headed,
I didn't want to go. But I was in observation mode. My
"action button" hadn't yet been engaged.

The more my daughters demanded, the more my
husband withdrew. He left for work at about 6 am
and returned around 5 pm, to take a long, hot bath—
something I greatly envied. Then he either disappeared
into the office at home or into the television. He emerged

from one or the other hours later. I could probably count the number of times he put the girls to bed on my fingers and toes. Emotionally he became colder and colder until one day I realized it had been three years since he had touched me, and I wasn't allowed to make overtures. My attempts at dialoguing about it were fruitless. My demands for counseling brooked only one worthless marriage counselor, who could have created divorce between the world's greatest lovers. I cried myself to sleep most nights, and he never noticed.

One day I recall standing by the foot of the bed. "Why don't you ever touch me anymore?" I asked, biting my lip, steadying myself for his answer.

"I don't find you attractive any more." That was all he had to say. He went back to reading then, and I went back to keeping the girls from bothering him, which is how I spent my evenings. He didn't like to hear them cry.

However, my business life was starkly successful, and we lived in the right town, and we drove the right car. And I had oriental rugs and antiques again! And the girls were in the very best nursery school and had been tested for Gifted Programs, which was de rigueur in Northern Virginia if you were anybody who dreamed of having successful toddlers.

Then the visitations began. I was asleep in my own bed one night, and I felt a finger prodding my arm. I turned over and opened my eyes, expecting to see Jennifer standing there wanting my attention. Instead I was shocked to see no one standing there. But when I looked at my arm, my skin was indenting in cadence to the feeling of someone poking me in the arm. I looked around the room and there at the foot of the bed was a large luminous shape, rather like the shape of a human body, but with no *body*, only a glowing, pulsing presence. It extended a firey "finger" and "whispered" to me, "Come and write."

And I got up and went into my office and began a series of poems I later called The Phantom Series. These poems desperately hungered to know what this presence was. It was a definitively male presence, a highly sexual feeling presence. I yearned to know who had entered my life this way, reminding me what passion was missing from my own existence.

"I have chased you across the paths of time. Through birth and death and birth and death. You ignite me and I burn," I wrote to him.

My childhood experience with the three lights visiting me in my room one night had left me with a great interest in the paranormal. I'd read a book on Edgar Cayce when I was quite young and fully accepted the understanding of reincarnation and karma. It just felt right, and my soul knew the truth of it, for me anyway. But it had been a while since anything had come to call, especially anything that had changed me so. After these visitations, which continued nightly for nine months, I began to write a newspaper column, and I moved back more deeply into alternative spirituality with a growing ferocity and commitment.

My previous interest had been in the paranormal, but now I began to contemplate God, and I knew that it was I.

My husband thought I was crazy.

But the visitations continued for nine months, long enough to birth a newspaper column, which I wrote for the next four years for the local paper. One of my first columns was about the first day Jennifer went to Kindergarten. It waxed quite poetic about a mother's hope for her child, intending to speak about the hope we have for all children, only using my own experience as metaphor.

I remember one line read, "May your toe shoes never hurt." It only appeared to be about Jennifer going to Kindergarten, but was much more about childhood and life and loss, all couched in a mélange of beautiful language. It spoke to all our hopes and dreams for all our children. And for whatever reason, people hated me for writing it. The editor was a friend, and he understood the power of columnists. He was delighted with the controversy I had created and featured the hate mail boldly in print.

I mean, how could they hate me for writing a sweet column about my daughter going to kindergarten and all my hopes and dreams for her? I have read and reread that column, and to this day I can only see it provoking tears, not hatred. But instead I opened the paper the week after it appeared, and there were two facing pages of hate letters about my writing. I cried all week. Next week the paper came out and there were letters praising my writing. I was up against my old issue of pleasing people. Why couldn't they all love me? One day I signed a check at the grocery store and the checkout clerk recognized my name and commented on my column, which led the woman behind to say how much she hated me, which led the woman behind her to say how much she loved me. I slunk out of the store and went home and cried again.

I told myself that if my five-year-old could grow up and go to school, I could grow up, too. Growing up, to me in this instance, referred to getting over my fears of not being wanted and "not being approved of." It was the same old, same old abandonment "why doesn't anyone love me stuff." And you know what? It was holding me back from being all I could be. I knew that as long as I cared what people thought, I wouldn't be all I could be. I was using all my energy trying to write pleasing things... please my husband...please my children...please my clients. I had no energy left for me.

My life is a series of stumbles and cracks. I stumble into something, and then I crack and get out. I guess I should have known that a fissure was opening a hole in my marriage large enough for me to fall through. We were traveling different roads and only meeting occasionally when we came upon a crossroads. But I don't give up easily, and I kept trying to make things work or pretend that it didn't matter that I wasn't happy.

One night we went to dinner with a friend who was in town on business. He always took us out to dinner during his visits, and on this occasion we were in Georgetown at a French Restaurant where the waiters wore roller skates and jumped on stage and did little musical numbers in-between courses. I'd had a drink, which was very unusual for me. It only takes one drink to make me very happy and very tipsy. Emotionally, I melted, remembering the man I had fallen in love with and married, the man I'd felt strongly enough about to have children with. And so I leaned over and ran my fingers along his neck, imagining deeply luscious thoughts of sensuality. He never looked around, but he must have mistaken my fingers caressing his neck for an insect, because he slapped his hand around behind his neck, like you would swipe at a fly to shoo it away.

It felt like someone had slapped me in my heart. It was, for whatever reason, the last straw, the last intimacy rejection of the hundreds I had suffered with him. I snapped. I stood up, slipped the keys toward him so he would have the car (God knows I didn't deserve the car myself!) and walked out the door. I had 25 cents in my purse when I hailed a taxi and asked him to take me to a bank machine so I could pay the cab fare the 30 miles out to Reston where we lived. The cab driver was an Iraqi student working on his PhD. We stopped, and I picked up a girlfriend along the way. She had a trumpet, and I stopped at the house and picked up my clarinet, and we sat together on the main plaza in town, and we played music, she on the trumpet and me on the clarinet. The cab driver was on tabla and vocals. We played and sang the blues on Lake Anne Plaza until sunrise. I sang about lost love. She sang about lost youth. He sang about the horrors of war. Why no one complained, I don't know.

I intended to leave that next night, but he talked me into staying for a few weeks, saying a mother with two small children shouldn't have to go out in the cold. He said if I just gave him a few weeks, he'd find a place. But he never left. I found out later that his father had advised him not to leave, fearing I might say he deserted and claim the house. He obviously didn't know me. I walk away from houses and antiques.

I don't deserve for anyone to take care of me. I take care of myself. No one loves me. No matter how much I give or how hard I work or how much I love, I am an orphan, and that is the way it will always be. And, after all, I am just a woman, and everyone knows we have no value. We cannot be Saints or Mystics. We are only whores. We can only serve a man. That we are necessary for the birth of children is only of temporary importance, and we about to be replaced biologically by test tubes and petri dishes.

I wound up staying almost another six months or so after that incident, but I took off my wedding ring and no longer considered myself married. And I began to work earnestly on my spiritual life, of which he wanted no part.

I rented a cottage on Chincoteague Island and spent two weeks alone with no clock and no phone. It was my first adventure into alone time since the back roads of Virginia. I soaked in it. I sponged it. I sopped it up. I reveled in it. I splashed it on my face and bathed deeply in it, sinking into myself, anointing myself with the space to breathe and think.

I made friends with a fisherman who saved me the best of his catch of the day, and I lived blissfully on a daily ration of one huge crab, one glass of red wine, and one artichoke.

As I walked the Atlantic coast beach of the sister island, Assateague, I had what can only be described as a life-altering experience. I began a dialogue with "words without a voice" that lasted three full days as I walked the beach during a storm. This "teacher" who appeared in my head was the most challenging and powerful presence I had ever experienced at that point, and I was both awed and humbled by the power and the presence.

These "words without a voice" taught me about the illusion of perfection and about the light spectrum and our creation through it as we *fell* into matter. I was taught about the physics of consciousness and about the perfection in what might appear to be imperfection.

He—it felt like a male presence—taught me about the physics of soul mates, how we begin the journey into matter as one light that splits into two lights, male and female/positive and negative, as we "fall" through the light spectrum to enter this electromagnetic plane of consciousness. He told me that almost never are these two original lights on the same plane even...that the reuniting of these lights is extremely rare, and that if it should happen prematurely, before each has finished its own individual work, they might blow each other up, so powerful are the magnetics of original lights. After these caveats had been delivered, this voice told me that my destiny lay in the reuniting with my original light.

A spark was rekindled in the little girl who had always believed in true love, who had always *known* there was another part of her somewhere out there, and though the spark had been relit with clear warnings, my heart leapt at the possibility. I looked deeply at my life and saw that the foremost issue for me had always been relationship. It was my *work*. It was my *love*. And the truth was, finding "this other half of me" was what my search had always been about. And—if it were true that you shouldn't meet before each of you had finished your own personal work, then I'd better go to work on myself. And so it was that I vowed to call forth any unfinished personal work, so that I would be ready.

I walked those three days through a fierce Nor'easter that blew a steady gale force at me, so that I had to walk leaning into it. I argued with this voice of God in my mind as I walked, railing about the inconsistencies and vagaries of life and metaphysics.

At one point, after I'd debated vehemently over a point, I was ordered to pick up a seashell that lay in my path. It was cracked and barnacle-covered, slick with the sludge of oil on one side. What had once been life was no more and in its place, only parasites and waste and pollution. The sky in my mind split down the middle, and for some period of time I can't describe—I saw truth. I saw it all. I saw the revolution of cosmos around cosmos, multi-leveled, multi-realmed worlds-within-worlds and layers of purpose.

Purpose and perfection were contortionists that could bend into anything they needed to be in the moment. It was *all* perfect. And even the concept of perfection was limited. And that was perfect. The imperfection was perfect!

I stayed in this place of sheer bliss for—I don't know, maybe only seconds. Maybe hours. After all, I had walked into a gale force wind for three solid days, sunrise to moonrise.

I had asked, "What's it all about?" And the Big Alfie had answered me.

I went back the fourth day at sunrise, and I asked to be able to write what I had been taught, as I had never heard such communication. I was told I'd have to "earn the words back," and that when I'd "owned" them in my own life, I could have all the teachings back—but they would come from my own mouth and heart then and not just be a repetition. And so it is that I can tell this story and not yet write the full teaching given by the wind in those three days.

Back home, I could never be the same. I had seen something, and I was different.

I loved my husband, but he was incapable of loving himself, and I should have learned one of life's great lessons by that point. You can't love someone enough to make them love you. If they can't love themselves, they surely can't love you. But I hadn't *gotten* that from my first marriage and wasn't to *get* it from my second attempt. Instead, I had lain awake at night, tears rolling down my cheeks for years, lying right beside him, and he had never noticed.

After ten years of waiting for a change in temperature, I figured he'd frozen to death and wasn't going to thaw, and so I left. I had reached a point in my growth where survival could not compensate for emotional freedom and truth. I refused to let the girls grow up in an environment that was a lie, perpetuating the myth of "mommy-daddy" based on common agreement to "stay together for the sake of the children." If this was my soulmate, he surely didn't see it that way.

And I had been called by an island in the northern sky and by a great teacher in the wind. A few months after my Chincoteague experience I saw a video that sounded a lot like my teacher in the wind.

And so it was that I packed up my daughters, closed my business, bought a van and packed it for a road trip. I was going west to write the teachings of this great Master and to work on my unfinished business, so that I would be ready.

There are memories I hold dearly from that cross-country trip with a six-year-old and an eight-year-old. We camped at night, our modest, older Volkswagen Westfalia wedged between huge converted buses and motor mansions. Linen tablecloths and silver goblets emerged from our turtle-shell, and while our neighbors stuffed themselves into plastic chairs outside their $200,000 motor homes guzzling beer, we breakfasted on eggs benedict and served our grilled cheese sandwiches with our crusts trimmed and drank our tea from silver goblets.

I sat in a pool of water beneath Horseshoe Falls in West Virginia the day my briefing was given to the Executive Branch of the White House, laughing under the pelting warm water. I could have stayed for that briefing, for the "glory" of saying I'd been there, but I chose the waterfall instead. It was the 4th of July, 1986, and it seemed a more fitting statement to make about freedom, to sit in a waterfall rather than sit in the Oval Office of the Reagan White House.

I experienced my first-ever migraine in Elk Creek, Kentucky. My head was pounding and I thought I'd better stop driving. It was early afternoon when we pulled into the Elk Creek Campground. I picked a campsite as the blinding pain sent me diving underneath covers for darkness. Next door to our camping site, Elsa permanently camped every summer. She strung Christmas tree lights and had fake grass laid out the entire breadth of her space. Her wooden sign announced her encampment to the constant stream of family and guests.

As I passed out from the pain, I held a vague memory of seeing Jenni and Adrianne wander over and enter Elsa's picket fence where she held court on a lawn chair picking beans, a little Chihuahua by her side.

I awoke hours later, electrically rewired, as I was to be for years, from these headaches that always took me down for what seemed like days. I was horrified. How long had I slept? Where were the girls? I had no intention of letting them out of my sight on this trip, having heard so many horror stories of children disappearing on their way to the bathroom at a campground. I pulled back the curtain on the van window and allowed the waning light of dusk to penetrate my optic nerve, only wincing slightly.

There were the girls, picking beans with Elsa next door.

"God," I thought. "What on earth will she think of me? I've been gone for however long, asleep in a van while my children roamed around." She was an older woman, and I had learned to be frightened of them, having been raised by one!

I stumbled my way out the door and over through the little gate beneath the "Elsa's Place at Elk Creek" sign.

The girls greeted me excitedly and begged to show me the trick Elsa's Chihuahua could do. Elsa agreed and they dispatched the little dog to "fetch a drink." The little snippet of short white hair raced into the camping trailer, and dragged out a can of beer. Ferociously, he growled and menaced and dragged the can back and forth across the fake grass, slamming it into the lawn chairs, clawing and scratching at it's pop-top until it began to leak beer. Gleefully he then lay back, pulling the can over him, catching every drop as gravity drew the liquid down his throat.

"So," Elsa said to me, "the girls tell me you're taking them off to some island way up in the Northern sky, smack-dab in the middle of nowhere. You got a good reason for doing that?"

Fear clutched at my throat. Was she going to judge me for this? Was I going to buckle under this scrutinization? Could I think of some lie to justify this action on my part?

"No," I heard myself say. "I don't have a good reason for doing this. I just want to."

"Good," Elsa said. "I never saw happiness come from anything done for a good reason."

I knew then we were on a magical journey of spirit, not mind. It continued from philosophical conversations with old folksingers on a riverboat along the Missouri to saving a frog in a whirlwind on the White River in the Badlands in South Dakota.

I liked Missoula, Montana so much that I got down on my knees in front of the van outside a Chinese Restaurant and cut it a deal. I promised my van that wherever it broke down, I'd consider that as a sign that we were supposed to stay there. Then I started the engine, silently hoping it wouldn't start. It started.

We continued until we ran out of land at the edge of a little town in Northern Washington State. We boarded a ferry on the way to the island whose call I had heard all the way back east. The three of us huddled against the wind on the bow of Kaleetan and sobbed at the recognition as home approached. Here—my heart sang. Here—my soul breathed with joy and recognized divinity. Here, where cliffs met the sea, entwined in a chain as ancient as memory, I found some sense of place I had never known before.

But no one was expecting us. There were no banners out that read, "Welcome. We have been awaiting your arrival. Sit down now and write the books you were called to write. Here's your paycheck." Reluctantly, we stayed as long as we could, but since no one made me an offer, we headed off, either to the Southwest or home. We would make that decision along the way.

But we were so close to a huge snow cone called Mt. Rainier that I couldn't see how we could be that close and not climb it. It was, after all, right there in front of us, begging for a pilgrimage. Alas, after climbing all the way up, the engine finally blew on the way down. And there we were, stranded. Or was it gifted? A blown engine would take a minimum of two weeks. I called home and had the same experience we'd had nightly when we tried to call. We got the phone machine. When I finally got through to the girl's father, telling him we were stranded, he didn't say, "Oh, let me fly out and take care of this. Are you all right? What can I do to help you? Let me fly you home right now." Instead he said, "So what does this mean to me?"

We never returned.

Through the next five years, I was a single mother, living with eagles and whales on an island in the Northern Sky. Since their father was on the other coast, he wasn't around to take them on weekends or overnights, so there were no nights off for me. No weekends alone. Life was full time. And the ear infections continued.

Through all the born-again virgin years, I had one mantra. I repeated this mantra over and over to myself. I repeated it in the bathtub, on hikes up the mountain, on the way to school to pick up the girls, everywhere. I must have said this at least twenty times a day for those five years.

"From the Lord God of My Being Unto the Mother/ Father Within, I call forth all my unfinished business. Bring it forward. Bring forward anything I have not looked at. Bring forward my fears, my jealousies, and my insecurities. Bring it all forward and let me work on it now. So be it!"

Occasionally, I must admit, I added a line to my mantra.

"From the Lord God of My Being Unto the Mother/ Father Within, I call forth all my unfinished business. Bring it all forward that I may finish it, so I will be ready to meet the mate to my being."

The girls and I were so close during those years you couldn't have gotten a sliver between us. We were all we had. We lived on $900 a month for most of those years. Once, I sat down with both Jennifer and Adrianne, and we talked about what to do. I worried constantly about money. I explained that we could move back to D.C., and I could make a lot of money again, and their clothes could come from Bloomingdales again, as they once did. Now their clothes came from Second Hand Rose. I explained that I wouldn't be as available as I now was, but that we could have help and they could take music and dance and have things they didn't have. We had managed to hang onto a nice winter rental, with large rooms and beautiful furnishings, but it was no longer in the budget, though we moved out of it every summer and sort of floated around until we could have it back in the fall. But it was still out of the price range now, and we faced a wall of expenses, especially if I was going to try to produce a book.

They listened patiently to my presentation of our financial situation, and they both intoned, simultaneously, "Oh, no! We came here so you could live your dream. You mustn't give up your dream. We can move to something cheaper. Nothing will ever work if you don't live your dream!"

And so it was that we located a deserted trailer, with missing ceiling panels that allowed insulation blackened with mildew to hang down into each room. To say the roof leaked was a gross understatement. We had no furniture with us and couldn't afford to move our furniture from D.C., so we acquired enough to "furnish" (loosely translated, please!) our singlewide on the beach. We got our queen-sized foam mattress from the dump. It was V-shaped, with a deep crevice in the middle. We all slept together, me in the middle, one little girl on either side. I slept with little arms and legs sprawled all across me. We turned as one tangled mass, sometimes getting caught in each other's limbs. I seemed to always have a little arm across my face. I loved sleeping that way.

Of all the things I felt anger at their father for, somehow every Christmas I resented him most. He had all the Christmas ornaments and lights in his comfortable four-bedroom home in Reston, Virginia, the one his father had made sure he continued to live in. He never used them after we left, I have since discovered. But he wouldn't ship them to us. And so we had no Christmas ornaments and certainly couldn't waste money buying any. One year our dear friend, the island doctor, brought us ornaments from his tree, so we would have something to hang.

One year we couldn't afford a tree, and so a friend brought us a tree from high atop a mountain on the island where he had logging rights. It was a hemlock tree, with beautiful green branches, much prettier than the trees of Christmas past. We hung our few little ornaments on it, strung it with popcorn and Madrona berries, admired it, and went to bed. When we woke in the morning, the girls ran out to see their tree, only to find it all over the carpet. Hemlock trees drop their "green" needles inside. We were picking Hemlock needles out of that carpet for days. That was the Christmas of the Madrona branch. I thought it was quite a statement for the environment myself. No tree had to die, and a dead branch got honored. I don't think the girls shared my altruistic opinion of that particular dead branch.

We fixed the roof and slowly repaired the ceiling tiles, holding back the deadly insulation finally, but only after dozens of ear infections, and one by one we had each thrashed in the boiling temperatures of viral meningitis. I remember slipping through dimensions and twirling through the underworld, a hell of sweat and burning. My head didn't *hurt*. Hurt doesn't even come close to what that agony felt like. It felt like my marrow was being boiled while I was still in the body, and I ached beyond this world and into the next.

Two horrific storms hit the island while we were in our "trailer years." Each was labeled a "hundred year storm," supposedly so ferocious it could only happen once in a hundred years. We lived on the North Shore of Orcas Island during both of them. Power was lost early on and water followed. We had a tiny Kent woodstove in the living room of the singlewide. I filled one wall in the kitchen with wood and sealed black plastic over the inside of the windows and the sliding door and taped us in. I forced myself outside in the wind only once a day, to restock the wood. I set an alarm clock to feed the stove every two hours through the night. But we survived in that trailer when everyone else fled the North Shore. Two other single mothers deserted their huge homes in the below freezing cold, and we laid mattresses across the whole living room floor, and three mothers and six children held together through the storm in an 8' by 8' area. We cooked soup and noodles for days on that tiny stove. We thawed snow for water on the same stove that boiled our potatoes and noodles. I will always hold a special fondness for Kent stoves. It not only kept us alive, it kept us warm and fed us.

Adrianne "celebrated" her eighth birthday toward the end of the worst, and we managed to drive into town to the grocery store. The power was still off, and the store couldn't even open its door without electricity. They pried them open and forced them partially separated so that islanders could buy what few things were left on the shelves. There was one box of Duncan Hines white cake mix and we took it home. We opened the box and passed it among ourselves with a shared utensil, spooning bites of dry cake mix while we sang Happy Birthday. It is, to this day, the best birthday party I've ever been to. Three women and six children survived that storm at the point on the island where the brunt hit, better than 90 mile-an-hour winds raging down from Alaska and below zero temperatures—and we stayed warm and well fed, with no help from a man.

Somewhere, somehow, in the midst of this struggle to survive with little income, I did manage to do what I went there to do. I edited and produced three books based on the material I believed to have come from the great teacher in the wind, a consummate accomplishment for a single mother living on $900 a month. Eventually I acquired the rights back to the first two, self-published the last one, and even got it on the New Age bestseller list. Adrianne still says this is the time period she remembers when she thinks about my power, those "trailer years" when we found out that nothing could stop us.

One of these books was on the subject of male tyrants, though I did not think I had ever experienced one at the time. One was on manifestation. And one was on super consciousness.

I wish I had known I draw into my life what I edit. I would never have done the book on male tyrants.

But it wears on you, you know—the aloneness with so much responsibility. The school was dreadfully inferior, and I worried about the girls' education. I could offer them nothing beyond the most basic requirements of life, though I had become a magician in a second-hand store.

Deep in my heart, I was still lonely.

I began to lecture about the third book, specifically because it addressed a subject I thought to be sadly in need of understanding. Many people I knew held deep respect, to the point of abject reverence and subjugation, for whatever presented itself within the framework of what we considered Deity.

Send a voice and call it God or Jesus or Mary or any "known" Master and people bow in reverence. But the same people who bow to what is considered Deity within religion scoff at people who have communication with information sourced outside our current historical frame of reference, i.e., aliens. How narrow!

I decided it was my task to bridge this chasm between spirituality and what is considered "alien consciousness" and began to speak on the subject.

I have never really understood where fate meets karma.
And if we create our own reality, what role does destiny
play? I may never know in this lifetime. I will surely never
understand how the same woman who left one man rather
than allow her daughters to grow up in a loveless home
could possibly get caught in what was to unfold.

I met a man at a speaking engagement who claimed
to be something he wasn't. But I believed him, because I
wanted him to be what he said he was...because I wanted
the world to have such possibility. I wanted *me* to have
such possibility.

He portrayed himself as a great teacher.

And he played guitar and he sang songs.

He told me he was Native American, a Medicine Man
who had studied with the great old Grandfathers and
Grandmothers. He performed ceremony and played the
flute and wrote songs. He carried a sacred pipe and con-
jured images deeply held within my psyche, and so began
my years with the Eagle, the Bear, Spider, Raven, and the
White Owl and the Black Fish. I hiked deeper into the forests and spent probably two nights of every week
carrying the stones into the Sweat Lodge, praying and
singing. The first two years we traveled with elders, and
I really did learn many amazing things. What I didn't
know was that he was learning right along with me. He
really hadn't known many of these things before we came
together, but then, I had never experienced a real con man
until him, and it took me years to figure that out. I did not
know how cleverly the dark could pretend to be the light.

Slowly he began a process of tearing me down,
demeaning me, cutting me off from old friends, and taking my power over a period of almost five years. Until one
day I awoke to realize I had become an abused woman. I
had allowed a man to hit me, while I supported him.

One day I was walking behind him, on the way to the
kitchen to make him a cup of coffee. All of a sudden,
he twirled around and pounded a blow to my left ear.
Pain so sharp it numbed shot through me, and I fell to

the ground from the blow. I spent the rest of that day in bed, holding my ear, curled in a fetal position from the pain. I was deaf in that ear for six months. And I told no one. He never said he was sorry. We just went on with life. After all, he was a "great teacher" and I was just a woman. What else am I left to think about my desperation for me to allow such treatment? Perhaps because the abuse was infrequent and came literally out of the blue, I excused it. Perhaps I was too ashamed to admit it happened. Perhaps my childhood wound re-opened.

I was in the fifth grade. Right after lunch one spring day, Charlotte, the teacher's pet, saw a book lying on the teacher's desk. Charlotte was the "room librarian," and so it was her domain to check all library books found in the room. Alas, it had not been checked out at all! Ever vigilant, Charlotte promptly returned the book to the library and came back to the classroom.

The bell rang, and the teacher walked in, took a look at her desk, and asked where her book was. The room got really quiet. Mrs. Brown was especially mean to some kids and particularly nice to others. There was never a reason anyone could determine that explained her behavior or her choice of victim.

On that particular day, Mrs. Brown walked across the room and stood in front of me.

"Judi, you took my book back to the library didn't you?"

"No, ma'am, Mrs. Brown," I said respectfully. To which she drew her arm back and slapped me across the face, propelling me out of my desk and onto the floor. I was stunned and humiliated. I had done nothing!

I couldn't wait to tell Ruby what had happened. She would take care of it. Mothers always take care of things.

When I told her what happened, Ruby said, "I'm sure she had a reason. I have to teach at the same school; there's nothing I can do."

I never forgot her response and lived out the repercussions for another 30 years.

If someone hits me, I must have done something to deserve it. If I was raped at knifepoint, it must have been because I had no business walking along that road that late at night.

Before I finally learned my lesson, he attacked my daughter and wound up stealing everything we had accumulated between us. In the very end he almost killed me—holding me against glass-paneled doors and beating me back-and-forth across the face until I almost lost consciousness.

The truth was finally clear to me. I had fought a five-year-long battle with the dark side for the soul of a man. And lost.

We agreed to separate after the girls and I returned from studying with an herbalist. Instead, while we were out of town, he wrote obscenities on the bedroom walls with magic markers, packed everything and left. He forged my name on documents that resulted in lawsuits and cleaned out the bank account. I learned the hard lesson of a male tyrant.

We returned home and found everything gone— everything, I should say, of value. He had taken the girl's new video player bought with their child support, all CDs, all my art, my sacred bundle, all the furniture of any value, all running vehicles, including a motor home in both our names, all paperwork, even my address book. He left behind 1500 pounds of wet insulation and trash everywhere. There were threats hidden inside jars and hatbands and a notice from the landlord that we had less then 30 days to be out of the house. The girls and I cleaned the house, sealed the walls he'd covered with obscenities, repainted, and moved within that deadline.

I know how much the insulation and garbage weighed because when we shoveled it off the rental truck at the dump, they charged me $180. When I looked shocked at the cost, they said, "Hey, lady, you just offloaded 1500 pounds of trash and that's what it costs." Without a penny to my name, that was a huge sum to be charged for dumping his trash, but insult to injury had become a way of life with him. He also deserted the two dogs he had brought into my life.

I put everything left into storage, kept out one good looking outfit and took the only living space offered us—a friend's tiny motor home. We boarded the dogs at the kennel and put three cats into cages stacked on each other and moved all of us into a space only big enough to sleep in, alongside the cat cages.

I borrowed money from Adrianne, who had saved every penny she'd ever been given, perhaps just so she could loan me that money, and I went to town looking for a house. A rental agent who had clearly lost her mind rented me an expensive old waterfront farmhouse on six acres of the most beautiful land on the island. I was a woman with no job and two teenaged children. To this day, I have no idea how I got that farmhouse, nor do I have any idea how I had the courage to rent it.

We moved in slowly and invited the owners to leave their old furniture in place rather than take it to the dump! *There is a Goddess!* Thankfully, this gave us beds, a sofa from the fifties, and a dining room table!

I slowly lifted my head from the paralyzing decay of shame and began to contact old friends, obtaining phone numbers one by one. I immediately discovered why he had stolen my address book. He had called many of them and told them I had stolen everything from him and left him with nothing. He told them I had taken all the money! He even told some of them that I had abused him! But here's the biggest shocker of all. Many of them believed him! He had told the most amazing lies I have ever heard. I had forgotten what a consummate liar he was! He had, after all, fooled me for years. And I had hidden the abuse from almost everyone for years. I don't know why. *It was infrequent so I justified it? I kept thinking I'd done some-thing wrong to make him hit me? It came so "out of the blue" it was hard to believe it happened?*

This was to be my first major encounter with betrayal, and I watched many people I called friends choose to believe him instead of me. Until that experience with him, I had always believed there were two sides to every story. Now I know better. By that I mean that I understand that there are always two experiences, and in the grand "metaphysical" understanding everyone has their own truth, but there is no mitigation for abuse, verbal or physical. There is no "other side" that excuses abuse.

The final shock for me was when a girlfriend visited me one day shortly after we got our new house. She was one of the few people who knew about the abuse.

She had lived near us and had seen his hypocrisy. She was also one of a handful of people who knew that I had stood by this man through his immense legal problems, paying for his lawyers with the profits from my own books to clean up his past shady history. She told me about a telephone conversation she'd had with his mother during the months of legal battles.

He had always claimed to be a Metis, a person of mixed blood, part Native and part Caucasian. So this woman had asked his mother which side of the family had the Native blood. His mother had replied that there was absolutely no Native blood on any side, only Italian. She had confirmed that he was actually full blood—full blood Italian!

In actuality, he was nothing he had claimed to be, and until the very end, I had believed him. I had believed his version of the legal battles, which portrayed him as a victim of the system. I had believed his version of why I found different names on paperwork. I had believed his version of how awful all the other women had been in his life, betraying him, and deserting him, and leaving him with nothing. (And I swore I'd stand by him and show him how wonderful *some* women can be!) I had believed his version of where he learned and earned his medicine. And in the end, I was to discover he was not Native, not even part Native. Not only was he not *what* he said he was, but he wasn't even "who" he said he was either.

I had wondered why he had a different name from his mother, and why his own daughter had a different last name, and why the name I knew him by was different from either his birth name or his only daughter's name.

He had been many different men in his life.

There is a dreadful shame that comes with being a "victim," whether it is of abuse, or ignorance, or both, as in my case. It is rather like being a rape victim. There is a terrible sense that you did something to bring it on, some horrible, awful feeling that somehow you deserved it. In my case, this was, of course, the result of my childhood with Queen Victoria, who had somehow always made me feel like I was very lucky she hadn't left me on a dung heap somewhere to starve when she took me in as a baby. And the ideal mating for terror is when a natural abuser meets a victim of childhood trauma. In that sense, we were made for each other. And, if you understand the perfection of imperfection, we both got what we chose to deserve, as harsh and awful as that sounds. As long as we allow it—we will be beaten. And when we value freedom above anything and everything else, we will choose freedom, even when it means the loss of what appears to be *everything*.

The reason he fled when he did is because in my growing suspicions of many things, I had began to call him on his hypocrisy more and more loudly, risking everything in doing so—and I threatened to let people know who he really was and who he really wasn't. Had I stayed subservient and obeying, he would still be dominating my life.

In the midst of escape from terror, I drew a friend to my cause. A remarkable and wonderful man literally flew to me and helped me through this crisis. He brought his white horse to America from abroad. He told me there was nothing I could ever do that would make him leave, that no matter how hard I tried to push him away, he was there to stay. I finally yielded to his pleadings, and I let down my long hair over the castle wall.

He was the antithesis to every man I had ever known. He was grounded, both in his business life and in his spiritual life. And, he adored me! He listened intently to my feelings, valued my opinion on all matters, and he loved to touch and be touched.

He held his hand over mine one day at a café in Santa Fe, took off his favorite ring which he wore everywhere, and said, "The next ring that will go on this finger is the ring that you put there, the same day I put one on your finger. It will be the ring that binds us forever." It was a moment from a movie, and I melted. Was I finally safe enough to trust again? I let my hair down further over the castle wall.

Slowly, basking in his love and his commitment, I began to relax. He helped me unravel the messes con-straining me. He defended me. I don't think anyone had ever defended me before. We began a new business together. He adored the girls, and for the first time in their life, they had a loving, generous father. He gave Jennifer money for guitar lessons, something I'd never been able to offer her. And he bought Adrianne her own flight headset so she wouldn't have to borrow one when she went flying.

He noticed little things and acted on them. He even drove to Jennifer's college to check out her potential housemates, lovingly interrogating them, qualifying them, to make sure she would be safe in that environment, ask-ing them all sorts of silly questions only a loving father would ask. She glowed in the attention. We all did.

Love and appreciation are beyond measure. There is no yardstick long enough to measure it's importance, no scale that can weigh its immense value. I began to heal.

And so when Christmas rolled around, I was determined to find the most special present I could, to thank him for choosing to be the amazing Being he had chosen to be. I wanted to give him something beyond a "thing" in a box, something beyond measure. I wanted to find something to bespeak my awed and humble gratefulness to him.

And that is how I met Tom Kenyon.

A little voice in my head said to me, "You must find the tones. Give him the "sounds" for Christmas." Hmmm. What on earth did that mean? I called all my friends who sing professionally to ask them to "sing" for him for Christmas, but they were all on tour or unavailable.

Then one night a girlfriend called and mentioned Tom Kenyon's name during the conversation. My heart jumped, and bells went off in my head, which doesn't happen often to me. For years people had told me how amazing Tom Kenyon's work was, and many had said we should meet. I had actually gone home several times during my "Medicine Days" with his phone number, suggesting a meeting, only for the Great Medicine man to snarl a refusal! (Later I found out why.)

Now I was with a supportive, loving person, and I could meet whomever I felt called to meet. The words in my head—the ones without a voice—were whirring and clanging and striking chords of recognition, telling me to act— this was the Christmas present I had been looking for.

I took Tom's phone number and called his office and actually left a message that embarrasses me to this day. I recall saying something like, "I know you don't know me, but for years people have said we should meet. I don't know if they have said the same to you, but anyway, I need to find the most spectacular present for a very special man. And I wonder if you'd consider being the Christmas present?"

He called a few minutes later, and we scheduled a "present delivery" at his home up near the Canadian border.

We drove up two days later to "take delivery" of the present. I didn't even know what Tom Kenyon did! I had no idea he worked with tones. I was just listening to my guidance, something I had avoided doing for years.

We were met at the door by the largest animal I have ever seen in a house. His name was Merlin. He barely had to raise his head to look me in the eye, scanning me from head to foot. His head easily reached

my chest. He was larger than a miniature horse, part
Bloodhound and part Great Dane.

Merlin ushered us in, and Tom met us shortly there-
after. Tom settled us on a sofa and unwrapped a crystal
bowl and began to call in the archangels. I had closed
my eyes, but when he began to sing, they popped open.
I had to see to believe what I was hearing! This music
of the spheres couldn't come from the human being sitting four feet away or from any *human* being. This was
the voice of God. This was like no other voice I've ever
heard, on CD, in a concert hall, anywhere, even in my
dreams. No one could sound like that. Tears poured out
of my eyes, and my body began to tremble. I have never
known such gratitude. I was grateful that a voice like this
actually existed on Earth and that I was lucky enough to
be able to be in the same room with it. Such voices are
locked away in cloistered palaces and hidden within opera
halls and protected by guards and security. No one gets
close to anyone with a voice like this, and there I was.

I slid further away on the sofa, not wanting to take
these tones away from my friend. This was a gift for him;
it was not for me. I was just grateful to be in the room.
After Tom called in the archangels, he began a process
of taking my friend into the eye of the Ibis, through it,
and into another dimension, all through tone and sound.
Sometimes he was an Eagle, sometimes he was a Whale,
and it was all coming out of Tom Kenyon. We were both
profoundly altered.

Then the Hathors came through and spoke to my
friend, as if they were old, old friends. When they finished their sounds and their information and directions
given through Tom, Tom himself returned for a moment
to announce, "The Hathor Goddess wishes to speak
with you, Judi."

I was dumbfounded. I hadn't expected any attention.
This was my present for someone else! I sat up straight-
er, feeling the intensity entering the room. I have no
memory of what she said to me, nor does anyone else

who was in the room. Someday the occasion will arise
for me to ask her, but I know it was deeply honoring and
very loving and intensely personal, so personal that none
of us can remember it. I know she made reference to my
recent battle with the dark and congratulated me for still
being alive.

When we left, Tom caught me on the way out the door
and said, "I have to tell you, I don't do this."

"*What* don't you do?" I asked.

"I don't see people privately at my house," he said
matter-of-factly.

"Then why did you let us come today?" It seemed to
be a legitimate question.

"The Hathors told me to let you come."

He closed the door and left me standing there, feeling
very strange and elated. I knew the Hathors as interdimensional beings who had been very active and beneficial in ancient Egypt, Masters of sound and love, but I
had never had an experience with them before.

Back at home on my little island I was a haunted person. I couldn't get those sounds out of my head. I had
this feeling there was a connection, a deep connection
somewhere. My friend had never been so affected by
anything in his life, and I was very proud of myself for
creating the most amazing Christmas present anyone
ever received! And the sense of connection grew inside
me. I was haunted by Tom Kenyon's comment, "The
Hathors told me to let you come."

So about a week later I called again.

"If the Hathors told you to let us come once, would
they tell you to let us come again?"

He laughed, and said he was sure they would, and
so another session was set, and we went back once
more. During this session I was given information about
our Egyptian connections, and at the end of the session it was clear that old friends had found each other
again, and I even understood why my former partner had
scowled and refused to ever meet Tom Kenyon. I had

been shown how I had walked a tightrope dangling above such a pit of darkness intent on destroying me that one tiny step to one side or another would have easily cost me my life.

I may not appear very logical in this very abbreviated version of my life, and perhaps I have not written the accounts of my logic, but I am a devout realist. I am logical, almost to a fault. And I am loyal, clearly to a fault, and was once very Pollyanna-ish, a trait I was quickly getting over now. I am a deductive reasoner. My greatest teacher, the friend in the wind, always used to say, "Master, reason it out." (I loved that he called us Master, rather than demanding that we approach him from a position of devotional enslavement. He always said we would never understand that we are God if we keep calling something outside of ourselves Master.)

I began to realize that the darkness isn't dumb enough to obviously look dark. It often looks like the light and discernment can be quite difficult. And when I thought about it, it made sense. If there were such a creature as the devil, where would he hide if he were smart? He'd hide in the church or some permutation thereof; he'd hide in spirituality.

And though I had long ago figured out that it was the devil himself, so to speak, at the helm of the Church of Rome and many governments, I had not looked within my own rank, within what I considered the truly sacred realms of alternative spirituality, where I was convinced the hope of the world truly lay.

And it was then that I realized that darkness was not dumb, just evil; and that darkness would, of course, attempt to permeate and use our own language to defeat our awareness in this attempt to subdue world consciousness. Darkness, the evil of enslavement, can no longer stop us from raising our consciousness through the ignorance of sin and guilt, so it has figured out how to creep, undetected, into our midst and stand alongside us, pretending to be one of us, luring us into confusion, beating us back once again from individual Christ consciousness.

Perhaps I should clarify what I consider evil. By the word evil, I refer to anything that thwarts the coming forward of the Christ Consciousness into the earth plane, anything that deters enlightenment.

My friend sat up all night that night, watching me. I went to sleep with him sitting on the edge of the bed, staring at me, tears streaming down his cheek. I asked him why he was crying, and he said he'd had no idea how close he'd come to losing me, and it broke his heart to imagine me so threatened. I woke to find him still sitting there. He swore that as long as he could help it, I would never be at risk again.

I remember the first time I met Pam Kenyon. It was several weeks after that fateful experience with the Hathors. She lit up the whole room with a glow that came directly like a light beam straight out of her heart. Her smile was sheer magnetism, her countenance pure Goddess. She was one of the most beautiful people I have ever known. She and Tom became dear, dear friends and when they moved onto the island, almost next-door, life felt really blessed, and our circle seemed complete.

Then my friend went back to Europe for a few weeks. I was to join him there soon. He called several times a day for a week, but then he discovered his European business associate had been draining the corporate funds. Then this associate emptied all the bank accounts and fled. My knight and I still talked several times a day during this crisis, and I only finally realized how serious the loss was when I asked him, pointblank, how much money he had left, and he told me he had $20 in his pocket, and since that wasn't even enough money to buy gas to get home, he was going to just leave his car in the parking lot and take a bus home.

And then, abruptly, the calls stopped, and the light in my heart went out again. This had been a very successful and powerful man who had collateralized everything he owned to the man who disappeared to get the funds to start a new business in America, so his loss was both financial and emotional. Many, many people were hurt when this occurred, and not only had my friend lost everything he had in the world, but he felt responsible for all his associate's employees who were now looking to him in their desperation.

I remember the last phone call I got from my white knight. I could hear the tension in his voice, and I could hear the only slightly muffled sobs of a man in the background. When I asked about the sobs, my friend said it was an officer in the corporation who didn't know how to make his mortgage payment, and my friend had no money to give him.

And then the phone fell silent. I slept with the cordless phone in bed every night, waking every hour or so to make sure there was a dial tone. Six weeks went by, and I was losing my mind with worry. He had come to my aid when I was at my worst. I had to do the same, but I didn't even know where to go. All the company phone numbers had been disconnected. Finally, in desperation, I called the only person I thought could get a message to my friend. I asked that he locate my friend and tell him that I was on my way to Europe to help, because he had saved my life, and now I must do the same. I just wanted him to know he wasn't alone. I asked him to tell my friend that no matter what had happened, we could work it out.

That got a response, but not the response I wanted. I got a fax that said he just couldn't be everything to everyone any longer. It said that he had taken care of too many people for too long, and now he needed to take care of himself. He said that he was going to take some time and go away and think. He said he loved me very much, more than words could say, and that someday I would look up and see him walking down my road again. He told me not to come. He told me he would come back for me, but that it would be a very, very long time before he could get here.

I have no words for the feeling of loss. I huddled on the floor, holding the slick paper in my hand. I remember it was daylight outside when night fell inside my heart.

The sun set inside me, and it would be a long time before dawn.

I had barely read the fax when Ruby's neighbors in Virginia, the good Christian ones who'd always been able to tell everyone what to do in the name of Christ, called to say that Ruby had no business living alone anymore, and that if I didn't do something to get her out of there, they would turn her in to social services. They said she was getting too mean and they couldn't be bothered with her anymore.

Adrianne and I flew to Virginia and packed Ruby's meager belongings and brought her to our little island farmhouse. I possess an immense inner strength and survival will, but I was reaching my furthermost edges, and I knew it. I was adrift on an ice floe, and it was my heart.

I had survived an abuser and the loss of what I thought was the love of my life, and now I had to caretake the 95-year-old source of my childhood pain?

One night shortly after she arrived I was over at a girlfriend's house, sobbing my heart out. I drove home around 5 pm to find Ruby sitting in the window, just like she did when I was 18 years old. I shivered, took a deep sigh and walked in.

"And where have you been, young lady? How dare you come home so late," her bony finger prodded the air near my nose. She harrumphed and made little spitting sounds and shook her head.

"Good girls don't go out this late. It doesn't look good! Or maybe you don't care what people think!"

There it was. There was the source of my entire life of caring what other people thought!

Something was gravely wrong with this picture.

The words of my old teacher in the wind ricocheted in my ears, "Look around you, Master," he used to say. "Look at all the people around you. Not one single person would step in front of a bullet for you. Not one person would die for you. If they won't die for you, why are you living for them?"

I hated having Queen Victoria back in my house, and my heart ached for my friend, for someone who loved me for just who I was, not for who I appeared to be, or for how I looked, or even for what I did for him.

Jericho came tumbling down; my walls crumbled underneath me. Nothing could support me any longer. There was nothing *there*. I had just begun to touch into the anger, finally, at the abuser—at all the abusers in my life. It had taken forty years, but I had finally found my anger—and it was to become a great ally.

Now I was to learn sadness with my friend's disappearance.

It was the first time I thought someone finally actually loved me.

Now the tears of 10,000 lifetimes came in torrents. There was nothing I could do to stop the pain. I had always been able to shore up my emotional dike, but these floods could not be assuaged. There was no comfort to be found. The Eagles screamed, but I could not hear them. The great Black Fish surfaced, but my eyes could not see the wake. Even the White Owl came to comfort me, but I could feel no loving stroke.

I walked with pain and the desire to die for almost two solid years. I cannot exaggerate the intensity of this anguish. I cannot find the words in any thesaurus which, when swiped on paper, adequately capture the depth of this pool of torture. Do you know what happens when you cry for hours on end? There is a point reached in sobbing where you can only wretch until you throw up, gagging and choking on pain.

Oscar Wilde's great ballad looped endlessly in my mind.

*"Yet each man kills the thing he loves, by all let this
be heard. The coward does it with a word, the kind man
with a sword."*

Cowards and kind men alike had killed me.

I begged the gods to let me die. I desired death. I
wanted death. I didn't have the courage to do anything
about it. But I wanted it. I courted the fantasy in my mind
and dreamed of having the courage to act on it.

I cut absolutely everyone out of my life except for my
daughters, and Tom and Pam. Tom and Pam enfolded me
in loving friendship, taking me into their inner sanctum
like a wounded bird. Three other friends stayed by me. My
daughters held onto me. Adrianne promised me that someday I would want to live again, a notion I couldn't believe.

And Jennifer said, "Mom, just imagine how amazing the next one will be. He's going to be even better." I
thought she was insane.

"I will never let another man within ten feet of me," I
railed at her. "Never. Never! Don't talk crazy!"

And so it was that I decided I needed some time
myself. I had processed a lot of emotional material
already it seemed to me, enough for one lifetime, and
now I could handle no more. Caught between pain and
anger, my death wish was growing.

I couldn't remember anyone who had ever kept a
promise to me. So many promises over so many years.
And so it was that a dream was born. If no one else had
ever kept a promise to me, I must keep one to myself. I
had always promised myself that someday I'd take the
girls to Europe, on a journey of spirit. Desperate times,
as they say, call for desperate measures.

I took what money I could scrape, hired someone
to care take my mother, rented a car on the Internet
and flew into Amsterdam with Jennifer and Adrianne. It
was potentially our last summer together. Jennifer was
going to India alone in the fall, and it was Adrianne's last
summer before her senior year of high school. But high
school could wait a month I decided. Nothing she would

learn in one month of public high school would ever equal what we would learn traveling Europe together hunting Goddess sites.

We landed in Amsterdam and were met by a friend of a friend. Ron took us home, determined not to let us sleep prematurely, so that we would become acclimated to European time more quickly. Adrianne fell asleep right away, but Jen and I pinched each other to stay awake. He put on a documentary video and promised it would entertain us. It more than fulfilled his promise.

It was the story of the Priory of Sion, the story of my name, and the story of a Priest named Saunier and treasure he found. One of the few remaining clues to the mystery he left behind was a parchment that read, "The treasure belongs to Dagobert and to Sion."

I flashed to the little shack in Appalachia where I was born and my birth name, Zion, which came from Sion. I laughed at the equally portentous name I was given less than a year later when I was adopted—Pope. I had always intended to take back my birth name when the woman who adopted me died. She was now 95 and quite alive, and I was caught between names, as she was caught between dementia and sanity, this world and the next.

The documentary unfolded a story I knew to be true, a story I knew in my heart and had shared with many people. But I had no idea anyone else would ever tell such a story. I had logically deduced the truth, from little things that strung together, and from a woman's heart, which always knows the truth, or at least knows *her* truth. But here was evidence, or so it claimed, of what I had *known* for so long and felt so alone with. This documentary mentioned one name I remember, Rennes-le-Chateau, and I swore we'd find it. That's all I had written on a scrap of paper, Rennes-le-Chateau. Somewhere in France.

We took off in the morning, and I had one goal, to find this place and solve my own mystery. We drove at break-neck speeds through Germany, assaulted by hail so heavy the roof glinted with dents in the sunlight of morning. We had much to cover before France and we found ourselves in Ancona, Italy where we jumped on a ferry to Greece. We literally followed a crescent moon to Delphi. We couldn't read the roadmaps. They were in Greek! But in the middle of the night, we ascended the mountains; and when the moon set, we followed our hearts. It's a funny thing; to stand on land you once lived on and not be allowed to fully explore it. We sniffed at a little chain that said, "No Admittance" blocking entry to the spring of the Pythia. How do you tell a swallow not to enter Capistrano!

Hungrily we drank the water and climbed the ancient stairs cut so deeply into the vaginal walls behind the spring. Then we went to Hera's spring, near Nafplion, and drank and bathed where, according to legend, she returned each year to restore her virginity.

But the most haunting experience in Greece was not at a pre-supposed sacred site. We were asleep in a campground somewhere near Isthmia, along the Mediterranean. At about 3 o'clock in the morning, Pam appeared and woke me up. She told me something, but I was too groggy and still half asleep, so she grabbed me and sat me bolt upright. I stared literally into her very face, in all her splendor. She looked absolutely beautiful, radiant and literally *she was there*. She said six words to me, and I slumped back down. She grabbed me back up by the shoulders, and this time she shook me for effect, until I woke enough to really hear the six words she repeated. She extracted a promise from me, and then she released me. I looked around to find myself sitting up on a Mediterranean beach in the middle of the night. I woke the girls and told them what happened. None of us could figure out what it meant.

A few days later we took a ferry back to Venice and crossed back over Italy and entered France to finally search for Rennes-le-Chateau, but there was no such place on any map we could find.

So we decided to go to Arles, to see if the light was really different there. Van Gogh had painted there, swearing the

light was different in Arles than anywhere else. And that's
how we came to be just south of Arles late one afternoon
as the sun hits a place of light unlike anywhere else I've
been on Earth. I guess you could say I just followed the
light after that. Arles itself felt too busy so instead of
entering the city, we turned south. The Mediterranean
wasn't too far according to the map, maybe a detour
of some thirty miles. As we drove, the land flattened
and marsh grass peeked up between endless fields of
lavender. Rounding a corner, we almost collided with
a man on a white horse, herding black bulls along the
road. He wore an old, sweat-stained Stetson and a pair
of Wrangler jeans. This was a working cowboy, no show
pony. Lathered chaps covered his front legs. We drove
on and the lavender fields yielded to full marshland with
rivulets of water, and galloping herds of white horses
were everywhere.

Barns on either side offered riding and we chose one.
Trotting along, we rounded a corner and spooked hundreds of pink flamingos, which took to the air, leaving us
behind in a stream of wind off hundreds of wings. The
horses took it for granted; we were startled. I was forever enchanted.

The road ended at the sea, and we got a room for the
night in a town where paella was easier to find than a
crepe, and a bullfighting ring was where the town parking
lot ought to be.

I hate churches. I always have. To me, they are houses
of hypocrisy. But I had read about a little church here
built on a Goddess site, as they almost all are, and we
bumped into it walking along. And so it was that we
entered the tiny church at St. Maries de la Mer. The art
depicted women in a boat, the Maries, and the story I
had carried in my heart for so many years began to have
a location and historical validation.

Magdalen had been here.

Through the years, Mary Magdalen had rather become
my patron Saint of sorts. I saw her as the lost bride, the

feminine not only taken away from Christ by the Bible
editors, but the woman shamed and vilified, the woman
made into a whore, and hence, all women in her stead.

Whenever I asked the woman who raised me about
my birth mother, she always cringed and sloughed off
the question with a shudder and a less than deft air
of inference as to the questionable morals of my birth
mother. So perhaps I know personally the damage that
can be done when a human being is so easily dismissed
by even the hint of impropriety, never mind the outright
label thrust on Mary Magdalen.

Somehow, miraculously, we had found the place
where Magdalen landed when she entered France after
the crucifixion. She had come in a boat with several
historically significant people, according to the legend
held there.

Among the people in the boat was a young girl, who
they call Sarah. (Magdalen says her name cannot be
translated into English, that it is very guttural, and that
spelling it Sar'h would be more correct.) Legend depicts
her as a servant. I knew her to be the daughter of Yeshua
and Magdalen, called the Dark One and presumed to be
Egyptian because she had to be hidden in the shadows
to protect her life.

We visited the tiny crypt where Sar'h stands, all but
one day a year, and were more enchanted than I ever
remember feeling in such a surrounding. It is actually the
only time I have ever felt holiness in a Church.

Sar'h is the patron saint of the Gypsies and every
spring tens of thousands of Gypsies come from all over
Europe to pay homage by taking her effigy to the sea
and bathing her in an Isis Ritual. All year they visit her in
her crypt and bring her new robes and gently layer her
until she swells with taffeta and netting and sequins and
rick-rack. They run their babies' fingers across her lips
and kiss her wooden cheeks, smearing their tears into
her wooden flesh. And then, on that one day, she rises
high above them on a litter, led by silver-saddled white

horses, snorting and prancing; and she moves through the throngs to the place at the edge of the sea where she landed with her mother.

In my brief time standing before her in the crypt, she called to me, and I found I wanted to spend time with her, waiting patiently for my turn to step close to her and honor her, over and over. I finally worked up the courage to touch her wooden cheek with my finger, and it brought tears to my eyes.

The only way I could tear myself away was to promise Sar'h I would return someday with the Gypsies, to watch her ride the clouds to the sea.

Nothing could keep me from finding Rennes now, I told myself, not after this high. You can't imagine how we felt, three women driving across Europe, sleeping at campgrounds, in the car, occasionally taking a hotel room, searching for history, for bloodline, for that which runs through the veins, driven by something beyond understanding. We had no tour guide, no maps beyond Michelin.

But Rennes eluded us, and we wound up at Lourdes, amid litters of sickness and palsy and aging, sagging bodies huddled together, shepherded by dozens of women in black robes. Sad, forlorn people shepherded by sad, forlorn looking nuns were everywhere! Hundreds more desperately held plastic bottles in the shape of Mother Mary under faucets, filling them, capping them, and stuffing them into shopping bags to be taken home like any souvenir. Holy water in a plastic Mary.

I was disgusted. Adrianne, who has never said a bad word about anybody or anything said, "This is the darkest place I have ever seen. You can stay here if you want to, but can you take me to the edge of town and pick me up on your way out?"

We survived Lourdes, and after exhausting myself looking for the light I never found there, we left that afternoon, leaving behind us in the rear-view mirror black-robed nuns pushing black draped litters and ancient wheelchairs back to hotel rooms and buses. There were no miracle cures in the waters of Lourdes that day.

My heart told me that Rennes was back behind us, somewhere so close we had almost driven past it to get to Lourdes. Our time was running out. Soon we had to be back in Amsterdam. There were planes to be caught and school for Adrianne; the woman taking care of my mother needed to go home; and Jennifer was leaving to study in India in just a few days. In spite of that, I turned the car back east and we headed back for the Pyrenees. Darkness overtook us, but the full moon sang to me as she wove in and out of hilltops. And then the moon began to disappear, little pieces of her eaten away by some invading force. We pulled over and watched the full moon go into total eclipse, somewhere in the foothills of the Pyrenees.

We fell asleep that night in the car, off to the side of a back road somewhere on the way, we hoped, to Rennes. I remember waking and stretching, amazed that I'd learned to sleep curled under the steering wheel. We woke to a chill, with dew still present and cows and the sound of chickens and roosters calling dawn.

All day we drove into villages and down country roads, stopping here and there and asking for Rennes-le-Chateau. Someone gave us directions that left us in the driveway of a deserted house in the middle of nowhere. I have no idea how it is that we wound up in a little town south of Carcasonne, but here we stopped to ask directions to a hotel. I needed a bed that night.

"Well, the only place to stay anywhere around here is the old castle right back there on the river." I should have realized that after a full moon eclipse, we might be privy to some magic.

Gripped by some sense of promise, we wound the turrets, climbing stone stairs worn by the ages. Thousands of feet had trod them until one step dipped to meet the other, like ancient tango dancers. The castle dated back to the days of the Templars, when the breezes blew stories of

knights and crusades through the air and mysticism filled
the homes and hearths of the Cathars, one of the most
persecuted sects, who were ultimately massacred by the
Catholic Church.

I felt the mystery slip into my mind and wrap tendrils of
a haunting that I had become so familiar with around my
heart, capturing me and carrying me into dreamtime. In
the morning I slipped back down the turret early and sat
in the courtyard, encircled by those high walls and sipped
espresso and a croissant. Life is good in southern France.

We packed the car and watched the willows weep in
the rear-view mirror as we chose a direction out of town.
I turned right and then left. I don't know why. I can't tell
you that I "let go" and something came and took the
steering wheel. I just turned left and wound up a hill,
round and round and up and up and up. Prickles broke
out all over my face and arms and legs and a feeling of
elation took me.

At the top of the mountain we pulled into the tiniest
of villages and parked. We walked in the only direction
that kept us from falling off the mountain and found ourselves passing a bookstore with the obvious markings of
esoterica. I cannot tell you how out of place, in the tiniest
village I have probably ever been in, an occult bookstore
appeared to be.

Our pace quickened. Up a rise and then there it was,
the tiny Church at Rennes-le-Chateau. The door creaked
just enough for effect and we stepped inside, right past
the Devil himself, or so he is thought to be by the religious
ignorant, about three feet high, carved in wood with cloven
feet and horns and bared teeth, holding the holy water!

On a panel, the Magdalen sat with a skull at her feet.
In a painting of the Last Supper she sits under the table
and as the Disciples toast Yeshua, she brushes her cheek
against his ankle, her hair wrapped around his feet.
The ceiling is painted blue with stars, like an ancient
Egyptian tomb. I quickly sat on a pew before my legs
could betray my quivering heart.

Beyond the Church lay the home of the Priest, Sauniere, and La Tour Magdala, which he built and so named, overlooking the Pyrenees. The mystery of what Sauniere found in his famous discovery was what the documentary was about, but it was not of consequence to me. I didn't want to know what he found or where he hid it. I had no urge to dig in the graveyard. My digging urges were elsewhere. I wanted the truth behind the mystery. I wanted the alchemical truth, and I knew it had to do with the Magdalen and her tantric relationship with Yeshua.

What could possibly have been so important that the Catholic Church destroyed a whole people and wrecked havoc on this entire landscape to keep secret?

That Yeshua was not celibate. That Magdalen was no whore, but the bride of Yeshua, a high Initiate, one of the highest in the Temple of Isis, well prepared for her sexual relationship with Yeshua in the Temples. That they had a daughter, and that her lineage was literally the rightful inheritor of the Kingdom, to those who believed in, or feared Kingdoms, as the Church did.

Despite the heights I scaled in Europe, despite my visions and visitations there, home ultimately demanded our presence. Life refused to be avoided, and we returned, deeply touched, but only momentarily distracted from my losses.

I suppose relationship is really not my life's work, I told myself. Perhaps I should pass the torch I carry for this work to someone who can bring it home; obviously I can't do it. I made peace with all my childhood advisors, said goodbye to all my dreams, and one night when Tom and Pam and I were driving through Hopiland, I realized what I had to do.

The love between them was the deepest and purest love I had ever seen between two people. I was thrilled to be close to it; absolutely thrilled that the closer I got, the more obvious the love was. It was real. It wasn't "put on" for show. They had loved each other from first sight. The exquisite depth of it had not lessened through the years and the experience of each other's flaws. They still held each other in the highest esteem on all levels, spiritually and emotionally.

"Maybe I'm not the one who is supposed to do this work in relationship," I gushed out from the back seat, gesturing blindly in the dark, nothing, if not dramatic.

"I've never seen two people love each other the way you do. It would be my honor to pass the Relationship Torch to you. Now I can relax and stop searching. I will never have another relationship. I pass the torch to you."

I don't know if either of them understood the depth within me from which my words came, but I leaned forward from the back seat and announced just that. I told them that I had never seen any two people love each other as they loved each other. And I babbled on that I had always been told that I came to work on balancing the male/female energy on the plane through living with my mate and through the day-to-day living/loving of each other in full and total harmony, in evenness, in truth. And then I thrust my hand forward, as if passing a torch, and summarily announced that I was out of the relationship business and that the job was henceforth theirs. Then I sat back and was quiet, to emphasize my point.

By this time, however, I had spent two years desiring to die, and I usually get what I want, in the long run. I've just noticed that I usually get what I want after I don't want it anymore. And so it was inevitable, I suppose, that the discomfort from certain physical symptoms would overtake the attention I was paying to my depression. Walking had become painful. My joints ached. I felt terrible. My strength seemed to have run out, along with my will. I had no energy. I couldn't sleep at night, tossing and turning, haunted by all the ghosts of my past.

I contacted Metatron, the archangel, through a remarkable and most genuine woman in Utah, who was also a medical intuitive. I had several readings and they, along with the information I had gotten from the Hathors through Tom, had been my only source of comfort and healing through those years.

Metatron had sharp words for me on this occasion, though. He told me I was in the early stages of Lupus and that if I didn't work immediately to counteract it, I would get my death wish. He then gave me a formula of anti-oxidants to take. I immediately called Tom and asked to speak to the Hathors. I needed corroboration or a different opinion.

When they "came in" I announced my unfaithfulness and told them that I had been seeing someone else. They howled with laughter and then, without me telling them anything that I had already been told, they launched into what was wrong with me and what could be done to heal it—if I chose to live. Then they gave me the sounds that I needed to release and heal. It was recorded, and I took those sounds home and played them over and over and over.

I credit Tom's Hathor sounds, along with the regimen of anti-oxidants, with healing me.

Now, I must tell you that though I'd had my personal healing experience with sound, I had not experienced Tom Kenyon as the teacher. Needless to say, I had issues with "teachers" and I had observed his impeccability as a human for a long, long time before I decided I would take a chance and see what he taught. But by now, the impact of sound on my life was significant, and when there was a local workshop, it only made sense for me to step in and help with registration and other facilitation needs, as a feeble attempt at "thank-you."

By the end of the first day I had discovered that my friend, Tom, not only had one of the most remarkable voices in the world, but was also the most erudite single human being I had ever experienced on a vast purview of subjects.

He understood the nuances and the intention behind the major streams of internal alchemy, including Tibetan Buddhism, Taoism, Hindiusm, Egyptian High Alchemy

and esoteric Christianity; and whatever his subject,
he taught with humor and humility, making the material both comprehensible and consciousness altering,
simultaneously. He had distilled the essence of how each
stream raises consciousness.

He literally understood the intention behind what was
held as sacred within each pathway; he understood the
mystery, without having to wrap the tendrils of dogma
around it. He had gleaned the kernels of these streams
of internal alchemy and taught both the science and the
physics of consciousness, carefully and gently with no
dogma attached.

By the end of that first weekend, Tom Kenyon had
earned my respect in a category where I never thought
I'd respect another human being—as a teacher. I was
different—literally and profoundly altered from both the
information and the sound.

I knew how he lived his life. I had been around the
house enough to see the impeccability with which he
attended his daily functions. I knew his honor. I saw how
much he loved his wife, how he served the feminine,
how the Mother was honored in his walk. Now I had
experienced the Master Teacher, and I wanted to help
him present his work to the world in the way it deserved
to be presented.

As I researched his life, I discovered he was one of the
pioneers in helping science accept the reality that sound
and frequency can and do shift brain states, having
formed Acoustic Brain Research to research the effect
of sound on consciousness in 1983. He spent a decade
doing the research that ultimately proved just how successfully sound could alter and affect brain states.

He had coined the word *psychoacoustic* to explain the
marriage of psychotherapy and sound.

How this translated to a workshop was actually quite
obvious and utterly brilliant. The left brain got the hard
information it needed from the psychotherapist/scientist
Tom, and the right brain got what it needed during the

"sound meditations" from the mystical Tom. Unspoken material was transmitted though sound codes that came through his voice during these frequent sound meditations. The combination of both "teaching in words" and "toning in sounds" was remarkable to experience.

My intuition told me this work was going to be critical in the next decades on planet Earth. We began to dialogue about how I could help Tom put his work into the world. My years in communication and writing could be used on something that made a difference again!

But then their beautiful waterfront rental house went on the market for sale, and since they had to move, they decided to move to the Southwest. I couldn't face any more losses in my life. We were all so close, I reasoned it was perhaps time for a change in my life as well, and I made plans to join them. The Three Musketeers couldn't be separated by anything so mundane as losing a rental house, and friends like we had become don't come along often in a lifetime. I held a garage sale, and sold my favorite things, and went east to handle some old business there. My mother's care had gotten beyond my capability, and I had finally placed her in a home. My daughters were both in college. I could move anywhere.

Pam had fought breast cancer a few years before, but she had successfully beaten it. She had chosen to live. I had work to do now that felt important and no longer spent all day wanting to die. I, too, had chosen to live. And so life began to feel like springtime. There were many places within Tom's work where my business background was sorely needed. I was going to help facilitate for him. And I was heavily involved in raising the funds to build a sound healing temple the Hathors had requested in New Mexico. There was much work to do, and I genuinely felt that getting Tom's work into the world was the most important thing I could do with my talent. His work is sound, and sound and music cut across all boundaries. Sound transcends language. And he was *real*. He was no hypocrite, and he loved and honored the feminine, the

Mother. And he loved and adored his wife. And that was what really mattered to me after a lifetime of men who either abused or ignored the feminine.

And besides, we were all best friends. We all had great times together. We moved through the kitchen with ease. We traveled together well. We laughed and watched bad television together.

Pam and I had cried over the mistakes we'd made with our children. We'd looked at our childhood photo albums and sobbed that we hadn't known how beautiful we were. We cried together that we had spent a lifetime thinking we were fat and ugly. I looked at her childhood photos and saw one of the truly most beautiful women I had ever seen. She swore the same was true of me. We held each other and told each other our most intimate secrets. She had given a girl up for adoption at birth. I had given a girl up for adoption at birth.

But Pam's shoulder had begun to hurt her. And when she went to the doctor on the island before they left, they told her it was a torn rotator cuff, probably from her previous surgery. They said it would take a long time to heal and there was nothing she could do. So she did nothing. But it was getting worse. And then, just before Christmas, Tom called me on the East Coast, where I was cleaning up old business. Pam's pain had gotten so bad that he'd taken her to the emergency room.

The Emergency Room had done bone scans, which hadn't been done on the island, and they showed that the cancer had gone to the bones. Tom was told that Pam was in Stage Four cancer. Allopathic medicine offered her nothing, only a death certificate. It was jarring news, but Pam swore she could beat it. Before I could join them, they began the process of moving back. Pam wanted to come closer home.

Then they called and asked me if I would accompany Pam to Mexico to a special clinic where there was hope through a new treatment. Tom had taken care of her alone for the last several years, since the initial diagnosis and expenses were mounting, and he needed to stay behind and work to pay the bills. It would mean being gone a month, and Adrianne had just gotten home for the summer and wanted me with her. But I had made a promise a few years before, on a beach in Greece in the middle of the night, and I knew I had to go. And so it was that Pam and I spent a month in Tijuana in a clinic that used insulin comas to suspend the body in a state close to death, allowing for maximum penetration of oxygen, which ostensibly could kill cancer cells. This process was highly experimental and was not possible in North America, not with the monopoly on death that the American Medical Association has.

In that month I watched the most remarkable, desperate and genuine people come and go. I watched miracles occur, and I watched people die. When Pam initially began the coma process, after weeks of preparation, the induction process caused a terrible struggle as she moved between the dimensions. This shifting of dimensions was as exhausting emotionally as it was physically; and after her first coma Pam swore she would never do another one.

The process of both induction and the return to consciousness were extremely altering. The sense of departure was so severe on induction that panic could easily occur. And when they injected the vitamin formula that brought her back, the body was subject to horrible sweats and spasms.

The morning she was due to appear for her second coma, she refused to go. The comas were, everyone felt, her only hope. There was nothing left to try. She had been doing all the other possible protocols for weeks, to build her system, but she was in Stage Four cancer. North America offered her no hope; this, at least, offered her *hope,* and as long as she had *thought* she could handle the process, she had *believed* she could heal.

I didn't know what to do. I was alone in Tijuana, Mexico with my best friend, and the responsibility felt huge. And so that morning I seized on the only thing I could think of. I offered to try to guide her through the dimensions during the induction process, to try to guide her into the coma and back out with my voice, to lay a trail she could follow when her consciousness left her body, and I promised her I would be there for her when she returned, singing her back. She liked the idea.

I spoke with the clinic director, as he had become a friend, and he approved. I had begun the process of rewriting their medical protocols and, for all practical purposes, I had essentially started working there. He supported whatever appeared to help a patient and offered the potential of making the process easier. I reasoned that whatever belief system the patient held should be honored, as the patient was, essentially, going through the death process with each coma, over and over. So if I could sing comfort to her, honoring the Deities she held sacred, that might create a safe platform for her.

So the next morning I took along the shamanic tools I had brought with me. I had Eagle and Hawk feathers and a Tibetan rattle and other simple Tibetan instruments. I had stones that had spoken to me and asked to come. When I wheeled her in that morning, the doctors who had become my friends moved aside and let me join them. They used one side of the hospital bed, and I used the other. We laid out our tools across the sheet from each other, syringe, tubes, stethoscope on one side, Eagle, Hawk, bells on the other. I was deeply touched by their respect.

They took out syringes and the bottles of medicine that would induce the coma and the vials that would bring her back. I took out the tingshas and rattle that would lay the trail of sound I hoped she would follow, just as I had seen Tom do many times.

They injected the insulin, and I kissed her goodbye and held her hand while the insulin sunk into her veins. As it traveled through her, her journey began. The process had caused her deep panic the first time, for as she slipped through the dimensions she encountered her own underworld and the monsters of her childhood.

I called the archangels and sang her chants that represented the Deities that she revered. She loved Tara, and so I sang her the Tara chant, over and over until she slipped deeply into coma with a blissful smile on her face, unlike the first time when she had jerked and moaned so radically.

I sat by her for the time she was gone, holding her hand, as I had the first time. Then the doctors motioned to me and began the process of injecting the vial that would bring her back, having held her in the near-death state as long as the monitored vital signs showed she could handle. I picked up my feathers and instruments and called her back. I sang her the Tara chant again and other chants I knew. Her return was peaceful, and she came back smiling, without the jerking and panic.

I was ecstatic. She came back with remembrances that would eventually help her heal many unresolved issues that had haunted her. These were early childhood abuses she had hidden from her worldly view, covered over with layers of acceptability. After all, there were people to please! These were the issues that were killing her, issues that could easily cause cancer, in my humble non-AMA approved opinion. This process continued every day then, until we left. When we left the CAT scans showed a remarkable reduction of about 60% in the bone cancer.

But a 60% reduction meant 40% was left, and the clinic didn't want her to go. But Pam needed a rest; and so we went back home, which Tom had moved back to the Northwest, at her request, while we had been gone.

Once back, though, it became very apparent that she needed to take the process further, and I couldn't go to Mexico with her this time. The summer was almost gone, and Adrianne was about to return to college, and so plans were made for Pam's son to go with her instead. Expenses were mounting, and Tom had to work. She was unhappy in the Seattle area, where Tom had initially moved them, and so while she was gone the second time, Tom moved all their belongings back where Pam wanted to be, back to the beautiful waterfront house they had left behind one year before, right back almost next door to me.

I was rethinking my life. Adrianne was about to go back to college. I loved working at the clinic in Tijuana, and they really needed me there. Through my time there I had discovered a strange gift. I am good with people in crisis. I loved the edge of life and death. No wonder I had been drawn to shamanism. I was really good at ushering people between the dimensions.

I began a dialogue with the clinic about working in Tijuana full time. I would be a North American shaman at a cancer clinic in Mexico! And as it is with small towns, so it is with small islands. Word went around the island that I might go to work in Mexico. And one morning as I dreamed about how it might be to live in Mexico, Tom called.

"So, I hear you might be going to Mexico."

"Well, I'm thinking about it," I said.

"So, I guess that would mean you couldn't help me get my work into the world then."

We had all been so busy taking care of Pam, I hadn't thought about what we set out to do a few years ago. I realized that with everything going on, Tom and I hadn't had any time for a business conversation in almost a year. His work had been put on hold, and the work I was going to do for him certainly hadn't materialized.

I sat at my dining room table, staring out to sea, and I realized what this phone call really meant. He was really asking if I was going to leave them. He was asking how much I believed in his work. And he was asking how much I really wanted to be with them. And I remembered the promise I'd made to Pam on the beach in Greece, and I heard my mouth tell Tom I wasn't really serious about going to Mexico. That was all that was said. We made no more of it.

I have never regretted that decision for one minute.

Then we got a phone call from the clinic that Pam's hip
had developed a hairline crack, leaving her unable to put
any weight on it at all. She wanted to come home, though
they pressed her to stay at the clinic where she could continue therapy. But Pam wanted to come back to the island,
where she could look at the water and the Eagles and
where ferryboats ply the great deep waters of Puget Sound.

Tom and I went to Seattle to pick her up. We hadn't
seen her in a month, and I remember how shocked we
all were when she got off the plane. She couldn't walk,
and she'd lost a lot of weight.

An incoming ferry had hit the ferry dock at Orcas,
and it was closed. There was no way on or off the
island with a car. I located a private barge that could
land without a ramp, and so we brought Pam home,
like Macarthur returning to the Philippines. The boat
pulled in and lowered its head gently onto the shore,
and we drove off.

I could write a thousand pages about the next few
months, and I could never fully or adequately tell the
story. You know, you go through life, and you think you
know someone from little experiences, little intimacies
here and there. A cup of coffee, a tear. And eventually,
you do know them, but not like we came to know each
other in the next few months.

I had known Pam Kenyon about five years then,
and I thought I knew her. And I thought I knew the stuff
of which Tom Kenyon was made. But the two people
I thought I knew became my blood in the next few
months. They both ran in my veins. I watched Tom give
everything he had to help Pam stay alive. He served her
day and night. He made her juices and when juice made
her sick, he made her grains and when grains didn't
taste good, he made her curried vegetables and when
they didn't taste right, he made her soup. He searched
through magazines and medical books and bought anything he thought would help. The living room swelled
with boxes of therapies and supplements.

In the next few months, we exchanged intimacies few people ever get the privilege to experience. I learned how to bath someone in a wheelchair. It took all of us to figure out how to dress her without putting any weight on her at all. We fell over each other learning to roll and turn the sheet as Tom and I figured out ways to move her around in bed. We propped pillows for comfort and told jokes and laughed and cried and shared deep secrets. And she had breakthroughs I will not share here. She remembered her deepest and darkest demons, the ones she had driven so far into her bones.

I arrived at their house around 7 am and I left around midnight those months. Tom handled the night shift alone, getting almost no sleep at all, for the nights were when she thrashed and relived her deeply painful child-hood. He simply never slept, and I watched his color turn beige and then gray. We were convinced Pam would live, but I wasn't sure about him anymore.

We hired several caregivers to give each of us a few breaks and Pam's other closest friends came in when he had workshops to teach. One by one, everyone she loved got to have cherished time with her. Remarkable people on the island came and sang to her and gave her massages and checked her vitals and did her hair. A doctor friend made house calls.

In retrospect, she lived with bone cancer for two years with no pain medication. Until the last weeks of her life, she took nothing. Tom held the pain off with sound and energy work, which he diligently delivered with love and humor.

One morning I went over early to find her sitting with the biggest smile I'd ever seen. Pam was bright and cheery and hungry, something I hadn't seen in quite a while. She drank a whole can of liquid food and asked for more.

Many friends stopped by that morning, and she greeted each of them with that smile that lit up their dark corners. But there was something different this morning. There was a power about her, a self-affirmed, self-assured presence I hadn't seen in her before. She told us what she wanted and how she wanted it. She didn't care what the people around her wanted this morning. She knew what *she* wanted.

Tom was in California teaching and was due to return later that day, and I couldn't wait until he saw this new, powerful Pam.

I bathed her and washed her hair, and we howled at the abject ridiculousness of it all, her sitting in a wheel-chair with me pouring water over her head and me sitting on the edge of the bathtub, wetter than she was.

Jennifer, my daughter, stopped by to visit. I don't remember now what Jennifer wanted to do, but I dis-approved and gave her my usual parent talk, recom-mending my vision for her future, which, of course, differed from hers.

When Jennifer left, everyone seemed to disappear simultaneously. Pam's grown kids all went into town, and Pam and I were alone in the house.

"You have to let go of your girls, Judi. You have to let them make their own decisions," Pam said to me, cocking her head to one side and narrowing her eyes at me.

"Oh, I know," I said, "but she depends on me being the mother. I'm *supposed* to disagree with her." I tried to laugh it off, but I noticed the air was different in the room. It had that wet appearance that I had seen in a room once before. The light transfigured differently; it was moist and pregnant looking.

Pam wasn't letting this go. "Look, I'm serious. You have to let go. They have their own lives to lead. Let Jennifer go. Let Adrianne go. *Let them go.*"

I thought I'd just cajole us through this. "Well, look who's talking," I giggled at her. "Aren't you the one who hasn't let your seventeen-year-old son out of your sight for the last two weeks?"

Her eyes lay on me like clouds, lifting and floating me.

"That was yesterday. Today I see things differently."

The very air changed density. The "light" in the air was visible.

"You have to drop your agendas for your daughters. They have their own agendas. You have to allow them *their* agendas."

She wasn't going to let this go.

"Everyone has an agenda," she looked out the window toward the sparkling water. "Even my caregivers have agendas. They all want to be the 'one' who helps me feel better, or the one who takes away the pain. All the healers want to be the one who *heals* me. There's nothing wrong with that agenda, but it's *their* agenda. Not mine."

We were at one of the major issues in Pam's life. She had lived her life fulfilling someone else's agenda most of the time.

"My caregivers even have agendas for what I see when I look outside the window! she laughed. "Yesterday," she said, "I was looking out the window, staring at the water."

"And my caregiver said, 'Pam, what are you looking at?'"

"And I said, 'I'm looking at the sparkles on the water.'"

"And the caregiver said, 'Pam, what do you see when you look at the sparkles on the water? Do you see God?'"

Pam shot me a cheesy grin and curled her lip.

And Pam had said, "No, I don't see God. I see freedom."

The silence cut the air like a knife. We were at some nexus point, somewhere to the left of the last star and closing in on forever. I knew what the next question had to be, but I didn't know if I had the courage to ask it. I don't think it had ever seriously occurred to any of us that Pam might die. She was *healing*. This was just a healing crisis. She only came home for her hip to mend enough to go back to the clinic and finish the treatments, and everything would be fine after that.

But this conversation had taken on mystical proportions sounding like last words, and I didn't want to think that.

But if this was her last conversation, and I didn't ask this question, how would I live with myself?

"Do I have an agenda for you?" I bit my lip.

"You used to, before you went to Albuquerque."

"What was my agenda for you?"

"You wanted me to live." She smiled a crescent that lit the whole room. Pam is the only person I have ever met who could light up a room like that.

My hand trembled as I brushed a strand of hair from her forehead and tears popped out of my eyes, like corks bobbing to the surface.

"I want to dance with you on all the great beaches of the world."

"We will," she said.

"What? In my mind and in my heart?"

"Yes, in your mind and in your heart."

"And what about after Albuquerque?"

I had just recently slipped down to Albuquerque, under directions from the Hathors, to sink the shaft for the tone-healing temple we were building there, and it had been a deeply mystical experience in which I'd had to own my power to make it happen.

"Now you're willing to allow me my own agenda," she said with a broad smile.

"Look," she continued, "it doesn't matter if I live twenty minutes or twenty years. It's the *process* that matters."

I felt transported to some realm I had never known before. There was a palpable luminous quality between the molecules around us. The air held moisture and refracted light differently than I'd ever seen before. It looked 'wet' and Pam was literally glowing.

"Give away your animals, Judi. Find a good home for Kola Bear. You have to be free to go."

She closed her eyes. I asked her if she wanted to take a nap, and she said she did, but she was afraid she'd wake up choking on childhood memories. I promised I'd stay in the room with her, and she drifted to sleep. I sat down and began to write down the conversation. I made notes to remind the caregivers not to press their agendas on Pam in the future.

Pam began to breath strangely. I dropped the note-book and stood up by her. I put my hand on her arm. She seemed to inhale, but she wouldn't exhale. She just held her breath.

"Breathe, Pam," I said, and she exhaled.

Watching her and coaching her breathing, I remem-bered a teaching Tom had done on the three gunas. He had used the breath as an example so we'd understand the role of each guna.

Raja, I remember him saying, begins an action. Sattva is the sustainer, that point of continuing inhale, almost in-between breaths, the place most of us live, where we get too comfortable, where we want to stay, where we hold our breath. And then there's Tamas, who ends an action. Like breathing out and breathing in. No one wants to think about destruction—but without destruction, with-out letting the breath out, Tom had said, there is no room for creation.

I was thinking about the three gunas, listening to Pam breathing. She looked absolutely radiant. Her skin was ablaze with an incandescent beauty, and I had never seen her look so powerful, even in her sleep. Her breathing evened out. But then it began to slow and became shallow.

I don't really know why I began to sing, but I sang the Tara chant, standing beside her, holding her arm. If this was what death looked like, it was powerful and mystical and deeply peaceful, and all I knew to do was to sing to her. And so I sang her song, Tara's chant, for what seemed like a long time, but was only a few min-utes. And then I thought about Tom, and I wondered how to let him know wherever he was, somewhere in the air nearing Seattle, that this might be the end. And so I shifted to a chant that I hoped would call his consciousness. But once that was done, I shifted back to the Tara chant. This was Pam's time, whatever was happening.

I was singing her chant when she stopped breathing, exactly twenty minutes after she said it didn't matter if she lived twenty minutes or twenty years—her process was complete. She was as free as the sparkles on the water.

The rest of the day and night are a blur of the intruding assaults that land when death visits, funeral directors, police. I wanted to scream about this mystical place I'd just been with Pam. I wanted them to know how serene and peaceful and exquisite her death had been, about how powerful she was at the end. But everyone had something to do. Late that night, exhausted and hysterical, I finally went home to an empty house. I sat by the window and sobbed. That's about all I remember of the next few days—sitting by the window in an empty house, sobbing.

We had walked the long, exhausting road to the end of her life together, laughing and crying at the mysticism of death and the insulting unexpectedness of it all. Life, the process—so unvalued one day, had become so precious in the end. Power, there for the taking, had been taken, finally, but not soon enough to save her life.

I felt Pam all around me. I felt her *in* me. I felt like I *was* Pam for days.

People came from every direction. I didn't know what to do with myself. I had known what to do every other day for months. I got up early and went over to Tom and Pam's house and helped take care of Pam. I was lost and purposeless without her, and there seemed to be no place for me in this new life Tom was pulled into. No one needed me.

One morning as I sat looking out the window crying, Tom called.

Hearing the tears, he asked me what was wrong, and I remember telling him, "I don't know who I am any more. I don't know what to do. I used to know what to do. I used to get up every morning and come over to your house, but I don't know what to do now." It blurted out without a breath, a continuous wail of exhaustion and abject frustration at the seeming hope-lessness of it all.

"Yes, you do," he said, matter-of-factly, "You go back to doing what we were going to do before Pam died. You help me get the work out into the world."

And I remembered what I was doing before Pam got sick. There was something to live for, something that mattered!

I could write whole books about the next few months; they were a textbook lesson in agendas. You'd be amazed at what descends on a man whose wife has just died. They came from everywhere to help him. I wondered where they had all been when we needed them; but my voice felt rather small in those first few months, especially up against all the raucous voices that all knew exactly what Tom Kenyon ought to do with the rest of his life. Everyone had an agenda for Tom. Everyone knew where he ought to move, where he ought to spend his time, what would heal him, what his grief should look like, what supplements he needed, who he should be with, and who he shouldn't be with—specifically me. I watched people circle and surround him with agendas. He was so torn in his grief; he couldn't see anything beyond the paralyzing pain of losing the love of his life.

As the parade came and went, I began to plan to move back east. I had just lost one best friend, and the way it looked, I was going to lose another, and I just couldn't watch that happen. Tom was completely unaware of what was happening around him, pulled this way and that, assaulted by so much grief, he just couldn't see beyond it. It was quicksand, and he wasn't even able to muster the strength to try to pull himself out, instead latching onto whichever branch was dangled nearby.

The more I began to plan my move, the sadder I got. I had my own grief from the loss of Pam, and the loss of "Pam and Tom." The hopelessness engulfed and overwhelmed me. And I felt rather lost in all the pro-cesses happening around Tom. He had just lost his wife.

I wasn't family. I had no idea where my place was in all this twisting.

So there I was, at the bottom once more, unsure where my next breath of air would come from. Some things just bring you to your knees, and if you don't believe in a bearded old God, to whom do you pray?

I can't tell you that I got a message or that a "light" appeared and told me what to do. I just gave up. I surrendered, and I went to Mother. Metatron has always told me that I possess certain powers, which I have done my best to completely ignore, one of which is the power to *call forth,* according to him. And though I have thought this not possible, I sank to my proverbial knees and asked for help. That's all I asked for; I asked for help. Almost immediately mystical events began to unfold around me. As I slid toward sleep each night, Isis appeared. She stepped forward from a circle of ancient women, all cloaked in robes with hoods, so I never saw their faces.

She took my hand and waved us through swirling mists and what were, I can only presume, dimensions. We appeared, from this "flight" in a variety of temples. In each temple we visited, a group of Priestesses stepped forward and took me by my hand. While Isis waited, they dipped me, first in one pool of oil and then in another. Night after night this bathing ritual continued, from temple to temple and pool to pool. I was always returned about dawn. Slowly my skin began to feel softer, and I think my heart rate quickened. I began to be conscious of my breathing. It seemed deeper and more audible, and I swear I could *hear* my heart beat.

One night they bathed me as usual and wrapped me, mummy-like, in long strips of fabric. Then they lay me down on a huge bed of giant crystal points, with dozens of different stones underneath my chakra points. I remember my "mind" thought it ought to hurt, to lie there on these crystal points. Perhaps it was the fabric wrapping that so protected me, or the careful way I was positioned, but I don't remember any pain. This specific

process occurred several nights. They changed the locations of the crystal points against my body and the stones
from night to night. Some nights the rose quartz was
against my back at my heart. Some nights a ruby pointed
directly at my throat chakra from beneath. Some nights a
great blue sapphire pierced my heart from the back.

And then one night as I lay in bed a thick fog licked
its way across the floor, and a giant cobra seemed
to ride in on the fog. Somehow it didn't frighten me;
though I remember thinking I ought to be afraid. It
slithered under the sheets and across one leg and down
under the other, then looping back over and under
again, holding me in a human Mobius strip. Then it
rose high above me and spread its hood, still firmly in
control of my body.

I told no one about these new nightly visitations of Isis
and friends.

I observed that I acted differently when Tom called.
I caught myself twisting the phone cord, staring off into
space when I talked to him. Once I blushed and giggled
for no good reason.

The people telling Tom what he ought to do with his
life began to bother me. I got edgy around them. I didn't
trust them. I saw their agendas and began to worry
that I might have one as well. I struggled to remain
his friend, no matter what the price, without prejudice,
without personal agenda. Leaving the island and returning East was the only solution I could imagine for the
swirling emotions washing over me. I had learned to run
away before the hurt, if at all possible.

I made lots of phone calls east; preparing what friends
I had left there for my imminent return.

One day I drove Tom to the ferry landing, so he
could take the boat to a nearby island to visit a healer.
We sat in my car, waiting for the ferry to dock. It was
pouring rain, not the usual spotting we get out here, but
a real east coast downpour. It added to the solemnity
in the air. We sat staring at the ghost ferry slipping into

dock, shadowed by the rain and gray so thick it licked the land like dragon's breath.

We sat in silence. Then Tom reached over and placed his hand on my heart, and he said, "I pledge you my truth."

I felt my heart tremble in response, and I placed my hand on his heart and said, "I pledge you my truth."

It is the greatest commitment ever made. It has sustained us through everything. It has held us, like a great cord. When I think I can't possibly talk to him about something, I realize I won't be in *truth* if I don't. When I want to let something slip by and not address it, I realize I can't just let it go, or I won't be in total truth with him.

Months later two old friends went to the southwest, to see if we could assuage the pain with a dose of sun. When we returned, Tom suggested I not go back to my house. And so I moved my chair closer to his piano at his house, and he wrote a song.

"Sometimes when I am near you, I feel like I am floating on air.

And it still amazes me that I do not even seem to care.

Sometimes when I am beside you, I feel like I am falling, tumbling into space.

And it seems to happen most often, whenever I see your face.

What is this feeling I'm feeling inside of me?

What is this grace coming down from above?

I don't know, but I feel like singing with the turtledoves.

Could it be that I'm just falling in love?"

And I wrote a poem, "I long to know your taste as well as I know your song."

And I can't, and I won't, write any more of our story. It is too precious, too magical, and too potent to put in words.

Now we are living my childhood dreams, living the prophecies I have shared with no one all these years, until now. Once a psychic dodged traffic rushing across a

busy street to "give me a message about my life's work."
It had to do with Sacred Relationship.

One night in a restaurant in Washington, D.C. I felt
someone staring at me across the room. I saw him write
a note on a napkin out of the corner of my eye, and I
watched it get passed from table to table. I knew it was
headed for me, and I knew what it was going to say—the
same thing the "words without a voice" had said in the fork
of the pear tree when I was five. And I had given up hope.

Some days I feel like an old, old crone now, an ancient
woman who has seen it all, and all these memories are
like the pages in a detached book of life. I can view them
from a distance, but they seem to belong to someone
else. I feel immune from my own life story. After all, it's
just another story. And I've heard them all by now. And
they're all the same. And they're all different.

I know what it feels like to think you are finally safe
and to step inside a car for a ride home from a long
night of running from danger only to find yourself looking once again into the eyes of torment, to have the edge
of cold steel pressed against your neck. I have listened
to screaming and realized it was my own. And I have
gasped for breath in the terror of childbirth and not slept
for days on end when a precious little girl needed me
much more than I needed sleep.

And I have chosen love over and over and over again.

I have fought a long, hard battle with the dark side
over the soul of a man and lost.

I have laughed over dinner and shared my soul and
my best red wine with a good friend, only to be fed back
betrayal in his climb for what he wanted. I have been cut
with knives and words. Sometimes betrayal looks like
your best friend. Sometimes it looks like your lover. It
wouldn't be called betrayal if you had seen it coming.

I have screamed in pleasure in a long night of ecstasy
and climbed the greatest peaks of the world in another's
arms, and those are the nights I will never regret. That is
the closest to God, to the Goddess, I have ever been.

I had dreams for my children and forgot they might have dreams of their own. My respect and the love I hold for Jennifer and Adrianne grows by the day as they teach me about strength and integrity. And the child I gave away has found me and that sweet piece has found that vacancy in my heart and filled it. I am truly sorry I didn't have the courage to raise her, for it was only my own cowardice that made me give her up. She is exquisitely beautiful, physically and spiritually. She is Laura and I love her.

And I have held the arm of a good friend when she died and had her tell me what freedom looks like. It looks like sparkles on the water on a sunny day, like diving into shards of diamonds and becoming one of them.

I have loved and desired from such a place of desperation that I have allowed someone to hurt me, my back shoved against a door, unable to breathe or twist or contort into a direction where there wasn't a blow, fists and blood tangled in a web of horror. I have prayed and sweated and begged and intended and hoped and owned and hungered and believed and *known*. And I have wanted to die, to find freedom in the sparkles on the water on a sunny day—more than anything.

And just when there was no more breath, no more hope in me, an angel said to me, "Just imagine what the next one will be like. If you're still alive, there's hope. Remember where you come from."

I remember a place where Beings swim in blue-tinged liquid love. Where the most beautiful Fairy Princess in the whole world wears Pink Lady Slippers, and she and Jack live in the Pulpit, happily ever after. And horses can fly and so can I.

I stopped believing. But I never stopped *knowing*.

And just when everyone around me had died... and there are many ways to die...when death of another hue hungered in the far corner, salivating for more, my best friend put his hand on my heart and said, "I pledge you my truth." And I pledged mine to him.

And truth is beauty, as all great poets know.

There is no "happily ever after" in a world where beings don't yet swim in liquid love. But there is work to be done, and I have found the most dynamic and quickest way to God Realization, just where I thought it was. And I have found my Goddess, the mother of all time and space. She is returning in this, the beginning of the ending of time. And if *you* really *hear* these words, well, that is enough.

A few years ago I was sitting in the back of a workshop, running the video camera. Tom asked everyone to find a partner and tell the partner his/her life story in five minutes. No cross talk. Whatever comes out in five minutes is your life story.

I didn't have a partner so I shut the camera off and sat down, as far away from everyone as I could get. I didn't want anyone to think I was listening to their private story. I tried to hide in the wall actually; I felt so obvious and so alone back there. But no matter how far I backed away, I could still hear the stories being told around me. So I turned and buried my head in my hands so I couldn't possibly hear, but the stories around me got even louder. I looked up to see how this was possible. There was no logical way this could be happening. Then I began to hear the stories at the far end of the room just as clearly as those near me and again I tried to bury my head deeper into my lap.

I heard every story in that room.

My father wouldn't let anyone pick me up so I lay there for months and months. They fed me and changed me and put me back, but no one was allowed to hold me...when I was three I got so sick, the doctor came and ordered them to take me to the hospital...I almost died...then she hit me and kept hitting me...and he held me down and I could feel him over me and he smelled bad, God, he was my father...and she died when I was six and no one has really loved me since...I lost my father and he was the only one who ever really loved me and I've felt so alone since...my family lost everything

*in the fire and we just had the awful cans of food they
give you from the food banks...when my dog died, my
life ended...I still miss my mother...I made millions but
I wasn't happy...I was so hungry and cold...I always
thought I came to do something but I don't know what it
is...and he left me for her...and she left me for him..."*

I pressed my middle finger deeply into my ears. I
was afraid everyone knew I could hear their stories, and
then the sound waves of the Cosmos parted. There was
a swoosh, like air moving through a huge seashell, like
waves pounding the shore, and it seemed to open a portal of sound, and I heard it *all.* I mean, I heard everyone
in the room, *and* I heard the litany of every story from
the beginning of time. They spiraled out of an invisible
tunnel around me. Birth, love, hope, betrayal, mistrust,
anger, pity, judgment, loss, joy, laughter, tears, sweat,
hard work, millions of story bubbles burst inside me. I
heard it all. And it's all the same. We all have the same
story. The details are different, but it's all the same
story, in a strange way. We're not just one Great Being,
connected divinely at a Universal level. We all have a
chapter in the same story. My heart burst and engulfed
everyone in that room, everyone from the beginning of
time, as we know it.

Underneath it all, I'm still the little girl who believed in
love. The one who knew that the secrets of the universe
lay in the love that can unfold between two people. And
I'm the same little girl who knew that you can get further
along in the search-for-God-business if you draw to you
a partner, a mate, and if you *evenly* stay in complete
truth, day-in-and-day-out, in the bedroom, in the bathroom and in the kitchen. And I'm the same little girl who
always believed that if you don't have a partner, you just
need to stay in complete and even truth with yourself.

It doesn't matter if I live twenty years or twenty minutes.
It's the day-to-day process that matters. What are you
doing with your time? It may be all you have...this minute...this day. Would you rather lie in bed with someone

you love for ten more minutes or get up early and jog?
Do you smile on the way out the door or just turn your
back and walk away? Who is your God? Is it a fearsome,
jealous thing that calls you a sinner? Darling, that's not
God. That's the patriarchy talking; it's either a religion
or a government or an unevolved alien! It's the voice
of enslavement. We have been held by such insidious
entrapment for eons, through the threat of ostracism and
derision, through the conjoined efforts of the ignorance
around us—through lies!

My story doesn't contain any hard truths. It doesn't
contain alchemical processes that if stirred and carefully
followed will produce the love of your life or enlightenment. And I don't care how sophisticated we all appear
to be—I know what we all really want in our heart of
hearts—someone to love us and someone who will let us
love them.

It is our potential.

"Time—as you know it—is running out, and I have
received permission from the Goddess herself, indeed,
I have been asked by the Goddess herself, to reveal to
you some of the most closely guarded secrets of all times.
These are revealed to you in hopes that you will elevate
yourselves in time...

And so it is that I reveal one of the lost secrets of the
ages—that Spirit, the male principle, in order to return to
itself through its journey into Matter, requires the assistance
of the feminine principle, the Intelligence of Matter itself.

But from the solar, light-filled perspective of the masculine principle, the feminine principle carries within her
a dark, moist and dangerous abyss. The solar principle
feels threatened by the darkness of the lunar aspect. But
it is in the joining of the Sun and the Moon, the joining of
the masculine and feminine principles, in equilibrium, in
energetic balance, that true illumination is attained."

—Mary Magdalen

One night, very early on, as we had just begun to ever so gently unfold our new love, right in the midst of other people's agendas, Tom and I stood at a precipice. We stood alongside a seawall on another island. It had been a rough day, and the sea monsters were after Tom. All the sirens had turned up their volume, and I couldn't hear the pounding waves for their cacophony. They pulled at him, luring him into the sea, out, way over his head, and he was blinded by the light. Just because something appears to look like light, doesn't mean it is light. I have learned that lesson the hard way.

And he walked away from me. He just walked away with palm trees swaying gently in the night air; he left me there. Standing alone in the middle of the dark night. And I looked around and there were campfires burning all around with men huddled, drinking, and partying. I didn't want to admit I was afraid to walk home across that darkness alone. And my pride stung fiercely. I had been left along a seawall on a strange island by someone who was numbed by a spider's bite and couldn't tell the light from the dark in the moment.

I'm fine. I will not ask for help! I don't need anyone! I know how to be alone. I have rather perfected that. I love being alone. I do it well. I don't know how to do relationship perfectly. That's the one I have to learn. And so I swallowed hard, and I called him back. And he hadn't walked so far that he couldn't hear me. And he *chose* to come back. It took both those steps. I *chose* to call him back. And he *chose* to come. In every moment, in every circumstance, from the simplest to the most sublime— it's all just choice.

In the coming years I suspect we will face choices the likes of which have never been posed to humanity. Choose freedom. Choose love. And if there is any way you can bring total, complete, *even* truth into your life— at all levels, please do it. The truth really will set you free, and there is nothing without freedom.

And to my Beloved, I adore you. May it bring tears to anyone's eyes, as Magdalen's love for Yeshua did to me, to read how it is that I love you for your willingness to cross the moist, dark and dangerous abyss to live in the portal of the feminine, in the Holy Grail, with me. Your integrity and your honor shine above all and your song will echo in the halls of forever. Thank you for allowing me to be both the Initiate and the woman in love. To me, you will always be the little boy in the back of the bus whose face I never forgot, the one I knew would grow up to play guitar and sing songs. The one I knew was my soulmate. You sing my heart. Yours *is* the voice of God.

AfterThoughts
A Diary After Mary Magdalen

The following entries were all written the year after we received the *Manuscript* and all the way up until publication. We felt they were pertinent, as they show a process of what this material and our commitment to truth brought forward in our lives. Be warned! It isn't always pretty. But it's the truth. It is a diary of what happened for me in living this material the best I could.

Back on beautiful little Oudish, just as Magdalen was nearing the end of delivering the *Manuscript,* I went through a torturous process, and we felt it important enough to share, to show that it isn't always the bliss that comes first.

First the man and woman come together and out of their love a child is born. In Sacred Relationship, there is always creation, a third energy is always birthed—and birth is painful. But there is a reward; a new life is created, whether it is a child, or an energy. In our case, our *work* gets birthed into the world. I'm afraid love is like that. It's

a process, like all of life, and you know what Pam said—
it's the process that matters.

By the way, Tom never saw what I was writing in my
story until it was done, and I read it to him. When I read
him the first part about when I saw the little boy's face in
the back of the bus, he crooked his head and interrupted
to tell me that when he was really young, maybe eight
or nine, his family was traveling through Virginia along
Route 1 on a bus, and he saw a little girl in a car. And
the car and the bus traveled alongside each other, and he
and the little girl stared at each other until the vehicles
parted, and he never forgot her. It's a long shot, but I
believe in long shots.

An Obscuration to Flight
My First Entry
December, 2000, Oudish Island

The storm lasted at least five, maybe seven days.
My storm lasted almost fourteen days, maybe more. In
my paranoia, I even wondered if perhaps, somehow, the
external storm had been called up by my own boiling,
stewing, festering watery depths.

Externally, the sea lashed out at the tiny island with a
fury akin to my own boil. Hurricanes and such identified
storms are horrific, but they have a beginning, a middle,
and an end. This storm blew in and swirled and stayed,
blowing at my back even now as I write.

In the beginning, it was worse at night, so that days
were still somehow manageable. Midway through, it
was constant, with no place to go in the limestone
house to escape the howling. We put towels underneath
the door to stop the scraping of wood and metal on
limestone, a sound akin to fingernails on chalkboard.
But the wind still found enough spaces to enter, so that
it whorled through the bedroom, into the bathroom,
and resonated down the bathtub drain, creating such a

banshee sound I could never describe. We were driven downstairs, into the spare bedroom, and it took the wind longer to find us there. In Marsalforn, it escaped the sea wall in it's fury and threw huge boulders across the street, aiming for the houses that encroached on the beach and bouncing them off the limestone, like a mad bowler. They lay in such litter on the street that it was undrivable. Between Zabbat and Marsalforn, on the back road by the sea, the waves leapt at such heights that they were turquoise at the very tops as they turned to froth, pounding the rocky beach, then dragging the rocks back to the depths from which they had escaped. I had never seen turquoise illuminated waves and hope to never forget the color or the cause, or the sound of thousands of rocks being dragged to shore and dragged back into the sea with each thrust of turquoise.

Internally, I suspect this material and the timing of the presentation of this material. By that I mean that we all have little fissures, mortared over, spackled, painted a pretty, acceptable color, with throw rugs covering even the hint of anything not perfect.

A simple incident occurred, innocent and simple, but it dug down into my foundation and found a sympathetic fissure and began a process of disintegrating everything I thought I knew and believed. It grew and grew in proportion until every moment of every day was engaged in examination and torture of some aspect of this little, tiny fissure. I do not write this, nor do I choose, to detail this very personal incident, but to show how the process can work, so that I did not just rip up the very foundation of my being for only myself.

What do you fear? It will come to your door if you choose the path of the Initiate.

I feared betrayal and abandonment. I was in one of the safest places in the world, surrounded by people who love and adore me, and my fears still found me.

It was not fear of the wind. I only saw the mirror in its turbulence. And I'm certainly not saying I created

the storm. I am only noticing the reflection of its fury
out of the calm. And I am aware that it, like my storm,
will have its season. The question for examination was,
what had caused the storm? Was there a change in the
barometrics, and could I determine what had changed in
the pressure around me so that my own storm, the internal storm, might have its glory and then allow me to go
back to my blissful state of relationship?

The incident had just occurred and it was insignificant,
though it carried a message to my ears that sounded
louder than it needed to have sounded. And why was
that? Magdalen had just given the information about how
crucial it was for the woman's *floor* to be strong and safe,
how she needed to know that she was loved and that she
was safe. And I had reveled in that information, knowing
how sweet and clear that message would sound to such
weary, tired ears as we women have. I knew we needed
to feel secure to fully blossom. The poppy does not look
the same that has been beaten by the wind and dashed
against rocks. But look at the tall poppy that has stood
in the field alongside other such poppies, flanked by sup-
porting stalks, safely looking into the sun, with just the
right amounts of moisture and sunlight and darkness.
She is all she can be in that environment.

How many of us are ever safe and secure enough to
be all we can be?

I was told as a little child that I would have every
experience a human could have, so that when I spoke, it
would be from experience and that I would have something of value to say. It was a strange thing to be told
while sitting in the fork of a pear tree when you're five
years old. And I never forgot it.

And so when I talk about how you can't perform
under the stress of abuse, I speak from the horror of
experience. I spent five years with a horribly abusive
man. The abuses were slow to appear at the beginning, or I tell myself I would never have gotten caught
up in such a situation. And in the beginning, they were

mostly verbal. Then he began to systematically cut me off from my friends, though I didn't detect any danger in that. Then, when I least expected it, completely out of the blue, not attached to an argument or disagreement, he would strike me; leaving me almost disbelieving the event had occurred. It is demeaning, demoralizing, paralyzing, and almost drove me mad. It is beyond dishonoring. The word dishonoring is so trivializing to the degree of shame and degradation that abuse creates.

I examined every aspect of every move I had made prior to those blows. What had I said? What had I done? There was nothing I had done. Did I dream it? And I was much too ashamed to let anyone know it was happening. I was far too evolved to allow such behavior and besides—thank you religion—it must have been my fault. We are, after all, such wicked creatures filled with guilt and created in sin and shame.

But that horrible relationship had ended with me still alive. I had put years and a lot of work between these incidents and *me*.

And now, here I am, in the most amazing, powerful, loving, honoring, fulfilling relationship I have ever even read about, much less experienced, and I'm feeling frightened and insignificant and jealous of nothing and every insecurity has moved into my head and taken up residence, haunting me, hounding me. All because of one tiny, little incident.

I should tell you that "nothing" happened. No one did anything to me. There was a simple communication in an email between Tom and someone else, and I took the message and extrapolated it. I boiled it, dissected it, reassembled it, recarved it, served it to all the voices in my head and published my report.

I was wounded, perhaps fatally wounded.

"But I can handle it. I'm an Initiate. I'm living a dream life," I reasoned.

So I tried to put a tiny, barely visible, throw rug over the insignificant dent in the linoleum.

And then the Magdalen delivered these words, *"The next level to understand has to do with the emotional tuning of the female Initiate. For the female Initiate's receptivity is dependent upon her emotional state. This is part of her nature and cannot be sidestepped if these techniques are to work."*

And she went on, as if that wasn't enough to stir the soup.

"Essential to the female Initiate is the authentic feeling of safety and love, or appreciation at the very least. When these are in place, something within her being lets go and allows the alchemy to occur. The alchemy is created by the joining of the male Initiate's Ka and the female Initiate's Ka. As they make love, the Ka bodies interconnect and this causes the female to open her magnetic floor."

I froze as she continued to speak.

"This is a strange term. It comes from the language used in the Temples of Isis. The floor is the foundation upon which one stands. When we set something to be secure, we place it on the floor. So the floor was used as a type of slang within the Temples, referring to the very basic piece that is required. So when I say 'the female's magnetic floor,' I am saying that this is the fundamental piece that has to occur."

The light winds turned to gale force, the sea whipped, and the throw rug was blown away.

Something greater than my timidity had ripped up my floorboards to inspect the tiny fissure. Where I want to go, there can be no weakness, no fissures, and no fears. I knew some of the secrets of the ages lay in this simple, short material given with so much power and clarity. I say the word "secrets" and any woman reading this *Manuscript* will tell you she knew this. But we have been shamed and quieted for so long that we have long ago stopped trusting those inner knowings.

Magdalen was rousted from where she lay within the soul she shared with her Beloved, Yeshua, by Isis and Metatron and asked to come and tell us her story. And

I had put a throw rug out to greet her. I have only two commitments. One is to the truth with Tom, and the other is to look at all my unfinished business. I have called that forward now for almost two decades. I just didn't think I could possibly have this much unfinished business.

The Feminist Rises
Second Entry
December, 2000, Oudish

This material was given over a period of time between Thanksgiving and Christmas of 2000. Mary Magdalen first came through one night in Zurich, Switzerland in a small hotel in the old section of town. She continued her delivery as we zagged across the breadth of the Mediterranean, triangulated Sicily, and wound up living on Oudish, the smaller Malta Island. Magdalen completed by editing her portion herself, word by word, shortly after the above-described physical storm passed, just before Christmas, 2000.

She had chosen each word before she spoke it through Tom with a sense of power and clarity I had never heard before from any human or Spirit. She had neither anger nor pity nor any common emotion through-out the telling, but over one thing. When she spoke of the love she felt for the man, Yeshua, her heart trembled. And I cried every time she brought up how hard it had been to take the role of the Initiate, for which she had been well trained, and still be a woman in love with a man, for which there is no training under the sun.

And he was a man on a mission!

How many of these have we known?

And the job he came to do was more important than his love for her?

How many of these have we known?

And in the retelling, he is remembered as the Christ, the Redeemer, the Only Son of God; and she is remembered as a whore, though it was she who filled him?

How many of these have we known?

And she, as the unlimited vessel of energy, gave him the strength to do what he came to do. And so he did it, and then he left?

And my little, tiny fissure cracked down the epi-center, and by Christmas the fault line was above ground, visible to anyone who came near.

Bah Humbug
Third Entry
December, 2000, Oudish

December continued to howl across the sparsely treed fields of Oudish, and the chill wasn't only in the air. I was still hounded by the innocent incident of the email. It was a simple, innocent email to Tom, to and from an old friend—but it happened to be an old friend who'd had an agenda for Tom, one that included a little more than friendship. This person had hurt me and almost cost us the relationship. I couldn't understand why this person was still in our life, since the original experience had brought such intense anguish.

Sacred Relationship—the way I want to do it, the way I believe it *must* be lived—must be the most important process ongoing in life. Reason is out! If I am God and my mate is God, then why would any god outside of us—any practice, any devotion, any being, anything—demand greater obedience than our love. It must be night and day, always at the heart of life, always the most important aspect of life. It must stay in total truth. No dust can be swept under the throw rug. No throw rugs covering the slight, tiny flaws. And unless it is held as the most valued and sacred experience, it will dwindle and succumb to the tendency of all relationships. This is the truth I hold in my heart. And it is the truth which no man I have ever known could handle or remain in honor to—and here I was, back at the point of truth. I felt like a jealous, scorched woman, a banshee with no compassion. I felt I *looked* like that. I didn't really think that's what was going on, but so deeply devalued is my self esteem, that I questioned my intuition. Still, if it were not so, if Tom really loved me, would he still be communicating with this person? If he knew that communication with this person hurt me, why would he continue the communication?

Perhaps I should leave.

I am impossible to live with. My price is too high for anyone to pay. I demand too much. I give no slack. I have no slack to give after where I've been. But who on Earth can stand up to the demands of an unrelentingly demanding woman who carries a picture of relationship with colors from another universe? And I cannot find the old "governors" on my thoughts and mouth; the tricks of the southern woman have deserted me, and I cannot help but say what I think. Goddess, help me!

Perhaps I should leave.

Oudish is said to be the island where Odysseus was held captive by the siren, Calypso, for seven years. I am captive here. There is nowhere to go. It's a tiny island dotted with fields and Catholic Churches and the sweetest, most honest people you will ever meet anywhere, and there is no escape. I am trapped here in my swirling.

Perhaps I *should* leave. Tom doesn't need this after what he's been through. He needs peace, not a shrew. I am a shrew. But I'm right. I'm a *right* shrew! Sigh.

Do you want to be right? Or do you want to be happy? But at what price does happiness come?

We went for a walk—a long walk. It was time for truth.

Each farmer on Oudish has a tiny little plot, maybe a acre, maybe a 1/2 acre. They are all appropriately "fenced," as it were, in oddly shaped walls of stone, hand-piled through the generations, each generation unearthing small boulders that continually rise to the surface and adding them to the stonewall. So the terrain is zigzagged by these stonewalls, like patchwork lines on a quilt of soil.

I am like a steam kettle, appearing quite quiet and passive and easy. But if something happens, like the email, I *used* to begin a slow boil, which took years to turn to steam. Now I just boil over, right away, and then I hold that boil. I mean, I can really harp over something that seems mildly out of place. I don't mean to; I can't help it. I don't see other dimensions, but I don't miss an energy exchange on this plane. Too many years in politics, I guess. I don't miss much happening energetically around me, and I could feel the difference in the air between Tom and me since I questioned this email. He was withdrawing from the dark, moist and dangerous abyss of the feminine. Her price was *pretty* high these days; I had to admit. It demanded total commitment and total truth, which he also demanded of me.

We began to talk about it all.

I thought I would die. I had to admit I was jealous of an email. I felt disrespected. I felt hurt and abandoned by an email. I thought I would die. I mean, when you cut yourself wide open to another person and talk about your fears, your jealousies, your inadequacies, your weak floor—you just *know* they can't handle it. You know your "stuff" is too ugly, too confining, for anyone to stomach. Besides, surely your stuff smells like tuna fish! No one could possibly love you through your truth.

I was afraid that it might appear that I was confining Tom, and for whatever reason, I cannot bear the thought of anyone ever confining Tom Kenyon again. I had refused to be like the people around Tom when Pam died, all vying for confinement rights!

But Tom doesn't see agendas like I do. He sees Deity and Spirits and Beings from other dimensions, and he talks to them like I talk to the waitress at a restaurant. I see agendas and politics and my prophetic abilities are limited to the human beings around me. I hear what they *don't* say, and I see what they don't think anyone sees. I see their true motives and am cursed with feeling crazy over my oddly unappreciated ability. I saw the *meaning* behind the message behind the *written* words in the email...not the one Tom wrote, but the one he received.

We walked for hours that day, over walls and fields, all the way to the Cliffs of Dwejra, a dizzying ledge of limestone hundreds of feet above the Mediterranean. I knew Tom was thinking how nice it would be to live alone. I was thinking how nice it would be to live alone. This was work!

But the love is so intense! He takes my breath away!

We talked it all over and over and over and over and over and over and over. Exhausted from the walk and the talk, we turned to head back. Perhaps it was time for us to part company.

Then I spotted something on the ground near my foot. It was a carved pottery shard of some kind, almost buried in the sand. It had a design, like a petroglyph, on its surface. Tom and I both stopped to look at this treasure. I reached down and dug at it with a rock, and it yielded to my pressure. We had found an ancient symbol from one of the hundreds of Goddess Temples all over the island, perhaps a message for this place where we were stuck—to love or to leave.

We almost fell down laughing when we brushed it off and discovered not an ancient amulet or shard of pottery, but the cover from a clutch pedal left in the sand decades ago. Our ancient pottery shard was someone else's old clutch pedal cover!

And so we took it as a great sign and we shifted into neutral. We had each told our truth. We stood there, in the light of that long day, and just stopped. We went home and just held each other. In truth, in total truth, no one has ever stopped my heart like Tom Kenyon. And he will learn to see agendas, and I will learn to see other dimensions. But if I don't ever see other dimensions, it's OK with me. I've got Tom to tell me the truth of what's out there. And if he doesn't ever see other people's agendas around him, that's OK, he's got me. And as long as he *appreciates* my gifts and *listens* to me, and I *appreciate* his and *listen* to him, we have total sight between us. Magdalen was right—appreciation, at the very least, is required.

Hauntings
Fourth Entry
July, 2001, Paros Island, Cyclades, Greece

I am haunted by many things as I contemplate placing this material in the world at large. The responsibility for putting such information into print weighed so heavily this particular night that sleep deprived me of her peace, and I find myself sitting at the small kitchen table, palmtop in hand, so to speak, braving the mosquitoes of the Cyclades. They are small but ominously dangerous in their predatory nature; humless, they are deadly in their silence. They are truly among the little things that can really make a point in life.

The Magdalen consciousness is upon the Earth plane now, as we realize the truth of the emotion and physicality of passion and welcome the return of the feminine principal. In your journey you may encounter some of the many other visages and the voices claiming to speak for the Magdalen, or even to "be" her.

They tell different stories, these different Magdalens.

Some channels I have great respect for have been given the story that she and Yeshua were together as consorts, but had no children. Some have been given the story that there were many children. Some say that Yeshua died on the cross during his crucifixion and that Magdalen carried on the teachings alone. Some versions say he did not die on the cross, but lived with her for many more years and that the crucifixion was nothing more than a hoax, to earn his freedom, a real "crock-of-fiction."

Some say he ultimately died in Masada, during the siege. Some claim his resting place is clearly marked

in India. One recent version says he is buried in southern France, in the Pyrennees. Some channeled versions
of the Magdalen story say she lived her life teaching in
her own mystery school in southern France and that
her bones lie there. Others say she found her peace, if
you will, in England. Others say there was no such one
person as Jesus Christ but that "he" was a composite of
many different teachers of the time, edited together purely
to create a new religion to quiet the masses under
Roman government.

I am not bothered by the discrepancies, though I
admit it would be far simpler if everyone were telling the same story. But they do tell the same story
over the significant issues—that this Yeshua and this
Magdalen were consorts and that the Church purposefully and maliciously mis-translated the word for whore
to dismiss the Magdalen, to impale all of femininity
with that brand, specifically to further the patriarchy
and discredit passion, so that, as Magdalen put it, no
one would accidentally stumble on the great truths that
lie in passion.

What matters to me in this *Manuscript* is the obvious
power in her words and the transcendent and palpable love
she has held throughout all time for her Beloved, Yeshua.

In addition to that, the practices she gave create elec-
trical shift. There is no doubt of that.

As I detach myself from the elation and personal
"high" derived from being present when this material
was given, experiencing the Magdalen first-hand, feeling
her strong and even presence, listening through tears to
much of her story, I find myself only now, months later,
able to do what I do best, be devil's advocate, questioning
it and its relevance today.

She had chosen each word with such calibrated preci-
sion. She was back to tell a story and to set the record
straight. Much of what she had to do was clarify the mis-
information, the lies the Church perpetrated. And Yeshua
had used language that had a meaning to only a certain

few, language which, when taken out of context, became supportive of something in total contradiction to what he really meant.

Just sitting down with the Master and having some bread and a glass of wine had gone from being something he loved to do with people, to eating his flesh and drinking his blood. And the Church calls others pagan?

And how would we avoid doing the same? How could we choose language and supportive commentary that couldn't/wouldn't, over time, be used to misconstrue the real meaning? Are people capable of understanding and choosing the divinity of Sacred Relationship? Or will they think this is just a great little manual on how to use sex to gain power?

And what about her role, in the light of feminism? Was she just another woman who gave her power to a man? In this case, literally *gave* her power to a man, who could not have done what he did without her contribution?

If you think this is a sex manual or the story of a woman who gave her power to a man, you have missed the point and will surely not attain the possible.

This is a story of what Magdalen called Sacred Relationship and the internal alchemies possible within the safety and devotion of Sacred Marriage.

We have been as careful as we could be in choosing words with consideration to their long-term meaning. We have tried not to use words or slang used within only certain schools of metaphysics, hoping that they will not be misconstrued, at least within our own lifetime anyway. Beyond that we can do nothing but *intend* truth and illumination.

Pondering
Fifth Entry
Orcas Island, December 2001

It has been one year since Magdalen gave us this
Manuscript. She gave it in two months. In two months she
gave what she wanted of her personal story and what she
wanted to share of her story as an Initiate of the Temple
of Isis. In her slim volume of exquisitely chosen words she
also taught what could be taught, what could be shared, for
those ready to hear the beauty of it. She gave us some of
the deepest secrets of the Temples of Isis and the secrets of
ecstasy that have been stolen from us. It has taken me one
year to come to terms with it, and to add what I have been
asked to add; and I am feeling deeply humbled in the job.
I have now worked with her energy on many occasions,
alone and with other people and my admiration, indeed, my
deepest gratitude for her beauty, her love and her genius
and power awe me and always will.

I don't know what happens to us humans. We are born
with all we ever need in life. We are born in beauty and
genius. We are born *of* God and with God fully infused.
We *are* God. There is no God outside of us. That doesn't
make me any better than the next person. That next person is God, too! That's the magic. We are all God. We are
all divine. We look around and we see enough land and
enough hard working people to be capable of feeding
everyone on the planet. We see enough bounty to take
care of everyone on Earth, all the animals, and all the
creatures. And we swear that when we grow up, we are
going to change things. We are going to make a difference. And then something happens.

I was lucky. I grew up in the strangest of circumstances, basically away from all common influences,
except for when humans tried to tell me something I had
experienced differently in nature. Although I had humans
telling me what to do, I had the counterbalance of deep
nature, deeper than anyone I've ever met. And I couldn't

see this "sin" we are all supposed to be born in. I saw beauty, despite what the people around me told me. I saw beauty in the love possible between people and I couldn't imagine how such beauty could be evil!

And then I went out in the world and I got hurt. And my *giving* nature was met equally by the *taking* nature of many around me.

And all the pain and hypocrisy and bigotry and judgment I saw growing up was caused by the belief in Jesus Christ! I didn't experience beauty coming out of the love people claimed for this Being. Then I grew in my own spirituality, and I came to understand that he was a Great Master teacher, one of many the world has been gifted to know, but indeed, a great Master, in whose name governments created a religion. How ironic then, that Mary Magdalen should use the phrase, "...were aghast that the Master would help such a one." Since that is my experience of Christianity, how ironic that this material would come to "such a one as me?"

Fear of Flying Returns
A Closing Entry
Orcas Island, December 31, 2001

Just as this book was going into final edits Tom and I encountered yet another "obscuration to flight," and because it brought about such major shift and wound up affording us such understanding, we decided we had a duty to share it. You need to be aware that prickles can lie beneath the beautiful roses when you undertake Sacred Relationship. And you need to understand that we work at it every day. We live in the alchemical furnace. The more I understand and experience what Magdalen means by true Sacred Relationship, and the more I live it, the more awed I am by the process, and the more respect I have for those of us brave enough to enter the catacombs of this process.

Something simple happened. Again. It wasn't a big deal. And it *was*. It was actually quite like the simple little experience that triggered our journey on little Oudish, when my internal storm out blew the external storm. But when one partner does something that hurts the other in relationship, intentional or not, it must be respected. If it doesn't see the "light" of examination, it will darken the door of love eventually, either through atrophy or eventually through revolution. When the safety net evaporates, so goes the alchemy.

Tom invited an experience of someone into his life, someone I felt was dangerous to him, and he did it without consulting me, or I would have at least warned him about the potential for danger I "saw" in such an encounter. I am cursed with seeing the machinations of people around us, people on the street.

I "see" agendas. He sees Deity. Sigh. I see his vision as a gift. I see mine, all too often, as a burden.

When he told me about the invitation, my gut twisted. My stomach flopped and my heart raced right out the door. I made the bed, dressed, packed my emotional suitcase, and left. I withdrew about forty years into my childhood. And I said nothing at first. I really tried to stuff my feelings back down. But my heart was making so much noise, I feared it would explode.

I have to tell you, I knew my discussion about this particular "obscuration to flight" wasn't going to be appreciated initially. After all, hadn't we had this experience already on Oudish? And so it was with great, heavy heart that I sat down and began to share what was happening within me as a result of his simple, innocent, but painful-to-me action.

Tom had simply invited someone into the relationship that I "saw" as potentially dangerous. It was an innocent action, and the individual involved would hardly be considered dangerous by anyone. Intentions were altogether well meaning. But I "saw" that inviting this person into our life potentially opened portals through which, shall we say, other presences might find entry. Magdalen actually called these other presences, these other energies, demons in her day.

So what does this mean? Was I simply being a jealous woman? Or was I so intuitive that I sensed anyone who was even inadvertently dangerous? Or was I so controlling that I couldn't allow anyone into our lives that didn't meet my stamp of approval?

My initial overtures regarding the subject brooked just the reaction I expected, and so I began my emotional packing job, ready to go out the heart door. Tom does what Tom does—he numbed. And there we were. The same magnets that usually draw us together flipped, and have you seen what magnets do when they are reversed, and you try to force them together? They repel. It's very hard to talk from your heart when you are repelled, and when you know you repel the significant other in your life.

I sat down and talked with him about what I thought had been created by this action and how I felt dishonored when he didn't talk to me before opening this particular barn door and letting this horse out, which has now become my mantra.

He was appalled at my reaction. Well, of course he was! I probably initially sounded like an insane woman again. (I mean, I thought I was right, mind you. In other words, I knew I wasn't insane, but I was afraid he would think me a bit daft. I knew I was even *right*, at least for me, but I have also learned the other great truth...do you want to be right, or do you want to be happy?)

I can't stress how life threatening this business of being in total truth is to the psyche. You really think you're going to die when you first begin to speak. And there is something deeply scary about the truth, the total truth, not the clean, pretty truth, but the truth that lies under everything, the truth that we hide from everyone.

And let me tell you—it's really easy to let all this go and not tell your truth, not stir the pot. I could easily just relax and let it go. We'd have been fine if I hadn't pushed this issue—on the surface. But I knew that eventually we'd wind up just like every other couple in the world today, together, but not really together, co-dependent to each other's refusal to look at truth. You can actually think you love someone so much that you never call them on their stuff, thinking it would hurt them too much. I'll tell you what hurts—not calling someone on his or her stuff. That's what kills and creates disease and compliance to non-growth and disillusionment.

I know in my heart that those little things, those little annoyances, those little nigglings, the little truths, when *not* shared between people in Sacred Relationship build brick walls, over which there is eventually no assault. When you do not share your truth, one morning you wake up and find yourself living with a stranger, a room-mate. Read my story again. I've been there, and it is not the road to Sacred Relationship.

And I wish I could tell you that we figured out the answer by ourselves without help. And the truth is, we asked for help. I was losing my mind, haunted by the image of myself as a fearful, jealous woman. I mean, I just wrote this whole section and admitted what my fears were and here they were again! I thought we'd gotten beyond all that!

The truth was, I had another ever-so-slight crack in my foundation, and it left me fearing for my safety and for Tom's safety.

And so I approached Tom with my concerns, and "our magnets flipped" as we call it, and the always so powerful attraction between us repelled each of us, and we withdrew to our corners. I felt wounded. He felt annoyed.

We shut everything down and we asked for guidance. This possibility for transformation through relationship is the most sacred and honored aspect of life to each of us. We have each chosen this, and it is our agreement to continue to choose relationship. And we were stuck and needed help.

I know we are fortunate beyond imagination in that we have such access to guidance. And it is because I know not everyone has such access that I share what we were told.

It was explained to us that "who" we are is forged from our childhood and a myriad of lifetime experiences. The swords each of us carries into relationship are forged in the heat of pain and out of terrific smelting; we are *set*, alloyed, from such experiences. It takes at least *equal* heat to re-forge us, to change what we are, to burn off the *obstacles to flight*, as Magdalen calls them, to burn off the dross.

I want that burn, though I admit I sometimes fear the heat, and it really helped me to be told that we weren't doing anything wrong, but that, in fact, this is the process and that this experience was an indication of where we were in the process.

Tom and I have chosen to share this personal piece of guidance in the hope that it answers some questions.

"The answer lies in the context of alchemical process. Are you showing the face of the jealous woman or the face of a woman who sees danger?

"It is the process between the two of you. You must speak the truth of what you are experiencing, and Tom must speak his truth from what arises within him—the conflict or the harmony. Those are the two faces. And this melding is the process of burning off the dross. So the two of you are in an alchemical process, and you are doing everything quite accurately.

"We understand it is a very difficult situation, and you are looking for an answer that keeps you from the heat. But the heat is required! There are psychological patterns within each of you that you might call negative, or less than resourceful, and they are melded with aspects that are positive.

The jealous woman is bonded with the person who feels danger, because when you make steel you bond,

you make an alloy. And what made you was your childhood. You are taking the swords of your identities and
sticking them in the alchemical furnace, and there is no
answer to make this easier, other than to understand
that you are in an alchemical process that you willingly
chose to enter. When your swords begin to dissolve, it
feels like you are losing your identity.

"The answer is for both of you to speak the truth
about what face you have on, in the moment.

"When the furnace gets so hot that the magnets flip,
it is because the heat is so intense that it is changing
the structure of the magnets. The magnets are created
through polarizations in each of you. You are drawn
to the polarizations in each other, so there is a match.
There is a magnetism that pulls you together. When the
heat is turned up, the magnets reverse and with all the
intensity that usually pulls you together, you are then
repelled. This is temporary; just ride through it; don't
read anything into it. There is a part of you that search-
es for evidence, for clues that you are in dangerous
territory, and you need to escape. There is no escape in
these times, only truth.

"Understand that you are in alchemical process when
you are in Sacred Relationship; and you search for pictures, and sometimes when the pictures don't match,
you get scared. You are in alchemical process. As this
heat gets turned up and you can't take the heat, go to
another place where the heat is not so strong. Pause and
let the world stop; and take each other's hands, though
the last thing you want to do is touch each other in these
times; and speak the truth about what face is showing
itself. Understand that telling the truth is not going to
break apart anything.

"Don't let anything come between you. You must
live in a fluid environment so there are no demands, so
if the heat gets too hot you can stop everything and go
through the truth process. You must live in a free-floating
environment so you can go into mystery.

*"When the feminine nature has discovered something
that she treasures, she becomes a fierce protectress, and
she wants to protect it at all costs. Jealousy is a face that
presents itself in the course of life experiences. The problem is not with jealousy; the problem is not speaking the
truth of what one needs. To go out on a limb is to speak
the truth, facing the possibility that the other one may
not be willing to give what you want.*

*"Relationships are rather like poker games, with
everyone bluffing about who has the higher cards.
When you go into Sacred Relationship, all the cards are
laid out on the table for each to see. Whatever arises,
it is simply put on the table; because the clarity of two
people looking at all the cards allows for the possibility
of transformation."*

Let me sum up.

Always stay in truth.

It's going to get hot.

Don't give up. Buy a clutch pedal cover and put it
on your altar. Hold hands and walk across the burning
coals. And I promise you—you will think you are going
to die. And you won't.

Post Partum
An Afterthought

This is a story of what Magdalen calls Sacred
Relationship and the internal alchemies possible within
the safety and devotion of Sacred Marriage.

We do not live in times of light. "We are," as Magdalen
says, "at the beginning of the ending of time." And time
is short and so secrets are being revealed, in the hope
that more people will wake up and make the relevant
changes necessary to make a difference.

I am reminded of the story of the young man walking along the beach. In the distance, he sees what looks
like tiny dots all over the beach and the shape of an old

woman, bending down and then walking to the edge of the sea, and tossing something into the sea, then walking back, and bending down again, and picking something up, and throwing it into the sea.

As he approaches, he sees that the beach is littered with starfish, left behind by a quickly receeding tide. There are hundreds of star fish dying on the beach and one old woman, picking one up at a time, walking to the edge of the sea and tossing one back, and then picking up another.

He is astonished at the impossibility of her task and says, "Why on Earth are you doing that? Why are you bothering? You can't save enough of them to matter!"

She threw one more starfish into the sea and yelled into the wind, "It matters to that one."

As Magdalen said in her final transmission, "I realize in the sharing of my story that only a handful will understand, but that is enough."

In sharing One Woman's Story, I realize that many will criticize me. Some will be jealous of me. Some will call me names. Many will judge. I chose to honor the request from Mary Magdalen that it be included because I have come to, unflinchingly and without hesitation, adore her and trust her wisdom beyond my fears.

May you find your own Sacred Marriage, in balance, evenness, and ecstatic devotion with another and with yourself.

What will happen when

one woman writes

the truth about her life?

The world will split open.

—

Addendum

We entreatied Mary Magdalen with numerous questions after she delivered her *Manuscript*. There were certain questions we knew we would be asked when we presented this material to the world. Some of the questions we asked were personal, but we felt it important to ask them when presented the opportunity. She answered some of these questions, but often her answer was, "Tell them Mary Magdalen has no comment." We share this with you to show you more of the personality of the Being we experienced. Her boundaries were clear. She had no difficulty delineating what was her personal business and what information might be of help in this time. She had no patience for questions that achieved nothing but reduce her story to idle conversation and irrelevant trivia.

Rather than write a dialogue we have presented these questions and answers exactly as they were asked and as they were answered.

Q: Were you and Yeshua married?

Magdalen: "Yeshua and I were married in a rabbinical tradition. In the Gospels they report that Yeshua turned water into wine at a wedding ceremony. What they failed to mention was that the wedding was ours. It was known.

There are two paths that sometimes overlap. One is Initiation and one is marriage.

Initiation is entering a higher threshold of understanding and ability. Initiations are given to solitary individuals.

Those in Sacred Relationship step into this through their mutual intention. Acknowledgement by another is unnecessary. That is a cultural way of doing it. Those who enter into the heart of Sacred Relationship will go through Initiations as a result of their entering into the mysteries. What is important is not the *act* but the *process* of Sacred Relationship."

Q: How does the Sex Magic of Isis change for women who have had hysterectomy or menopause?

Magdalen: "The sexual fluids of a mature woman who has gone through either of these is, of course, different from those of a woman who is fertile. So the interaction of semen and the woman's sexual fluids do not have the same energetic constituency. However, there is a reaction and more importantly all other aspects of the Sex Magic of Isis apply. The stroking, the touch, the nesting all create the magnetic fields which can be drawn into both Initiates' subtle bodies, and so while the act may not be as dynamic as in their youth, it is still effective."

Q: How does Sex Magic change with men who have had vasectomies?

Magdalen: "The possibility of vasectomies was not a consideration during my time in the Temples of Isis. From the standpoint of the Sex Magic of Isis, the truth of the matter is that the man must rely upon stroking and touch and nesting to create the magnetic fields. The question implied is, will the Sex Magic work for a man who had a vasectomy? Yes, but with one consideration. Because the magnetics of his semen are denied interaction with the sexual fluids of his partner, he must actually stroke and touch his partner more than normal, in order to build close to the same intensity of magnetics."

Q: In the *Manuscript* you said that the issues that men had with their mothers might affect the alchemy between them and their partners. Does the same hold true for women? Does their relationship with their fathers affect the alchemy?

Magdalen: "To a certain extent, yes; a girl's experience with her father, by necessity, colors her interactions with her partner as a woman. And so to this extent, the effects are similar. But what I wish to have pointed out in regards to the male Initiate is the unusual vulnerability that the male experiences in relationship to the female. A daughter was never "carried by her father," for he does not have a womb. Her body was not formed out of his elements.

The son, on the other hand, is carried within the womb of the mother and is surrounded by her during his development. And once he is born, he begins the process of separation. Once his development reaches a certain stage, and if there were issues with his mother that are unresolved as a man, he may find it difficult to *nest*—because to *nest* is to be surrounded by the feminine energy once again, as he was *in utero*. And this is a different situation than with the woman and issues she may have with her father."

Q: Do you have any comments about the other major alchemical streams that teach that a man should retain his semen during intercourse?

Magdalen: "You may say, 'And she laughed!'
My bias, you understand, is as a Priestess of the Temples of Isis. The alchemy I was trained in is *feminine based*, and we view some of these things quite differently than the other streams you mention.

For one, we hold that the Creatrix of all time and space, whom we call Isis, is enfolded in the natures of all women. It is a *part* of them. Just like the seeds of a fig are hidden within it. We also understood that alchemy was based upon the joining of two opposites, the male principle and the female principle. But in this way of alchemy, the woman is understood to hold the alchemical keys. The male is needed in order to turn the keys, and it is *in* the mutual joining together of these polar opposites embodied within the male and female Initiate that the Alchemy takes place. From our perspective, the withholding of the male's semen is just another playing out of his general tendency to withhold.

It is true that a male's vitality is related to the energetics of his seed and that reckless release of his semen can affect his vitality. However, when the male releases his seed into his Beloved and he nests within her energies, he is fed and nourished by the magnetics as the door to her inner nature opens, flooding both of them with life-force. This is a different alchemical path than the other streams on the Earth at this time."

Q: Did you form a mystery school or teach in France or England?

Magdalen: "Upon landing at St. Maries my first and foremost concern was the safety of Sar'h, and so we headed north with the Druids to the Glastonbury and the Tor. When Sar'h was twelve I returned to the reeds to do the water Isis Ritual. By then Sar'h was not in danger and our return to England was more leisurely. I formed some teaching circles. After Sar'h wedded, I made periodic trips into France and into parts of England where I did teach the mysteries of the Temples of Isis."

Q: Is Magdalen a title?

Magdalen: "It was a title of spiritual recognition. There is an Order of Magdalen. It is hidden."

Q: What is the reason for the use of the reptilian imagery as used in the Alchemies of Horus?

Magdalen: "These serpentine images were used to communicate the serpent-like structure of sekhem as it moves up the djed. As the energies released by the Alchemies of Horus rise up the djed, they are snake-like in nature, undulating in other words. As they enter the head, they often tend to spread out across the hemispheres of the brain, like a cobra that shows its hood. Thus, the serpent form is a metaphor, a symbolic element that points to the deeper structure and nature of consciousness as it moves in the subtle body (the Ka)."

Q: The Gospels report that Yeshua exorcised seven demons from you? What was that?

Magdalen: "Yeshua performed a rite of purification, clearing out what you would call negativity from my seven chakras. It was a chakra clearing. The "seven demons" are simply negative energies that we all carry from time to time in our fields. He cleared this from my fields in preparation for the deeper alchemy we were to perform together.

What is not clarified is that I cleared the seven chakras for him as well. I performed that same process on him.

The principal is this.

As one increases the power of one's illumination, or spiritual nature, one becomes a magnet for many energies that are not one's own. This is true when a person is in a lower emotional state and becomes open to negative forces or energies, which in Yeshua's time were called demons. This becomes especially true when one is intoxicated or altered through drug use. If one's emotional tone (or vibrational state) is low, one opens the door to these negative and sometimes destructive energies.

However, paradoxically, something similar occurs when one moves upward into higher states of consciousness, because one becomes a magnet (or attractor) for these negative energies. And we all have occasions when we are not aware, and sometimes places are frequented that are not in our best interest, and this is when these energies *ride in*, so to speak.

The process was simply an ancient practice that stretches back to the Temples of Isis. It was a process for the Purification of the Seven Seals that drives out any negativity that we may carry, that we may not even be aware of. This was accomplished through the use of secret mantras, prayer, and the direction of light through intention, or will, into these centers. It is a complex process that not everyone is capable of, so to give the methodology, so to speak, to the masses would be a dis-service, because distortions would occur. It takes a level of mastery to clear the seals in the method that I used to clear him and he used to clear me.

Yet, once again, we see in the Gospel account of this, a one-sided and manipulative perspective. That Yeshua came to me for this purification as well was never report-ed. And yet they knew about it."

Q: What is meant by "the return of Cosmic Mother?

Magdalen: "It is a shift of collective consciousness to an honoring of the feminine. It will show up as a global and collective understanding of the sacredness of the earth itself, so that instead of raping and pillag-ing the earth, there will be a co-creation of the earth. And women—those souls embodied as women—will be elevated to a place of equality, of appreciation along with the male principal.

As you can tell, this earth has a long way to go before it reaches this."

Q: Do you mean it will be a long time before this happens?

Magdalen: "No, I mean it's a big leap in conscious-ness from where humanity is now, collectively. So thus, we can see or understand the need for purifica-tion. The need for purification decreases as each per-son comes into balance with the male/female within and moves to a place of honoring those externally in embodied male/female relationships."

We asked Mary Magdalen if she has had other incarnations and she told us that she has had no other incarnations.

Mary Magdalen made several references in our conversations to "those aligned with the New Earth." When we asked her what would qualify those in alignment with this New Earth, she replied without hesitation, "No guilt. No shame. No regrets."

Glossary of Terms

Alchemy - the art and science of changing one form into another. Inner alchemy (like the Egyptian system) transforms the energy of consciousness and the life-force of embodiment into expanded awareness, imparting enhanced abilities to the practitioner.

Ammit - a mythical creature related to the djed or sacred pathway of the chakras. Part crocodile, part lion and part hippopotamus, the ammit is often represented with a depiction of the djed. It sits with its reptilian snout tucked between the third (power) and fourth (love) chakras.

Anubis - an Egyptian deity (part jackal/part man) associated with the Land of the Dead. Egyptian myth holds that Anubis was Osiris' guardian into the Underworld, and is thus associated with this subterranean level of the psyche.

Ascension - the process of raising the life-force (sekhem) up the djed into the higher brain centers, thereby activating the powers of consciousness (siddhis) and giving the practitioner access to the spiritual realms of being. The term also applies to the ascension of the Ka body into higher realms of energy and light.

BA - the celestial soul.

Black Serpent - a term used by the Magdalen to describe the lunar pathway up the spine (see ida). The Black Serpent embodies the feminine mystery of creation and is related to the Void, the source from which all things are created.

Chakra - an energy vortex within the subtle body. The word means "wheel" since chakras tend to spin like wheels. Science has documented the existence of the chakras, and they emit both sound and light.

Central Column - a subtle energy pathway that runs in front of the spine from the base up to the top of the head (see pranic tube).

Central Pillar - the same subtle energy pathway as the Central Column or pranic tube.

Djed - the sacred pathway of the chakras. The djed runs from the base of the spine to the top of the head (the crown chakra). This is the central pathway for the process of Ascension in Egyptian alchemy.

Glorious Spiritual Body - see Sahu

Golden Raiment - see Sahu

Gold Serpent - a term used by the Magdalen to describe the solar pathway up the spine (see pingala). The solar circuit embodies the male aspect of creation and is related to light.

Horus - the son of Isis and Osiris. Symbolically, Horus refers to the joining of spirit (Osiris) and matter (Isis). His story is allegorical in the sense that his journey is the same as ours as we rise up the djed to expanded states of consciousness.

Ida - a yogic term referring to a subtle pathway up the left side of the spine. Also known as the lunar or Chandra circuit, the ida runs from the base chakra up into the head and ends at the tip of the left nostril (see Black Serpent).

Isis - the mother of Horus and one of the most prominent deities of the Egyptian pantheon. She was considered to be the Cosmic Mother, and her cult spread through most of the known ancient world.

Incarnate - a priestess within the Isis cult who has been trained to embody the energies of Isis.

Initiate - one who has passed through a portal or threshold between one level of consciousness to the next. Generally speaking, an Initiate has been trained in a sacred science and has been given access to the spiritual lineage responsible for that sacred science.

Initiation - the process of stepping from one level of consciousness into the next. Initiations are like benchmarks, acknowledging the attainment of some level of mastery. They may be granted or given directly from a spiritual being, or in some cases by a physical person.

Ka - a subtle energy body described in Egyptian alchemy. The Ka is an energetic duplicate of the physical body and is sometimes referred to as the etheric double or *spiritual twin*. Much of the focus of Egyptian alchemy is on the transformation of the Ka body.

Khat - the dense physical body of flesh and blood.

Kundalini yoga - a form of yoga that focuses on the movement of kundalini shakti, a form of energy very much related to sekhem, up the spine. As the kundalini shakti makes its ascent up the spine, the various chakras are activated giving the yogi or yogini mastery in those planes of consciousness.

Maat - an Egyptian deity associated with the Land of the Dead. Maat holds a scale weighted on one side with a feather. On the other side of the scale is the heart of the person seeking entrance into spiritual paradise. If the heart is weighted by shame and regrets it will tip the scale and the person must wander the Underworld. If the heart is light as a feather, the person is granted entrance into the sublime realms of spirit.

Neter - these are subtle powers. There are 26 neters in classic Egyptian alchemy, but the term can also be applied to anything that has energy or power. Thus the term can be related to the concept of shakti or energy in yoga.

Pineal gland - a gland sitting roughly in the center of the head. Its function is not fully understood by western science though, esoterically, it is viewed as holding keys to higher states of consciousness.

Pingala - a yogic term referring to a subtle pathway up the right side of the spine. Also known as the solar or Sureya circuit, the pingala runs from the base chakra up into the head and ends at the tip of the right nostril (see Gold Serpent).

Pranic tube - the pranic tube can be viewed as the center line of force within the magnetic field of the body. All bipolar magnets, including our bodies, have a north and south pole. These two poles are generated around an axis, like the axis of the earth, which is also a bipolar magnet. Within the physical body, this axis runs from the crown down to the perineum and sits in front of the spine (see djed, central column, central pillar).

Obstacles to Flight - a term used by the Magdalen to describe the psychological impediments to spiritual illumination. One task of the alchemist within her tradition is to remove these Obstacles to Flight so that the Ascension of consciousness up the djed can take place.

RA - the Egyptian sun god. From an alchemical understanding, anything that is fire is a power of RA. Within the Ka body, there is an energy center or chakra that is fiery in nature, known as the solar plexus. A good deal of Egyptian alchemy deals with RA in its many forms as a source of energy to drive alchemical reactions within the Ka.

Red Serpentine Drops - a subtle energetic substance emitted from the crown that is related to the attributes of one's physical mother. These drops are generated from an alchemical meditation, given in the *Manuscript* using the Black and Gold Serpents. Interestingly, this practice is similar in many regards to a practice in Tibetan Vajrayana yoga using what are called the red and white drops. In this Tibetan practice, the drops are also used to generate bliss, but then the practitioner rests in this bliss while contemplating the empty nature or emptiness of all things. In the Alchemy of Horus, however, the end goal is different. While the joining of the drops also produces bliss, this bliss is then sent into the Ka body for the purpose of strengthening it. According to the Magdalen, ecstatic states of consciousness strengthen the Ka.

Samadhi - a yogic state of inner attention attained through meditation. In samadhi, consciousness is turned from the outer senses to the inner worlds. There are many ranges of samadhi, from light inner attention to profoundly altered states of consciousness. In the deepest forms of samadhi, perceived time comes to a standstill. There is no sense of it, and there is no sense of the world. Awareness becomes aware of itself, and from this deep inner recognition of the Self there is a spontaneous arising of bliss.

Sahu - the immortal energy body sometimes referred to as the Golden Raiment or Glorious Spiritual Body.

Sekhem - life-force. It means "that which makes things erect." In the process of Egyptian alchemy, one's sekhem, or life-force, is strengthened in order to be transformed into expanded awareness. It is the power of sekhem that raises the djed generating the power to *ascend* the ladder of the chakras into illumination. This highly potentized life-force is also used in specific alchemical processes to generate the powers of consciousness (see siddhis).

Set - the brother and murderer of Osiris, Horus' father. It is Set that Horus must overcome in the Osirian myths.

Sex Magic - the use of sex in relationship to magic has a long history that spans many thousands of years and numerous cultures and spiritual lineages. The Sex Magic of Isis, however, is not viewed in the same manner as magic in general. Rather than trying to affect the outside world through magical transformations, the Sex Magic of Isis focuses on the magical transformation of consciousness itself. Thus it is really a form of internal alchemy, an alchemy that draws upon the most primal and potent energies available to embodied beings.

Siddhis - yogic powers. These powers of consciousness cover a wide range of non-ordinary abilities. They include such things as clairvoyance (inner seeing), clairaudience (inner hearing), clairsentience (inner feeling), and clairgnosis (knowing something without knowing how you know it). These abilities also include the capacity to heal and limited powers of prophecy. The siddhis also include such truly unusual abilities such as bi-location (being in two places at once), teleportation (instantly transporting oneself over great distances), and levitation (floating in air). These powers of consciousness have been well documented in many of the world's religious and alchemical traditions, including Buddhism, Christianity, Hinduism, Islam, Judaism, and Taoism. In addition, many indigenous peoples report that their shamans also exhibit many of these abilities.

Tantra - a term referring to energy practices. The term is sometimes used in Buddhism, for instance, to refer to the energy practices of consciousness itself. However, the term can also be used for the energy practices of sexuality. This form of Tantra is based on the use of sexual energy for the elevation of consciousness and has many forms throughout the world.

Uraeus - sometimes referred to as "the anointing," the uraeus occurs when sekhem (life-force) is brought up the djed and into the brain. This movement creates a snake-like energy form, which may be why the uraeus was represented as a serpent by the ancient Egyptians.

White Serpentine Drops - a subtle energetic substance emitted from the crown that is related to the attributes of one's physical father. These drops are generated from an alchemical meditation, given in the *Manuscript* using the Black and Gold Serpents (see Red Serpentine Drops for a comparison with a similar practice in Tibetan Vajrayana yoga).

About the Authors

Judi Sion

Judi Sion's background includes communications and advertising, as well as political consulting. Additionally she has been a photographer, a talk show host, and a newspaper columnist. Her articles have appeared in numerous magazines and newspapers. She spent seven years in a Mystery School with her teacher "in the wind" and her books from those years, *Last Waltz of the Tyrants, Financial Freedom,* and *UFOs and the Nature of Reality* are published in English, French, Spanish, and German. Her interest in Native American traditions took her into five years of intensive study and apprenticeship with the grandfathers and grandmothers of several tribal groups, including the Hopi. She has lectured on UFOs and Spirituality and taught women's mysteries both in North America and in Europe. Along with Tom Kenyon, she is taking *The Magdalen Manuscript* around the world.

Tom Kenyon

Musician, researcher, author, and therapist, Tom Kenyon has a Master's Degree in Psychological Counseling with over seventeen years in private practice. In 1983, he founded Acoustic Brain Research (ABR) to document the effects of sound and music on consciousness having realized its vast potential in his therapeutic work. For ten years he conducted brain research in the area of psychoacoustics (a term he coined, meaning the effects of sound on the psyche) and as a result developed numerous psychoacoustic recordings to increase creativity, insight and spiritual illumination.

He is the author of *Brain States* (New Leaf Publishing), a critically acclaimed guide to the brain's unused potentials. He is also co-author of *The Hathor Material* (SEE Publishing). His book *Mind Thieves* (ORB Communications) is a visionary sci-fi novel that deals with the intricacies of quantum mechanics and consciousness.

Tom regularly conducts trainings and seminars throughout the world on the topics of sound healing, consciousness and spiritual illumination. He joins Judi Sion in taking *The Magdalen Manuscript* around the world.

Tom Kenyon's Psychoacoustic Recordings, Books, and Videos

For free information about Tom Kenyon's vast library of personal growth tools (including the ABR library) please visit the web at *www.tomkenyon.com* or, for a free catalog and newsletter, write **Tom Kenyon, PO Box 98, Orcas, WA 98280**

The library includes a diverse collection of CDs, audiotapes, and videos. Most of these recordings use Tom's nearly four-octave range voice as part of sound meditations or inner explorations of consciousness. These recordings are well known for their highly transformational effects.

Workshops, Trainings, and Sacred Tours

Tom and Judi regularly conduct seminars and trainings throughout the world. These cover a wide range of topics, reflecting their interests in many areas of human potential.

Occasionally, they conduct tours to sacred places to be immersed in the culture that birthed a particular practice or spiritual tradition. On these tours, intensive inner work is part of the experience.

If you would like to be placed on their mailing list to receive yearly schedules and occasional updates, you can email *office@tomkenyon.com* or write: Tom Kenyon, PO Box 98, Orcas, WA 98280

Their schedule of events is also regularly posted on the web site at *www.tomkenyon.com* for your convenience.

Mary Magdalen Energy Meditations: Alchemical Practices to Elevate and Balance the Serpent Power Within

Tom Kenyon brings you five practices of the "Cosmic Mother" on CD as they were revealed to him in *The Magdalen Manuscript.* With *Mary Magdalen Energy Meditations,* he teaches you the techniques he has restored from Egyptian alchemy for transforming your life energy into a powerful force of creation. Through step-by-step guidance, Tom shows you how to channel this energy up the spine into precise areas of your higher brain centers. With each technique, you will strengthen the power of your "Ka body," your energetic self that is the key to accessing the higher realms of insight, creativity, and awakening.

Songs of Magdalen

"These songs were forged in the foundry of my heart. May they bring you comfort and solace on your journey home to the exquisite light and unimaginable beauty of your soul."
—Mary Magdalen, received by Tom Kenyon

Songs of Magdalen reveals through music the eternal love, poignant solitude, and transcendent grace of Mary Magdalen—priestess, mother, and beloved of Yeshua ben Joseph. Through his special connection to her spirit and his astonishing four-octave voice, Tom Kenyon transports you into the very heart of Mary Magdalen. Hauntingly beautiful, these songs are "a lightning bolt from the heart of the Cosmic Mother." Features three toning tracks, soul therapy meant to transmit healing energy to you directly from the source of the divine feminine.

Mary Magdalen Energy Meditations and *Songs of Magdalen* may be ordered either directly from Tom Kenyon or through Sounds True: www.tomkenyon.com or www.soundstrue.com.

The path into the New Earth
is simple.

No guilt.

No shame.

No regrets.

So be it.

—*Mary Magdalen*

SOUNDS TRUE was founded in 1985 by Tami Simon, with a clear vision: to disseminate spiritual wisdom. Located in Boulder, Colorado, Sounds True publishes teaching programs that are designed to educate, uplift, and inspire. With more than 600 titles available, we work with many of the leading spiritual teachers, thinkers, healers, and visionary artists of our time.

For a free catalog, or for more information on audio programs by Tom Kenyon, please contact Sounds True via the World Wide Web at www.soundstrue.com, call us toll free at 800-333-9185, or write

The Sounds True Catalog
PO Box 8010
Boulder, CO 80306